Trika

the Kashmir Śaiva Essence

Tej Raina

I dedicate this work to Maheshwara , (also known as Mahendra Raina), my father and friend , who , with a tender smile , always prompted me to unfold .

Acknowledgement :

I take pride in acknowledging the patience of my wife Usha, who always, lovingly stands all my manifestations.

I appreciate how Anubhav - Prerna and Bhavana - Kailash, my children, always look up to me, for whatever I am.

I enjoy, quite often, the excitement of seeing, the glint of sparks at the distant horizons, together with my friends Arvind Gigoo, Tej Zadoo, and Veena Pandita.

I am indebted to my brothers, Bhuvanesh, Chander shekhar, Pankaj, and (late !) Kshemendra; sisters, Usha, Kalpana, and Prerna as also my mother (late) Mohini, who all, form a multi-dimensional world for me, and interactions with whom enriched me always.

I received from Himanshu Koul handy help, whenever my computer had any hiccups.

My special appreciations are for Anubhav, my son, who took extra care in managing and smoothening all the hassles of the publication of this work.

I express my immense gratitude to all the above persons.

Tej

Contents :

Pronunciation Key for *Devanāgrī* vowels

Given below is a tabular guide of Devanāgrī vowels, along with their symbols, and their denotations in English alphabet used (generally in *italics*) all through, in the text of the book for transcribing the words of *Sańskṛta* origin in the Roman mode of transcription. English words, communicating phonetically (nearly) similar sounds are cited to provide an idea of their pronunciation. Examples of their actual use in transcribing *Sańskṛta* words in roman mode of transcription is also provided .

vowel	*symbol*	*Denoted as:*	*Sounds as the magnified letter in the given words (English and Sańskṛta both).*
अ	ऽ	A, a	*akula,* (अकुल) , *tato-api* (ततोऽपि)
आ	ा	Ā, ā	*tar* , ; *ābhāsa* (आभास)
इ	ि	I, i	*sit rEmain ; idam, tithi,* (इदं, तिथि)
ई	ी	Ī, ī	*see , thief ; īśwara, bīja* (ईश्वर, बीज)
उ	ु	U, u	*pUt ; umā, mukt* (उमा , मुक्त)
ऊ	ू	Ū, ū	*brUis ; ūnat, rūpa* (ऊनत , रूप)
ए	े	E, e	*HAte , sAi ; dEha* (देह)
ऐ	ै	Ai, ai	*eye , I ; vaikhari* (वैखरी)

ओ	ो	O, o	*BOar , grOw ; mOha (मोह)*
औ	ौ	Ao, ao	*B OW l , l OU d ; kAOshala (कौशल)*
अं	ं	Ň, ň	*HUNt ; Ahaňkār (अहंकार)*
अ:	:	Ĥ, ĥ	*Ah! ; pratah (प्रात:)*
ऋ	ृ	ṛ	*kṛšna ; pṛthvī (पृथ्वी)*

Next is the table of additional vowel-sounds (specific to Kashmiri Language,) introduced into *Devanaagri* Script* with their symbols (for illustrations, almost matching equivalent sounds in English, wherever possible, are provided, along with some usages in the Kashmiri language).

[* *For complete study of the whole regime the book 'Mātṛkā_* pūrna-devanāgrī *lipi' (A complete script for the phonetic transcription of Kashmiri and several other languages and dialects of India) by the author,* may be *consulted.*]

Kashmiri usage

Vowel	*Symbol*	*sounding key*	
अ꣡	꣡	*FErn , fIr*	कच (how many) गर (watch) नर (arm)
अ꣢	꣢	*HErtz , pErt*	असु (mouth) मल (appetite)

अ॒	◡	*Kr̥śna* *	चु (you) सुच (tailor)
अ॒	⌒	*No matching sound in English available*	त्र (cold) सत्य् (along)
अि	ि	*cOmmunicate*	कित (where) दिर (hard)
अि	ि	*vOcation , bOy*	विथ (get up) दिद (milk)
ए	⁄	*sEmi*	र्ख (eat) र्ष (six)
एं	⁄	*yEt , hEckle*	सँख (sand) छँन (separation)

(*) In the word Kr̥śna , r̥ does not sound as अ॒ *but actually it is the stress of vowel sound on r that has phonetic feel of* अ॒ .

Key for the transcription of consonants

Consonants in *Devanāgri* script are classified in *vargas* according to the mode of delivery of the (Sanskrit language) words out of the oral cavity during speaking. Roman script does not transcribe many such words or sounds, and therefore a modification in the transcription of certain letters is helpful for the adaptation of Roman script for such transcription. For instance, in addition to an *anuswar* vowel अं , there are three more distinct nasal sounds and also a half sound of *n* and *m* each, to be accounted for. We here shall be using three nasal-consonant symbols to cater to the nasal *varṇas* of different *vargas*. Symbol ñ and ṇ for *varga* च and ट respectively and only ň for k-*varga nasal* and also *anuswar* because of their marked resemblance, and therefore less discrimination in their verbal delivery. Since there is no symbol for the transcription of aspirated-sounds of different *vargas* in Roman-script, addition of *h* to the respective non-aspirated sound is resorted to, for instance, *kh* for ख when *k* is used for क . Again, since त *verga* letters are used more often than ट *varga* letters, *t, th, d, dh,* are used for त *varga*, and *ŧ, ŧh, đ, đh,* are used for ट *varga* letters for the discrimination of the use of *t* and *d*. There being no ष and श sounds but only स sound of this class, in Roman mode, *s*, the letter indicating स is used as š , ś respectively for ष and श sound, while simply s is used for स . Similarly there being no च sound available, ć is used for it and ćh for its aspirated sound छ . Again since क्ष is a compound *varana* of क and ष , it is therefore indicated accordingly by *k* and š together as *kš* and as ज्ञ is a conjunct of ज and अ and pronounced generally as '*gya*' (and also as *gny or jny*), it has been indicated here simply as ġ , word *gyāna* (ज्ञान) is therefore written as ġāna.

(In addition to the consonants used for transcribing Saňskṛta and Hindi there is yet another *varga* that follows ć-*varga* (and is uttered by touching the back of the upper frontal teeth with the tip of tongue during the oral delivery of its *vaṛṇas*. These sounds are peculiar to Kashmiri, Marāthi etc. languages and are denoted by putting a dot under ć – *varga vaṛṇas* with which these have a resemblance. These are not indicated here.)

A tabular layout of all consonants of *Devanāgri* letters in different *vargas* is given ahead. Under each letter, the corresponding equivalent Roman mode of transliteration used in the book is shown. This table, in addition to the one's given earlier for the vowels can be a useful key for grasping the method adopted for such transliteration.

क　　ख　　ग　　घ　　ङ

k　　*kh*　　*g*　　*gh*　　*ň*

च　　छ　　ज　　झ　　ञ

ć　　*ćh*　　*j*　　*jh*　　*ñ*

ट　　ठ　　ड　　ढ　　ण

ŧ　　*ŧh*　　*đ*　　*đh*　　*ṇ*

च　　छ　　ज　　झ　　ञ

ć　　*ćh*　　*j*　　*jh*　　*ñ*

त　　थ　　द　　ध　　न

t　　*th*　　*d*　　*dh*　　*n*

प	फ	ब	भ	म
p	*ph*	*b*	*bh*	*m*

य	र	ल	व
y	*r*	*l*	*v*

श	ष	स	ह	क्ष	ज्ञ
š	*ś*	*s*	*h*	*kš*	*ġ*

Abbreviations

Some abbreviations have been used in the book on certain occasions. These refer to certain sources and publications. Following are the actual referred titles along with the abbreviations that have been used in the book.

1) (IPKV) : *Iśwara-Pratyabhigana-Karika vritti.* (see Ref. 5)

2) (KSTS) : *Kashmir series of Texts and Studies.*

3) (MLBD) : *Motilal Banarsidass, Publishers, Delhi.*

4) (NTU) : *Netra Tantra* with *Uddyota* by *Kšhemaraja,* (see Ref. 7)

5) (Pbh)-x : *Pratyabhijñāhṛdayam* [with Sūtra number] (see Ref. 16)

6) (PT)- x : *Parātrīśikā* [with Sūtra number] (see Ref. 12)

7) (PT)-x/y : *Parātrīśikā –Vivarana* [page/line number] (see Ref. 12)

8) (Sp.S) : *Spada-Sandoha* (see Ref. 6)

9) (SS-x)-y : *Śiva-Sūtras* [with chapter and Sūtra nuber] Th. Jaidev Singh. (Pub. MLBD, Delhi.)

Trika

The perspective

Preface

Śaiva wisdom of Kashmir is very ancient, and was communicated down the centuries through oral traditions, but recorded in texts giving details of the delicate philosophical perspective, the clues about the actual experiences the sages had, as also the guidelines for the genuine aspirants of the reality, discussing the appropriate ways for such pursuit into the exploration of their true self. Such manuscript-information dates back to about eighth century A.D. with Vasugupta's documentations. Later writings and compilations continued from time to time. Foremost amongst many others mentioned in line are the names of Somānanda, Utpaldeva, Abhinavgupta, Kshemrāja, Bhāskara, Varadarāja, etc. The literature comprises basically three kinds, namely *Āgma*, (believed to be direct revelations, handed down orally from *guru* to *Śiṡya*, in utterances as crisp *Sūtras*), *Spanda*, the doctrines sorted out and elaborated upon in detail with interpretations, and thirdly, the *Pratyabhiġa shastrās* comprising discussions, arguments and counter-arguments, with logical interpretations.

My aim in documenting this modest title, '*Trika , the Kashmir Śaiva Essence* ', a humble presentation of the most profound truth, is simply to trace, in a coherent continuity, the basic, the essential communication of *Trika* wisdom, as I conceive it, and put it before the readers, only to motivate them for seeking a broader and more comprehensive perspective of it. I have attempted to present in this book, how, a contemporary, scientific and rational approach of looking at the mundane reality projects certain baffling aspects of it and raises some nagging questions demanding answers. The very questions that led me to seek answers from the *śaiva* wisdom, which, layer by layer peeled off most of the dross my thoughts had gathered and the notions I had installed in my within. I have precisely documented the same line of approach that opened up a perspective for me, substantiating each move with *Sutras* from different *śaiva* sources. I invite the serious reader to probe deeper and contemplate without any resistance of prejudice to partake of the lofty wisdom of *śaiva* !

Tej Raina, Jammu.
(Dec. 2012.)

Introduction

Immense cosmic emptiness (space) is represented by nothing, no known thing at all. We know it as empty, but that does not mean we know it. It truly is unknown. Presence of something may be recognizable, but the absence of a recognizable may be the presence of something else, not discernible by the known means and understanding. Any visible solid is after all not so solid and continuous as it looks, and we believe it is, because, it does not show to our eyes the hollows; it harbors in the most of its within, with sparse punctuation of molecules, and within them similarly, the (so-called) elementary particles. And an invisible odorless gas is not without any content, as it looks. A floating iceberg, in an ocean, on a hot summer day, is a system of three different entities, the ice, the water and the vapor, all of which are objectively the same content, presented differently at the same time. Different is not the content of the three but the placement of their building blocks or rather the *empty spaces* within them. It is the relative spatial layout of the elementary particles they are made of, which gives them the distinctness of their features and qualities. And what after all, ultimately, is this matter that forms these materials? Who knows! Is vacuum truly empty? Studies in the domain of quantum theory have shown that even at absolute zero (-273° C) temperature, when it would appear that an oscillator has no energy reserve whatsoever, it continues to perform zero-oscillations, with the residual half-quantum reserve of energy, which it always retains, and cannot be taken away from it. This zero-point energy[1] (manifesting in Casimir effect, and Lamb-shift perturbations), is an intrinsic property of vacuum. Investigations into subtler objective aspects of vacuum may reveal a lot many, yet unknown, features of it, but, indeterminacy will still persist at the level, where there is non-differentiation between non-objective and objective states. A keen, discerning mind may be able to lay hold on the subtlest of the thoughts or feelings, even when they are just emerging into distinctness of their form, or exist still in their earlier, somewhat vague, formative stage, but can never perceive them in their nursery of un-differentiated levels. On the arrival of a new thought, decay of the earlier thought in its cognitive stage, is clearly succeeded by a seemingly blank, no-thought, mental-space, that precedes the new thought. This blank space provides distinctness to the new thought, as much as it acts as a bosom for the old thought, to go into a sleep of oblivion, but not annihilation. This indeterminate, blank mental space, without any objective character or form, acts like an indefinable and inaccessible field, for the sprouting of the new, and sinking in of the old, discernible feelings and thoughts. Teeming with infinite number of all the un-differentiated thoughts and feelings, that ever existed, or shall ever come into existence, this level of consciousness is indeterminate for mental reach, as it does not possess any discernible thought in it, although, any of the feeblest of the most feeble probes, whatever, can cause any of them to flower forth. Rationality, idealization and other like terminologies, after all, refer to our perceptions of finding an order in the known, and a visualization of the unknown. The known is always limited by the means of knowing, and the means are always objectively defined. Idealization also is possible within the objective references, because our mind cannot perceive except in objective terminologies. This sets a barrier for our resolving faculties mentally, beyond which our *known* faculties cannot operate. In objective phenomena the means of knowing re-express and re-orient their horizons from time to time. If our 'known' shuffles its presentations, what do we hold on to? What changes have not occurred in our concepts about our own physical world around and within us in just a few past decades, or a few hundred years! And then, how aware are we of the lots of *very well-known* things, or the most intimate things around us! How aware, for instance, are we about the air surrounding us all the time? An occasional sudden whiff of any aroma, or else, a pressure wave in air presenting itself as some kind of sound, any time, may briefly make us conscious of the medium around us. But do we see the ever-present patterns of the gas molecules laid out all around us in a strictly disciplined mutual relationship, even in the seemingly chaotic flow of all the gases, as also, all the other so-called, abstract things in air that comprise our atmosphere? Can we see or perceive the chaotic crowd of the multitudes of the wave phenomena drowning us every time in them? A beam of light passing just across my field of vision does not make itself visible to me unless its presence is felt only when intercepted by any material, even dust, that is brightened up by it. Even then, I don't see more than a glare or glint. I don't see the procession at all of the infinitely various packets of energy (if they are packets), the quanta as they are called, in extremely unflinchingly, disciplined patterns, parading in front of me. I do not admire the perpetual dance of an unending host of infinitesimal energy packets, of a specific kind, that presents itself as a colored patch of green in a leaf or red in a petal of rose. What image patterns, the invisible tiny rays of light shooting in the space all around me, carry in the placements of their energy packets mutually, or rather the placements of the gaps in between the energy packets, or actually, the mutual relationships of quanta and gasps remains shrouded in mystery. This objective and non-objective presence of the energy in each of its wave-fronts is not at all visible to me. Only when, an appropriately interacting interception occurs, something may show up. A beam of light starting from an incandescent source of light, and passing through a slide or an exposed film will reveal the image it carries of the slide, if it hits a white opaque screen which acts temporarily as a non-interfering witness to it. A beam, on the other hand, that has just kissed a face or a panoramic view, and carries its imprint, will not reveal anything even to a white opaque screen, or an appropriately interacting chemical screen, (like an optically sensitive film inside the dark chamber of a camera and in absence of any other interacting input) unless resolved and focused on to it. Such a film acts as a pure witness, retaining the image temporarily, as a memory in a chemical pattern, as long as no other input interferes, distorts it or destroys it; or else a fixing chemical alters its composition to a permanent, chemically structured pattern, similar to the look of the basic pattern borne by the beam. Alternatively the beam may be tapped for information by an electronic device, to recreate an electronic memory in a digital pattern, which can be viewed as an accurately faithful replica of the original information carried by the beam. This orientation or re-orientation of patterns is an exchange of energies, a re-orientation of energies in the realm of invisible. The tender lightening up of everything at dawn, or the magical folding of an enchanting panorama into soft darkness gently at the dusk, the delicate lights and shades, the soft and harsh hues, that beautify or light up the surroundings, as much as a poet's visualization or a lover's mind is actually a play and interplay of tiny packets of energy. The tiniest of a pencil of light emerging from the sun, or any other source of light, carries unimaginable and stupendous information, in the complex patterns of photons, of all infinitely varied energies, present and absent, in the source, or, about all the various media it has encountered and passed through. A lot of such information can be harnessed, by the means, and the knowledge available to us at present, while so much still remains, and shall remain, forever obscure. We may not lose much, by not having all the information available to us, but we do lose the experience of greatest ecstasies by not being aware of the indescribable cosmic dance of these feeble and delicate energy-pattern entities. A tiny ray of light meeting our eyes and entering our pupil excites numberless switches[2] before and after reaching the screen of the retina of our eyes. The processes involving identification, classification, rationalization, or the storage of the memory-record, or our responses associated with them on physiological and psychological levels, comprising numberless neuron signals and biochemical activities, all expressible in their structural patterns are extremely profound. They remain un-witnessed and unappreciated by a normal state of our mind. Any visual-probe may sometimes initiate a flux in our thoughts and feelings, which can provoke some specific response from us, or even cause a change in our personality matrix. Sometimes, even our determinative faculty may get altered. If considered keenly in its entirety, we can find that a probe, a signal, a pattern of energy input, can alter the chemistry of our feelings and responses, or even the chemistry of our personality or our determinative faculty. All physical, chemical or biological expressions, all experiences, activities and thoughts, are expressible in patterns. Our feelings and urges, our knowledge and rationale, our desires and perseverance, and the totality of our personality, all, are woven in the fabric of patterns, with defined boundary conditions, self-limiting and self adapting. So seems to be the rule in the inanimate also. Alteration of a boundary condition, say, the electric potential of a conductor changes the distribution of its surface electrons, realigning them to move in a particular order as an electric current, and simultaneously, manifesting as associated magnetic properties. Subjecting an electric current to constrictions in its flow by narrowing its path or by altering the composition of the conductor makes it exhibit different incandescence (emission of light or heat) properties. Decrease of the surrounding temperature to the neighborhood of absolute-zero value can make a conductor, a super-conductor with hardly any resistance to the flow of current, or make certain materials to behave as super-fluids with properties contrary to those exhibited according to the normal laws of physics. The intrinsic adaptability of the materials is inherent in the materials, as is interaction, within the living things, coded within them. A single sperm cell, on contacting an ovum, fertilizes it to produce an embryo which grows systematically into a full-fledged young one, complete, like the bearers of the sperm or the ovum. Each step in its growth is meticulously regulated and accomplished. Not a single cell in its developmental phase divides more or less than that needed for the appropriate development of each system, organ or unit. Such in-built programming, for switching in and out, of any activity, like the response, interaction, adaptability, etc., are subtle and marvelous features of the entire objective world, all coded in the basic matrix of each unit. Our being able or unable to explain it, through the patterns of our models of understanding, does not matter. The truth is, that *it is*, and the truth of its being an inherent potential with appropriate information for continuing that way, is the most outstanding feature of everything. The structure of each living and non-living unit is a pattern, and therefore the creation is expressible in a matrix of patterns. And what are patterns? The definitions, the boundary conditions, the specific information, all scaled into specific potentialities needed for their defined modes of being, expression, and interaction as empirical individuals. It is all coded in their matrices intrinsically. In simple terms, all objectivity is potency, in a multitude of intensely accurate matrices of expression, __the potency *in operation* for its *objective expression* ! What this potency is and how it expresses itself as an objective existence, animate and inanimate, or living and non-living, at micro and macro levels, as the entire objective world of the strata of discernible, is not known. Spatiotemporal references of the dynamical properties, and other behaviors in the domains of cause and effect fix the attributes of the objective world, but pursuing the studies of these manifestations to the extreme limits make their comprehension intangible. Classical physics describes most of these attributes in non-relativistic dynamical states and normal macroscopic domains fairly well, but micro, the subatomic, and the outermost fringe levels of the universe project enigmatic and un-resolvable challenges. Scientific studies reveal that structures and forms, as also all attributes of matter, are a manifestation of the internal spatial relations of the constituents of materials, the molecules or the basic elementary particles. But then what these constituents are basically made of themselves, and how do these correlate for their expression as living and non-living entities is an enigma. What were believed to be the most stable and irreducible constituents of matter at nuclear level, namely protons and neutrons, are now found to be able to swap their identities, for instance, via the exchange of an electron and a neutrino, and are also actually an outcome of the manifestations of internal spatial relation of some other entities. Theoretical postulations, and later, actual deep inelastic scattering experiments conducted in high energy particle accelerators have transformed the status of the fundamental constituents of all matter. All stable and unstable nuclear particles, *hadrons* (protons and neutrons being the most stable ones) are found essentially to be formed out of *quarks*[3] and *leptons.* Quantum mechanics has changed the concept of deterministic correlations and approaches, with respect to the micro-world to statistical correlations of events and things. It is established that measured outcomes and preconditions do not explain or interpret quantum behaviors. Say for instance according to quantum descriptions *any* conceivable event has a probability greater than zero, which means that *everything* is possible. This certainly does not correlate to our tangible world, but all the same it has yielded new approaches to the handling of many illusive problems. We know now that the existence of objects hinges on the *fuzziness* of the relative position and momentum[4] of their basic constituents. Mathematically rigorous and philosophically sound way of quantifying a fuzzy observable is to assign probabilities to the possible outcomes of a measurement of this observable, which projects their existence as formless and attribute-less entities. This lack of form and specific structure in the *truly elementary* particles creates a picture, that this manifestation of form and attributes, is formed out of a formless existence. The question is whether these formless (and therefore attribute-less as such) entities are truly the constituents of matter, or just a stage, only instrumental, in the evolution of material objects. Again since these formless *particles* are not discernible, they represent a *single entity* capable of *multiple presentations*, as the true constituent of the manifestation. The question, what these *formless* entities, the so called *elementary particles* are made of, thus becomes irrelevant as much as that, if the differentiation of space gives rise to the forms that are objects, to what lowest physical limit can the differentiation happen. It seems that, not space, but an *unrestricted* and *limitless* *potency*, actually differentiates itself into a multitude of spatial-orientations with itself, to produce the forms and structures, and thereby all the visible multitude of objects with all various attributes, and their inter-related causal diversity. Therefore, the manifestation of space, (space being the totality of the spatial relations of forms) and matter (the entire multitude of quality-bearing forms), even up to the domains of formless and attribute-less entities, with no internal spatial relations, are only self-differentiations with itself, of some unique absolute potency ! Theory of Relativity has already established the inter-dependence of time, space and mass through the dynamical aspects of the latter and thus their relativity. Truly does all this attribute-full immense variety of matter, with baffling behaviors of space and time, seem to be the manifestation of some ineffable existence, not accessible through the material means, and beyond the causal interpretations. *How then do we find the truth of the totality of our being (?)*, an enigma that evades any objective solution !

And the greater still enigma is: *what is it* which perceives and discerns all these objective phenomena? *What* is the *subject* , that perceives all this objectivity? If the subject is also objective in nature, then all perceptions become an object-object interaction, and then, no perception would be a true perception but a variable, perpetually differing, indistinct statement of a phenomenon, and then, a subject as a pure witness only, wouldn't exist. But, as we believe, if it is consciousness that discerns, then the question arises about its location and the process of its functioning. Is consciousness every individual's separate personal reality, occurring as multitudes of consciousness aspects, (in which case perceptions would again be variable), or a singular and uniform reality that provides similar perception of an event to all individuals, (only individual responses depending upon their mental approaches would then vary), thus giving consciousness the recognition of a pure witness. Then again, the location and nature of consciousness is a problem staring in our face. Looking at a tender (colorful) flower, or a charming beautiful face, that presents many aspects of its being in color, texture, curvatures and charm, with an overall balance and symmetry, relating to our vision, and also to our feelings and responses, initiates very many activities in several different centers of our brain, in terms of specific neurobiological manifestations. *What* coordinates all these processed inputs, and to *what* is this entire perception presented for the final discernment and response? If it is brain itself, then the *subject* is an aspect of brain, and the consciousness only a neurobiological activity, and all of it actually an objective phenomenon. This raises a question whether 'brain, the material' is conscious, and also, whether 'consciousness is material'. The fact is that any object, whatever, presents information, say through visual signals, which is received by various optical receptors and coordinated by various neurobiological processes in the brain into a coordinated and comprehensive report which is presented to the subject. 'What' *is* that subject ? And where ? There are channels between the things 'out there' and the brain, all various objective entities, gross or subtle, that connect the phenomenon out there, to the brain. But how does the brain then connect to the *subject* that has not to be an objective entity. Or is it, that there is no need for that connection at all? Does *subject*, the *consciousness*, in fact not accessible to brain, *itself* look *through* the brain(s), at the objective phenomenon (that registers *similarly* and uniformly to all). If so, why does it not then *look* directly (rather than through the brain) at the phenomenon, whatever, that occurs in the domain of objective, out there. Why does it need the brain to process all that information in a specific way for its perception that way, or does consciousness *need to look at it all, through the brain to perceive it that way?* Why does consciousness need to subject itself to all these conditions and confinements of perceiving through the material entities, when it is not a material entity itself? Is it that, if the consciousness looks directly at the objective phenomenon, it will not see what we see, (as we see through our perceptive faculties aided by the brain). Is it because the consciousness wants to see the material phenomenon as we the material existents perceive it, or is it because our material being will not perceive anything at all, in spite of all the neurobiological processing by the brain unless the consciousness gets linked to it. We are, in fact, actually confronted with the most subtle question of all : *What is consciousness? And ' how ' does the perception of the 'objective' and its attributes happen to it ?* Also, *has it any bearing on the reality of our true being ?*

We all know that the perception of any objective entity needs the *presence* of the subject with that. The event has to be *in the present*, with the subject, the consciousness. Even a memory or a thought, only when linked *in the present* to the consciousness is discerned, or else it has no existence. This means that the objective *finds* its existence only when consciousness discerns it, recognizes it. The question is: are the two, the objective and the consciousness, two *different* entities? If so, then, how does the consciousness know the objective? (And why is the objective unable to know the consciousness?) In fact how can any *one* actually know the *other*? Or is it that the two are basically *one*, and differ only in the state of their *being*, their *presentation*? In other words, *one* being *a* different expression of the *other ;* consciousness a purely attribute-less, un-confined, witnessing-existence aspect of the infinitely attribute-full existence of the *form* and *structure* of the same reality. In that case, consciousness is *'the always witnessing'* reality and the objective the *witnessed reality*, in whatever perspective, of the *single existence!* The witness simply links with the event by giving attention to it. Unless the attention links, the experience doesn't happen. The consciousness is there, *ever there*, (it has to be ever there, or else no experience can ever occur, no objectivity ever register). It may link itself or remain in abeyance, it may be attentive or not attentive, but it is never absent (else, no call to attention could ever commission it). On its being directed to the objective, the attributes of the objective become its focus, therefore, if directed to itself, it should *be* only itself. *Witness, witnessing Itself!* Awareness aware of the pure *being* of *itself!*

Scientific postulation or experimental investigation may not reveal except up to the material, the objective borders, limited by its own boundary conditions. What we are left with then, is tapping for all the answers about the consciousness from the consciousness itself, by penetrating into *it*, consciously, attentively !

This is what *trika* (त्रिका) approach is all about. *Trika* holds that an ineffable reality with unrestricted potency manifests out of itself everything that is manifest, remaining itself ever, the foundation and the faculty inherent *within*, and providing the means for continuance, change, or adaptability for all that is manifest! *Trika* is the triad of *Śiva*, *Śakti*, and *nara* (नर). *Śiva*, is the *being* aspect of the reality, ever in the transcendental (*parā*, परा) plane as a completely non-differentiated (*abheda*, अभेद) and indeterminate *reality* ; *Śakti*, the *unrestricted* and infinite potency of *Śiva* (the means, mode, and material, for the manifestation as *everything*, its maintenance as also the withdrawal), and therefore both the transcendental and the immanent (*parāparā*, परा-अपरा), or in other words differentiated and non-differentiated (*bhedabheda*, भेद-अभेद) reality, thus both indeterminate as well as determinate in its aspects; and *nara*, the empirical existence, representing the manifested objectivity, the entirely differentiated (*bheda*) and therefore determinate, and thus an immanent (*aparā*) reality. In essence, *Siva* is pure *Consciousness*, absolute and un-altering, while *Śakti* is the *Dynamic-Consciousness* (the consciousness '*in action*') both in the transcendental as well the immanent domains of existence, and *nara* is ultimate terminal in the immanent existence of *that Śakti*, 'the Dynamic-Consciousness'. All the three aspects exist in absolutely undifferentiated state in the totally ineffable point (*bindu*, बिन्दु) of *Mahā-satta* (महासत्ता), the absolute reality of *Ćinmaya-puruśa-sattatva* (चिन्मय पुरुष सत्तत्व), which is *sarvaġa* (सर्वज्ञ, all knowing), *Sarvakṛtatva* (सर्वकृतत्व , capable of doing *everything*), and therefore entirely autonomous and sovereign (*swatantra*, स्वतंत्र). Termed therefore as *vimarśamaya-prakāśa*[5] (विमर्शमयप्रकाश), it is an all-knowing, all-doing *will* in *being*, the unsurpassable (*Anuttra*, अनुत्तर) also called *parā-Bhairava* (पराभैरव) , or *parama-Śiva* (परमशिव) .

This approach is unlike the *Vedantic* that holds that the ultimate *brahm* is only *parkāśa* of existence, which to a *Śaive, a trika*, means only an inert entity that leaves doubts and question about the validity of creation and other several allied aspects, unexplained. For a *trika*, *Vimarśa*, the awareness of the potency of its being, provides *Siva* the aspects of *sarvaġata*, (all knowing-ness) and *sarvakṛtatvta* (all doing-ness), and thereby the complete *swātantrya*, the greatest bliss of complete autonomy and sovereignty. This lands the ineffable *Śiva* in a state of absolute indeterminacy. What can be known about that *infinite* and *unsurpassable* by the limited means of knowledge and understanding that we posses. No qualities or attributes can be associated with it, because, each of such *knowns*, would put a catch in it, define it, and thus put a finite limit to it. As an indeterminate, it can present itself as anything in any way, being itself, the source and the sustenance of everything conceivable. And that is what provides an empirical being a means of touching that truth beyond all the borders and reaches. Since that forms our reality, the reality of everything, the penetration into our own being may provide to us the recognition of ourselves and our source the *Parama-Śiva*. And that is what *Śaiva approach* into the *trika reality* is all about. It is not an armchair philosophy conceived in mind and presented on paper or in a discourse. It is an approach to experience the reality in all its multi-dimensional perspectives and in essence too. It is about a true recognition of one's reality and a complete, consequent transformation of the concepts and pursuits, rather an actual enjoying of the sovereignty and freedom of *being.*

Anuttra, the unsurpassable !

त्युथ मे करनाव युथ नु आसि करनुय कंह !

"Make me do *such*, that I need to do nothing else," prayed Kriśnajū Rāzdān, a highly revered Kashmiri *Śaiva* saint, not long ago. What was it that he aspired for? What need be done so that nothing else is required to be done?

Seekers even from the remotest past, as they began to come with grips of exploring the entire manifestation desired to find out:
' What is that, by knowing which, one needs to know nothing else?' Knowing *such*, that nothing *else* need be known! Is it a statement that smacks of arrogance? Knowing too much! Or in fact, was it a desire for freedom, from both, the *known* and the *knowing*? What needs be known, so that one needs, not to know *anything* else, or that, there is no *need* to *know* anything at all? Is it to *recognize* the *knowledge* and the *need* for it, both, and therefore have freedom from both? Freedom _ the eternal quest, the *mokša!*

"मोक्षो हि नाम नैवान्यः स्वरूपप्रथनं हि तत् "
(tantrāloka. I, p-192)

Said Abhinavgupta[6] : "*Mokša* is nothing else but awareness of one's true nature, real *swarūp*." True nature cannot be the one that is assumed, taken on or considered in terms of an identification with something. Being aware of oneself needs no props to justify it. Knowledge can be acquired, awareness is intrinsic. Knowledge can be true or untrue but awareness is the being of it, in actuality and in entirety. The discernment through awareness has to be unique and not comparable. How then can awareness of oneself be duplicated. Awareness therefore gets a pedestal higher than *anything* else, in fact the highest, because only awareness can recognize itself. Awareness thus is the ultimate judge, the absolute subject that has the ultimate knowledge of oneself intrinsically and not through assumptions or in patches, by definitions or categories, classifications, or descriptions, but beyond all that, in actuality and entirety, with all the authority at command. Awareness is *being*, without props and justification! Free ! In mundane considerations too, freedom and confidence rule as long as one does not try to live what one is not (even by worldly evaluations). Once the posing, or behaving as what one is not begins, the whole life becomes a muddle. It is crushed within a vicious circle of falsehood and misery. Precisely, the empirical individual suffers in all the multifarious ways, only due to false identifications with what one believes oneself to be, and thus gets involved in a host of complex and endless apprehensions, pursuits and miseries, in the world. Being oneself, is being the master of one-self, and therefore being truly free. Nothing else needs to be known or done, as everything is encountered in actuality, and thus dealt with naturally, as it happens, effortlessly and spontaneously. In the mundane world this truth is no less valid, although with some boundary conditions, (since the mundane life is after all, defined by boundary conditions), but for sages like Abhinavgupta or Krišnajū Rāzdān, being oneself has spiritual connotations. It refers to a transcendental state of *being* also, sovereign and *swatantra*, because, although to us they are visible *as a body*, they themselves *are aware* of their *true* being at the same time. In fact, if *awareness* is the ultimate judge or the subject, then what else can be the actual *self*. Being aware is living the real *swabhāva* , the true self.

चैतन्यमात्मा

(chaitanyamātmā)

...Sūtra-(ss -I- 1)

" Awareness is (our) true (self) essence. "

The very first of *Śiva-sūtras* (चैतन्यम ~ आत्मा) declares that *ćaitanya*, the awareness, is *ātma*, the true essence, the core of our being, the self. ' *I* am ' is an assertion of my being. ' *I* ' represents or refers to my entity, conceived in whatever way, as body-mind, as personality, a composite of name and shape, or concept, visualized in terms of thoughts, whatever, but *am* is the essence. 'Am' need not be imagined or thought of, or given a name or shape. *Am* is awareness of being. No one need to tell me *I* 'am' . No thoughts or logic need to justify it. 'I am' is the awareness of my being. This awareness fixes my subjectivity, my presence! It is the light that switches on my presence. *What* I am, *is* my belief, not the truth. The truth is only that I 'am', the *vimarśa*, the sense of अहं, the awareness of being present, which is not there when I am fast asleep, (everything *else* remaining as usual). Would this awareness persist, even when body functions were in a slowed down state of deep-sleep, with all the thoughts in abeyance, then alone, could I start recognizing myself, not through the agency of, or in terms of, thoughts, and all the maize presented by them (all those being then, in abeyance), but through pure awareness. Awareness has the freedom of being anything, because *being* anything is the awareness of its being. It is the pure awareness *itself*, in actuality, without having to become anything, and that *is the essence*. When it becomes anything, it is *sṛṣṭi*, in any of its innumerable aspects, into which it is manifested. It is the *Śakti* in action, the *Kriyā* aspect of *Anuttra*. *Anuttra*, the un-manifest, the pure undifferentiated awareness, is the entirety of the transcendental as well as the immanent reality, while anything manifest, is actually a partial commitment of the awareness, the consciousness of an empirical aspect only, (within some defined boundary conditions). It is in fact awareness focused on certain boundary conditions. If the awareness is turned on itself, it is *Anuttra*. No analogies can define this profundity, as the analogies are conducted through thoughts, which would be, an objective definition of the subjective role. Referred to, as *Baindavi kala* in

Śaiva, it would be like an attempt by a person, moving away from the sun, to set his foot over the head of his own shadow !, futile objective exercise ! The attempt need not be dismissed by tagging it as impossible, which only refers to the objective aspect of investigation. If it were the only way then an empirical being could, in no case know the truth or realize his *self.* No, there is a way. The Awareness! This is the only link. Each individual, although a committed soul, is after all, *soul*, the consciousness, or else he wouldn't be what he is. He would be, not even nothing, because there is nothing, not even the absence of *any-thing*, that could be perceived without consciousness. This consciousness when directed on itself is nothing but pure awareness, the *Anuttra. Ćaitanyam-ātmā* (चैतन्यम ~ आत्मा) is the way. Each individual self actually, is awareness. And by being aware, of one-self purely, one touches one's core, one's *self*, recognizes 'it', and then subsequently, recognizes the *pure*-awareness (पर्मात्मा), the *Parama-Śiva!* No description in words, or fabrication in thoughts, even the most subtle, can lead any one, any way, near this intimate realization of the actuality, the ultimate reality. All such attempts are illusory. It would be making love through an interpreter ! All the knowledge is just the husk, or the shell, or even the kernel, but the core is the potency of creation in it, the *awareness*! Knowledge is, only definition or information of a specific and particular structure, of thoughts or some tangible and material existence, relevant only to *an* aspect of existence. This is precisely what is declared in *Śiva-sūtra – (2).*

ज्ञानं बन्धः

(Ġānam bandhaĥ)

...Sūtra-(ss -I- 2)

This *Sūtra* actually is very subtle, only two words *Ġānam* and *bandhah* making one sūtra, the very second *Śiva-sūtra*, and that too, following at the heels of "*Ćaitanyam ātmā*", the first *sūtra*. It has to be very profound, and needs to be seen very cautiously. If *Ġāna* is knowledge, any knowledge, regarding whatsoever, the transcendental or the mundane, and *bandhaĥ* is bondage, that inhibits freedom, then one needs to know which *Ġāna*, the knowledge of what, is a cause for bondage. To find a clue to it, it may be worthwhile to consider the *Sūtras* (*1 & 2*) together in continuity, as : (चैतन्यम आत्मा ज्ञानं बन्धः). Considering three of the four words चैतन्यमात्मा ज्ञानं, (*Chaitanyamātmā Ġānam*) we get a communication: *knowing* that '*awareness is the true-self* ', is *Ġāna*, the true knowledge ; and then, like चैतन्यमात्मऽज्ञानं बन्धः (*Chaitanyamātma-aġānam bandhaĥ*), the four words mean that '*lack of knowledge*' that '*awareness is the true-self* ' is the cause of bondage. The *Ġāna* here need not imply the awareness in actuality of it, but even an intellectual or intuitive knowledge only, since *Ġāna* implies the acquired knowledge also. Even then this understanding is potent enough to cause a strong motivation for the realization of the truth ultimately. If various other dimensions of the meaning of word *bandhaĥ* are considered, a very many new dimensions of the communication of the sūtra come to fore. *Bandhaḥ* means (also) a construct, a framework, an arrangement, and this aspect of the meaning of *bandhaḥ* brings up a different communication from the two *sūtras* "चैतन्यम आत्मा ज्ञानं बन्धः" as: " *awareness* is the core, the *self* (of everything), and *Ġāna* is (only) *structured knowledge* ". Also, the essence, the core of anything is pure awareness of its *being* in actuality, without any specific constructs of words or forms to define or present it, while knowledge is its 'info' presented in any form. Knowledge could even be the inherent, *intrinsic knowledge* like a programmed data within a specific construct, to coordinate or direct its functioning. This could apply to any and every construct or *framework*. Awareness is free and sovereign and therefore unbounded foundational core of everything, which on assuming a pattern (specific and bounded), remains inherent in it as its limited knowledge. *I am,* signifies my 'being' in the word '*am*' , the presence, which is the sense of being, undefined or unbounded, without a name and form, while '*I*' can be anything, a man, a child, a father, a lover, a conditioned entity with definitions and boundary conditions. My functionality is defined, guided, and coordinated by *that* concept or structure. There is nothing wrong in being *this* or *that,*__ a father or a son, even simultaneously, it is owned. I act and interact accordingly, as a specific entity. Knowledge is committed awareness, and not a bondage. It is a specified understanding in a specific framework. It has not to be the totality of awareness, but only a *directing* awareness, [*directing* is another of the meanings of the word *badhaĥ*]. How else otherwise, does each infant, every animal, including a microorganism, as also every herbaceous living unit, and even for that matter, each individual constituent cell of all living phenomenon, *know* intrinsically, and exactly how to respond to the probes and stimuli, and even to adapt to a changing environment. Intrinsic knowledge, as specified awareness, does it all ! Even a stone *knows* its boundary conditions and remains as a stone, as water behaves as water and obeys the laws of the physical world. Isn't it all structured in the constitution of everything, right from the inaccessible macro-systems to the known (and unknown) limits and domains of the most illusive, the so-called elementary particles. All our classical, or even the latest of the quantum understanding, has not been able to understand the writ, which these extremely minute entities intrinsically understand and obey every moment. The profound phenomena, of endlessly varied, living and non-living objective manifestations, coded with breathtakingly subtle, organized, and coordinating understanding, wedded intriguingly with the structure matrix within each unit, is beyond our possible comprehension. And it goes on, unfalteringly, re-organizing and re-adjusting perpetually. Nothing is isolated but well knit, inter-related and self-adjusting. This all because, it is all sustained by the infinite and ever-vibrant pure *awareness* that breaths in every unit as its inherent *Ġāna*, the intrinsic knowledge. Without this intrinsic knowledge, no unit matrix, no unit manifestation, can ever be expressed. It is lucidly clear therefore, that the basic truth, the un-definable pure awareness, the endless, ever *alive* and unique awareness-existence (*ćaitanya-swarup*), the absolute autonomy and sovereignty, (and therefore all-bliss, the *ānanda*), conceives it all and cherishes to *see* itself in the infinite number of matrices of '*Ġāna–confines*'. These *Ġāna-confines* are certainly not bondages, but windows into the ultimate pure awareness, and also out of it. It is a matter, only of getting limited, into believing oneself to be a confine, and basking in its limited knowledge, or else, withdrawing the attention from what one *knows* (and believes as the only reality), and remaining just *attentive,* without any specific choice ! This *attentiveness* is the *ćaitanya* within *Ġāna*, because *ćaitanya* is the core, the true self of everything !

Śiva-sūtra - (3) actually provides a perspective of these *Ġāna-confines.* After declaring so far that the *awareness, when pure, is the essence, and, when committed, is only knowledge*, the *Śiva-sūtras* unfold to make it clear, what after all these confines and commitments (*bandhaĥ*) are:

योनिवर्गः कलाशरीरम्

(yonivargaĥ kalāśarīram)

Sūtra-(ss -I - 3)

"The source, the class or category, the segment and the specific construct of all the units, (are the different aspects of conditioning)."

This *sūtra* pertains to the knowledge that brings about the sense of differentiation. It is only the sense of differentiation that establishes the objective existence. The indeterminate or the transcendental reality is indiscernible because of the non-differentiation. It is the difference, or a sense of some quality, that gives identification to things. Objective existence is determinable due to the quality of each existent. Quality of each existent is the projection of its intrinsic knowledge matrix, which gives it, the internal constitution and the outer quality. It is because of their quality that all objective existents are classified. Classification is made in consideration of the data available with regard to the source, class or category, segment and other specific details concerning each unit broadly. Living or non-living entities all, can be classified on such lines, and all the knowledge gathered on these lines definitely is based on the projection of the internal knowledge matrix of each unit. For instance water is considered as a chemical compound formed due to a specific kind of bonding of two gases, hydrogen and oxygen, which are believed to be an outcome of two different patterns of the (so-called) elementary particles. One of the two gases, the hydrogen, can burn spontaneously with a very slight excitation (ignition energy), and the other, the oxygen makes burning happen, or supports it. Water at normal temperatures can dampen or suppress burning and also behave as a trough for heat, storing it within, even after changing its liquid state into gaseous state of steam. Steam can store a lot more amount of heat energy than water. Water can even act as a source of heat and give it away till it changes its state into a solid, the ice. We find from this common observation, that a structural change, caused by the variation of the co-relations of some elementary particles, projects different behaviors. The elementary particles *know*, as do the compounds they form, how to behave and perform in different conditions. True, it is their property, but isn't it *coded* in them all. In the world of hydrocarbon materials, astonishing variations are encountered, which explicitly are due to all the coded knowledge within all of the constituents and resultant products, the most illusive and unknown, being the transition point from non-living to living domains of existence. Classification with respect to the origin, lineage, groups and units, living and non-living, flora and fauna, solids, liquids and other states, terrestrial and extra-terrestrial, and all other classes, and sub classes, of the minutest units and their constituents, etc., is useful in various activities of life. All these infinite *Ġāna*-confines are structured and coded, specifically and exclusively, to perform individually, as empirical units, or co-relate with others. These coded structures, define their empirical existence in *yoni, verga, kalā, or śarīr,* and project a diversity of *Ġāna*-confines, with their core, the consciousness scintillating as their specific *Ġāna,* relevant to their specific confines. It is no bondage, it is the absolute sovereignty, and *Swātantrya* (autonomy) of awareness, expressing in infinite ways. We are not outlaws, nor underlings, condemned to the isolation of bondage. We are each, a specific *swara,* in the marvelous divine outpourings of the melody of manifestation, perpetually being created and cherished, as the throbbing music of bliss, by the unsurpassable ! Our bondage is in *our believing* ourselves to be different and separate, underlings, and deprived, condemned for seeking. Seek we must, but not the petty, nor the illusory, but the kingdom of real. We are *paśus*, as long as we believe ourselves to be *paśus* , content or grumbling, in the mire and mud we believe we are in. We have to break-through, and trace our *self*, by piercing through the channels of knowledge within us and without, in this enchanting *sṛṣṭi*. We have to contact the core, the awareness, and recognize that we are *pati* not *paśus*, and cherish to sing the song of bliss with the eternal !

Śiva-sūtra - (3) is more meaningful than we considered yet. Digging deep into it, yields immense communication. Going by the broader connotation of the meaning of the words of the *sūtra*, say, *yoni* (origin, source, repository, race etc.), *varga* (class, category, division, group of similar things), *kalā* (a part of a whole, a segment) and *śarīr* (the body, the unit, the construct), we resort to the gross classification, which *locates* various aspects of the objective existence. A keen or thorough investigation provides a subtler perspective, of the whole of the evolutionary phenomena of the objective existence, and validates the '*Ġāna-confines* view' interpretation for the *Śiva-sūtra* (2), more fundamentally. If we consider the first three *Śiva-sūtras* in continuity, we discover the complete and profound philosophy of the process of objective manifestation, as conceived in *trika* wisdom.

Looking at *Śhiva-sūtra - (1-3)* in the light of some initial *sūtras* of *Parātrīśika,* the greatly regarded (and extremely subtle) manuscript of *trika*, that has come down to us in line with the *Āgma* tradition of communication through sūtras, would be extremely interesting and enlightening. Starting with the *Sūtra-*(2) of *Parātrīśikā*, presented as *Devi* addressing *Bhairava*[7] (for) seeking a clearer understanding and grasp of the most subtle truth, for the inner satiation of her quest within. *Devi* speaks thus:

हृदयस्था तु या शक्तिः कौलिकी कुलनाकिा
तां मे कथय देवेश येन तृप्तिं लभाम्यहम्

(hṛdayasthā tu ya Śaktiĥ kaulikī kulanayikā
tam me kathai deveśa yena triptim labhamyaham)
Sūtra - (PT – 2)

" *kaulikī-Śakti* is *hṛdayesthā*, and even then undertakes to be the *kulanāyikā* ! Tell me O' lord of lords, (all) about her, so that *I* find true satiation".

Hṛdayastha, is that which dwells in *hṛdaya*, (the innermost core of everything) as its essence, as the ultimate reality! And what is that which occupies, or '*is itself* ' the innermost core ? *"Ćaitanyam Ātma"* (awareness is the core !) Declares *Śiva-sūtra* (1). The ultimate core of everything, all transcendental and immanent existence, is awareness. It is *kaulikī-Śakti*, the *Śakti* belonging to *kaula* , the *Śiva*, the *ćinmaya*, the *akula.* It therefore is indeterminate, transcendental reality, having nothing to do with objectivity, and is beyond the domain of immanent or the manifested totality, the *kula*, the *whole-lot* of the universal phenomenon. *Kulanāyikā* means the ultimate lord or ruler of the *lot*, the one that has the ultimate authority of taking any action. *Kulanāyikā* is also the guide of the whole-lot, the one that enlightens, leads, shows the path. *Kulanāyikā* means also the mistress or the loving partner of the lot, the one with whom one has full intimacy, and the one that provides delight and fulfillment. *Devi* refers to the enigma, and seeks to know as to how awareness, the transcendental reality, forming the core, that dwells not in the objective domain, can be the guide, the lord and the lover that fulfils all the desires, and provides delight in all walks of life, of the whole of the objective manifestation. This *Sūtra* reveals another dimension of what *Devi* says. There is also an intrinsic answer in her query, if we consider the word *hṛdayastha* in a different way. *Hṛdayastha* is also *hṛt* + *aya* + *stha* ; where *hṛt* means heart, the core, the supreme awareness, *aya* means spontaneous knowledge, manifold and of all varied things, and *stha* means abiding as. Word *hṛdayastha* therefore connotes, that 'supreme awareness is the core, abiding as manifold, spontaneous and intrinsic knowledge of everything, in all the varied objective manifestations', as was precisely the interpretation given earlier, while considering the communication in the *Śiva-sūtra* - (2) [*"Ġānam bandah"*]. It forms the core of everything yet it is not explicit as core, but as *kulanāyikā*, the lord, the guide, and the beloved or the mistress. It is actually (the *kula bhave - akul rupa,*) the *Śiva-rūpa* essence of everything, the *kula*, the whole-lot of the immanent manifestation. It forms, manages, guides and counsels as well as provides all fulfillment, as the intrinsic knowledge, to all the *Ġāna*-confines of the existence. But *Devi*, representing our innermost state of *madhyama*, where the sense of differentiation just begins, wants to know more, and comprehend fully as to how the *hṛdayastha*, is also the *kaulikī-Śakti* that abides as *kulanāyikā*.

In *Sūtras* (3) and (4) of *Parātrīśikā*, *Bhairava*, the *parā-Saṅvit*, (the absolute awareness), which, is *hṛdayastha* in everything, dawns through the *paśyanti* state, to reveal the secret of the riddle, by declaring Her (*Devi*) to be the ultimate answer to the whole riddle. *Bhairava* explains how She, the *Parādevi*, the core of His being, the *vimarśa* or the *swātantrya-Śakti*, is the cause, the course, and the lord of all that is. *Bhairva says* :

श्रृणु देवि महाभागे उत्तरस्याप्यनुत्तरम्
(*Śṛṇu devi mahābhāge uttarasya-apy-anuttaram*)
Sūtra (PT - 3)

कौलिकोऽयं विधिर्देवि मम हृद्व्योम्न्यवस्थित:
कथयामि सुरेशानि सद्य: कौलिकसिद्धिदम्
(*kaulikoyam vidhirdevi mama hrdyomny-avasthitaĥ*

kathayāmi sureśāni sadyah kaulikasiddhidam)
Sūtra - (PT - 4)

Bhairava addressing *Devi* : *'Śṛṇu-devi, mahābhāge, uttarasya-apy-anuttaram'* is an extremely subtle communication. *Śṛṇu-devi,* (listen *Devi*) is seeking attension for listening. *Bhairava* asks *Devi* to invoke the *Śakti* of listening for creating a link between *Devi* and Himself. This is a profound communication highlighting the channel of 'the *Śakti* of listening'. Listening is, paying attention to any sound emanating from any source in the form of *vaikhari-Śakti.* Listening also refers to attending to a mental flux originating from within one's own mind, the *Śakti* in the *madhyama* stage. Listening is not only just receiving sound energy through the ear, or touching a mental flux in the mind. Listening is a highly profound activity in its actuality. It is a subtle operation which forms a channel from immanent to the transcendental. Listening involves receiving a specific input from within the hotchpotch of noise, of a physical or mental domain of the objective world, in the form of a determinate objective entity, and routing it through the subtler realms of *Madhyama* and *paśyanti,* to the absolutely indeterminate *parā-vaikhari, parā-madhyama,* and *parā-paśyanti* domains of *parā,* into the presence of the absolute awareness, for the complete identification, comprehension and appropriate response *instantly,* and then, routing the response back again, through these very channels of indeterminate, to the determinate domains of mind, and on to the *vaikhari,* for its expression as speech. Else there would be no instantaneous grasping, analyzing and appropriate response, accompanying the phenomenon of listening. Attributing it all, to a bio-electric expression of a chemical activity of the brain would be an ultimate folly, because in spite of everything else happening, but in absence of attention or awareness, linked to the whole affair, listening doesn't happen. This *Śakti* of listening, the profound bridge between the immanent and the transcendental existence, acts as a womb, wherein an eager egg of a question, or a quest as an input, gets impregnated by the seminal truth of the ultimate awareness, and results in the manifestation of an answer, or an understanding instantaneously, providing also, at the same instant, an inward thrill, like the joy of an orgasm, associated with the getting of an answer, a concept, or satisfaction of a curiosity. It acts as the supreme Divine *Śakti parābhattarika*, an expression of absolutely free manifestation of the bliss, of the union of *Śiva* and *Śakti*. The transition of *Śakti* from *vaikhari* to *parā*, the inversion aspect *ma-ha-a,* from *nara* through *Śakti* to *Śiva,* the *samhāra swabhāva* of *Bhairava,* resulting in the union of *Śakti* with *Śiva* ; and then again, the instantaneous projection from the *parā* to *vaikhari* aspect, that is, from *Śiva* to *nara,* as *a-ha-m swabhāva* of *Anuttra,* is, how *Śravana-Śakti* manifests. *Bhairava* declares *Devi* as *mahābhāge,* the one who is the partaker of *mahā,* i.e, *ma-ha-a* journey, the one who enjoys with Him this blissful *samhār*-journey into His *hrid-vyomny,* (the *ākaś* or space of his core,) for unraveling the truth that she seeks. *Bhairava* lauds her as the greatest, such that even *mahā(n)* , *(*the *anaśrit-Śiva)* is just a fraction of her being.

Bhairava says further that she is *Uttarasya-apy-anuttaram*, knowable yet un-knowable and therefore puts *Devi*, the *mahābhāga*, in the very subtle realm of tangible and intangible, accessible and also inaccessible (*parāparā*), an answer, yet no answer! She is perpetually manifesting yet transcendent, being *ćaitanya*, the very core of *Anuttra,* thus indeterminate, yet pregnant with all possible manifest-able determinates. *Bhairava* calls her '*kaulika*', the *akula-Śakti* expressing as *bimba*, the *mahā-sṛšṭi*, (the *swarup- sṛšṭi* in the transcendental domain,) and as *pratibimba*, the entire *sṛšṭi* in the immanent domain, in the form of all the different subjects, all the different objects or knowables, and all the knowledge therein and there-from. He calls her also *Vidhirdevi*, the goddess governing the means and procedure of creation, the Devine-matrix, that is the divine rule, the mode, the means and the actual instantaneous (*sadyaĥ*) accomplishment (*kaulikasiddhidam*) of the projection of entire manifestation (*kaulika - sṛšṭi – prasāraĥ*). "You", says *Bhairava*, " always reside in the space of my *hriday* (*hridyomny*), and (still) *I* relate it to you, *sureśāni*, the greatest of all the gods and goddesses!"

These *Sūtras* [(2-4) of *Parātrīśikā* and (1 & 2) of *Śiva-sūtra*] stress emphatically that the ultimate reality or essence of all that exits in any domain, whether determinate or indeterminate (immanent or transcendental), is the absolute and pure awareness, which forms the core (*hriday*) of the unsurpassable (*Anuttra*), as *His* ultimate *swātantrya* (*vimarśa*) *Śakti*, and expresses itself, by manifesting into all that can be ! This establishes not only the source (*yoni*), but also essential one-ness of the content of all heterogeneous distribution, of all the *vargas* (classes), and *śarīrās* (empirical units), in spite of their ability to perform variably on account of their internal structure-matrix formations.

Precisely the same is addressed through the *sūtras* [1-2] of *Pratyabhiĝāna-hradyam.* (stated below)

चितिः स्वतन्त्रा विश्वसिद्धिहेतुः

(Ćitiĥ swātantrā viśwa-siddhi-hetuĥ)
sūtra-(pbh – 1)

" *Absolute free will of Ćiti is the only cause, for the accomplishment of the universe.* "

स्वेच्छया स्वभित्तौ विश्वमुन्मीलयति

(sveććhyā swabhittav viśwa-unmīl-yati)
sūtra-(pbh – 2)

" *Unfolded, (or enfolded), out of its own Iććhā, upon the screen, (also) as itself.*

Ćiti is *ćaitanya Śakti*, the pure and absolute awareness, the core or essence of everything, the ultimate reality (ss-1), to which everything gets reduced, and out of which everything is fabricated into all the infinitely varied, composite and programmed units of creation, by *Her*, out of *Herself* (ss-2). An infinite potency, this *Śakti*, with all its sovereignty and autonomy, implies an absolute *will*, to express in any desired way. An infinitely vague urge, subsequently, but instantaneously unfolding as strong desire, with complete knowledge, plan and means, all within it (as there is no without), to become the fulfillment. Itself the foundation and the structure, the sustainer, and the sustained, as well as the beholder, *She* unfolds for itself, by itself and from itself. That is what the two sūtras quoted above communicate. We have already gone through a more comprehensive analysis of the same view by analyzing the *Sūtras*(2-4) of *parātīśikā*, where-in *ćaitanya-Śakti* is seen in many roles, including *Kaulikī, kulanaikā*, and *Vidhir-devi Śakti* aspects, and thus making her the totality of the immanent and the transcendental reality aspects, as also the worm-hole[8] between them. *Pratyabhiĝāna Sūtras*(1-2) become explicitly clear in the light of all that was considered earlier.

We need now to understand how *trika-śastra* explains in detail, the whole process of projection of the ultimate awareness, into various different levels of its manifestation as *Ġāna*-confines, and thus get a feel of the hierarchy of various realms of *sṛšṭi* conceived. *Sūtras* - (*5 - 8.5*) of *parātrīśīkā* expound this mystery in terms of *parā-vāk Śakti*, the most subtle philosophy of the profound relationship between the subtlest indeterminate levels of sound and thought, manifesting into the gross expressions of letter and word, and the grosser material manifestations of the universe. Before exploring those intricate and delicate aspects of creation, it would be very interesting to know first the *tattva*-description of the projection of the *sṛṣṭi*, put forth in *trika-śastra.*

Tattvas

Most of us should be able to confirm that sometimes, we experience a tender tickling of a very vague and undefined feeling, ecstatic like a thrill, which makes us feel excited, and inclined to act like children. Sometimes we even experience a kind of an undefined quicksand-like inward pull that makes us sink inside into a strange isolation and brooding. Although very vague and unclear in our mental plane, these feelings have an impact, and make us behave or act inexplicably. These vague but identifiable feelings occur, not in our perceptible sphere of mental grasp or expression, but somewhere in the channels of indeterminate. Such feelings are not differentiable, but seem to exist. Desires similarly bubble up very imperceptibly in the deeper layers of awareness first, and then on gaining momentum become identifiable at the stage of their expression as desires, demanding execution. The stages such feelings and thoughts pass through, range from very vague to distinct, in the process of their precipitation into the existence of the actuality of comprehension in our conscious mind. Their actual *being*, in fact, is beyond the mind, in the womb of their conception, where awareness begins contracting itself from its transcendental existence into a defined expression. What we experience in our mind refers to their objective field of existence. All such states of existence of an urge may manifest as thoughts feelings, or intuitive inclinations. It is profound unfolding of the succession-less transcendental urge into an objective form, full of succession, the indeterminate into determinate aspect of being. Discernible thoughts, feelings and inclinations have their own hue and character and represent a clearly differentiated world but their source is the absolutely undifferentiated reality of being in *parā*, where there is no reach of mind or any other faculty we may imagine to have existence. All our dealings in the objective world are guided actually by our true being at the *parā* level, through perceptions, feelings, understanding or logic manifesting at various different levels of our comprehension . All these guiding factors, comprehensible at the objective level of *vaikhari*, get referred to our source at *parā* (*parā-vaikhari*, *parā-madhyama* and *parā-paśyanti*) through the profound channels of *madhyama* and *paśyanti*, not as we know them in our objective domain of *vaikhari* but in successively changing presentations. This reinterpretation of the successive objective reality, from a completely determinate and differentiated existence known to us, after undergoing several transformations at various domains, into totally undifferentiated and indeterminate reality in *parā*, is the reversed journey of the actuality of the creation. The urge of creation beginning as an extremely subtle *will* assumes very many roles in the process of expansion before reaching the tangible level of this solid earth with its varied features, including our existence in terms of an empirical life. Termed as *tattvas*, this hierarchy in the *vāman-yukti* (the projection of the creation) is distinctly classified in *trika-śastra,* (as will be considered subsequently). From our experience in grosser objective world, we know that almost all solids can melt and occur in a molten state also. Two such states therefore, represent the same content at different temperature ranges, liquids possessing a higher level of intrinsic heat-energy in the form of the kinetic energy of the constituent molecules of that substance. With yet greater intrinsic kinetic energy of the molecules the same content may exist also as a vapor. The range of its intrinsic energy can therefore make a material manifest as a specific category of solid liquid or a vapor. These three states simultaneously also imply a modification with regard to the spatial orientation of the structural constituents of the material and thus the status of electromagnetic force associated with these constituents, dictating the form and certain other characteristics of the material. Domains of intrinsic electrostatic and nuclear energy content, gravitational behavior and total mass-energy (on relativistic considerations) of the material, form a more subtle aspect of the objective existence of things as can be discerned through our known objective means. The composite inter-expressible perspective of things comprising of solid, liquid and gaseous form of materials, their intrinsic spatial and energy orientations etc., is the signature of objective existence expressing itself as animate and in-animate creation on the tangible side. Earth, the gigantic expression of all such co-existing aspects of objectivity, represents an amazing dynamics of it all, bearing within it, different preceding, succeeding and re-expressing states of matter, spaces and energy-fields, acts therefore as the source and the sink of all living and non-living existence we know of. This furnace projects life in all the innumerable varieties, sustains it and also acts as the bosom where life retires into, for the eternal transformation into yet another aspect of its material expression. Conditioned by it, our perceptions flower into knowledge and thoughts, feelings and action, and a personality, which is sustained inwardly by specified awareness linking it to the pure awareness, the pure being, beyond the realm of all objective, and its bonds of definitions, forms, attributes, qualities and limitations, into perfect autonomy of *pūrantā* and *swātantrya*. It is this autonomy that assumes all the representative postures of categories in its expansion down this staircase of creativity, the *tattva-sopān*, out of its own pure *being* into its *becoming* from absolutely undifferentiated and indeterminate existence through successive differentiations and specific presentations up to the most tangible state, the earth. *Trika* holds that *Anuttra*, the unsurpassable, the fundamental and unique, (also called *Parama-Shiva*,) forms the essence of everything, the whole phenomena of creation, from its being to becoming, all that is and can be. What this *Anuttra* is, cannot be expressed, as it is like nothing known or imagined. It has no name or form (*nāma-rūpa*), since these are the attributes that indicate objectivity. It has no objective existence and thus possesses no attributes or qualities. Qualities would make it finite, define it, and provide a lead to explain objectively what is not objective. It is indeterminate and unbounded. The only thing *trika* tells us about it, is, that '*It is*' , and '*is aware*' of its being, and therefore it is termed as *vimaršmy-prakāśa* in *trika* terminology. *Prakāśa* (like light in objective domain), need not be indicated. It *is*, when it is, and its being is its proof. It has no dependence on any confirmation. *Discernment makes things accessible.* This is precisely what *vimarśa* implies. *Vimarśa* is awareness which enlightens, even the *prakāśa* of being itself, and everything else the *prakāśa* gives presence. Awareness is the 'sole-essence', the 'soul-essence', and the 'essence as soul', of everything. It is the sparkle of light, the throb of life, and the knowledge-matrix of things. It makes things *be* and behave, as what they are. It is the *Śakti* of pure-awareness and also the awareness-in-action. It is *kaulikī* and *kulanāyika*. It is the bliss of perfect and absolute autonomy of the *Ćidānand-ghana*, the *parama-śiva*. This bliss is the throb (*spanda*) of expression. It is the flashing (*sphuran*) in the core of the awareness. It is a spontaneous song bursting out of the elation of absolute freedom and sovereignty. It is the creative urge, the out-pouring of *Śakti* from *parama-Śiva*, becoming *srišti*. This urge for creativity results in the polarization of *Śiva* and *Śakti* aspects in *Anuttra*. These, the two *tattvas* necessary for the creation of *srišti*, the *being* and the *potency* (of knowledge and performance), the dynamic-expression of the bliss of *I*-consciousness, mutually indistinguishable, become distinguishable within *Anuttra* through its urge for creation, like a cream droplet within milk (grossly speaking), or sap in a branch of a tree aching for piercing out, as an infinitesimal point, to shape into an eye, on the bark of the branch. This is the first step in the perpetual *tāňđava* of creation! No, *tāňđava* is not the dance of *samhāra*, it is simultaneously the dance of creation and dissolution, both ! Which creation does not get assimilated in *samhāra*, and which *samhāra* does not bear in its bosom the secret of unfolding of a creation. The *ardha-nārīśwara*, the inseparable *Śiva* and *Śakti tattvas*, performs perpetually the dance of creation and *samhāra*. The creation of objectivity is the dissolution of transcendence and folding back into transcendence is the *samhāra* of objectivity. The projection of creation and its dissolution is the eternal waning and waxing of the transcendental aspect of the reality. *Śiva* remains the unchanging principle of being-ness (*tattva*), and *Śakti* weaves the patterns of manifestation, perpetually. The first manifestation is the *desire* to manifest as *something*. It is these two factors, the two aspects, the potency of *being* and urge of *becoming* at play. *Vimarśamaya-prakāśa*, the universal experient, the pure universal subject, *Anuttra* is a unitary state with no trace whatsoever of objectivity. Although creativity is its *swabhāva*, yet objective manifestation is not its domain, as it is no domain for objectivity. The *prakāśa* and *vimarśa* or *Śiva* and *Śakti* aspects are in absolute undifferentiated unity in *Anuttra*, the essence of which is *ānanda* of over-brimming *Śakti*, pulsating as creative impulse or *spanda* (सपंद) within it, and becoming the manifestation. This *spanda* initiates a kind of polarization within *Anuttra*, a kind of differentiation of *Śiva* and *Śakti tattvas* in the unity of the two aspects of the pure I-consciousness and the creative urge. This polarization of *aham-vimarśa*, a kind of prelude to manifestation, a vague (अस्फुट) visualization of the urge into *aham-idam vimarśa*, the *I-this* consciousness, called *Sadāśiva-tattva* (सदाशिव तत्त्व) is a state, with prominence of *I* - consciousness and just a vague sense of '*this*' beginning to show up. There however persists a sense of unity between the '*I*' and the '*this*'. This manifestation of *Iććhā–Śakti* is followed by the flowering into *Ġāna-Śakti*, the state where the visualization or recognition of this creative urge gets a clearer definition (स्फुटता). To become anything needs to sort out and *know* what to become. This urge therefore flowers into various *tattvas*, the various '*aspects of being* '. *Sadāśiva-tattva* is the desire aspect of *Śakti*-expansion, while its knowledge aspect that subsequently emerges, is the *Iśwara-tattva*. This is a state of *idam–aham*, the ' *this-I* ' (*this* I *must* become). In desire aspect, subjectivity dominates, while the objective knowledge dominates in the *Iśwara- tattva*, where ' I ' is more involved with the knowledge aspect. There is however no difference implied in the two aspects, both being transcendental or *parā-states*, of *desiring*, and *knowing* the desire. The fact is that *Parama-Śiva* has manifesting potency (*ābhāsana-sāmarthya*) of expansion into '*this*', of whatever kind, and self-repose (*ātma-viśrānti*) into its pure-self, simultaneously, as its *swabhāva* (no succession is implied in the transcendental reality), by virtue of its *swātantrya*, which bestows it with perfect autonomy and lordliness to repose into itself or project its potency into actualization of any and every kind of manifestation, or withdraw it all again into Himself.

In *idam-aham vimarśa*, (the *this-I-consciousness* of *Iśwara-tattva*), although the I-consciousness is still prominent, yet a breach in the non-difference between ' the *I* ' and ' the *this*' becomes significant, since an immanent (विश्वमयी) aspect of manifestation begins shaping itself up. This expansion is that of the pure, the transcendental (*parā*) and undifferentiated (अभेद) aspect of *Anuttra* and *ānanda* directly, as the phase of objectivity has not yet commenced. Further on, after the *Ġāna* phase, and before the actual onset of the phase of manifestation, the domain of objectivity, expansion of transcendental consciousness of *Anuttra* and *ānanda* ceases, and a complete polarization of subjectivity and objectivity, the consciousness of a kind of *differentiation-in-unity* (भेदाभेद, *bhedabhed*), takes over. This state is *parāparā* state that forms a kind of bridge between *parā* (the transcendental) and *aparā* (the immanent). This, the *śuddha-vidyā-tattva* (शुद्धविद्या तत्तव) of *aham-aham, idam-idam* (अहं-अहं, इदं-इदं) consciousness marks the experience of true relationship of the purely subjective aspect and the objective entities.

Parama-Śiva, the absolute reality, is conceived in *Śaiva* as *Śaktimān*, the supreme lord, the *Maheśwara*. This connotes being, not an incapable inert entity but, possessor of the *śakti* of being. *Maheśwara* implies possession of *maheśwaryatā* (*mahān* + *aiśwarayatā*), the supreme sovereignty and power. *Parama-Śiva* is *Ćidānand-ghanā* (mere awareness-bliss) in its pure *being*, while *Iććhā*, *Ġāna* and *Kriyā* are His *'Śakti of being'*, the sovereignty, the *sarva-Śaktitvata,* which bestows Him *swātantrya,* the absolute freedom of remaining grounded in complete self-repose as well as manifesting as anything (*sarvakartṛtvata*)! In fact this aspect of *sarva-Śaktitva,* is His immanence aspect of reality in its most subtle form. He can immerse within, into complete bliss of self-repose or open his eyelids to enjoy the bliss of *sarvakartṛtvata* which is His *swabhāva,* His *Iśwara-Śakti.* This extroversion into creativity is *ātma-viśrānti-virodha* (opposed to self-repose) and thus the absolute causality aspect of His being. This visualization gives *Parama-Śiva,* the *Ćidānand-ghana* three aspects to *His being.*

First, in its absolute sense of completely transcendental existence He is *Ćidekaghana,* the singular compactness of awareness. This awareness is one-ness of being and bliss, rather *being in bliss* or *bliss in being,* a complete immersion by Him into His pure being, the *ātma-viśrānti.* Secondly, the *spanda* of extroversion of bliss, an awareness of its autonomy in focus, is the flowering of *Śiva-tattva* awareness, 'the *sense-of-being* as the immanent reality', 'an identity to immanence' within the transcendental existence. Thirdly, the aspect of awareness of the potency of autonomy, the *'kartṛtvata'* in focus within that transcendental reality, is the *Śakti-tattva* awareness coming to fore. There is in fact oneness (*ekattva*) of that absolute reality, in all these aspects of transcendental awareness, such that, *Śiva-tattva* and *Śakti-tattva* represent the two aspects, the *'identity* of *being'* and the *'potency* of *being'* of the singular reality of immanence in the *Ćidānand-ghana*, the *Parama-Śiva* which remains in absolute, undifferentiated indeterminacy in His *ātma-viśrānti* state, but arises as *spanda* of creativity. There is no succession implied in these two phases but an eternal presence of Absolute singularity and one-ness of *Śiva* and *Śakti* as *tattvas* of '*identity and expression*' aspects of the immanence, in their most subtle of the transcendental existence in *Anuttra*. Throbbing as *nimeša* and *unmeša*, eternally and without succession, these transcendental and immanent aspects of His being present His *swabhāva*. *Unmeša* or the rise of the *spanda* of the manifestation marks the *nimeša* or fall of the transcendental awareness, and vice-versa. Since *Śakti-tattva* represents the 'expression' of autonomy, it is this, that subsequently tells the story of *becoming*, the immanence, the domain of objectivity, while *Śiva-tattva* maintains its identity as the 'immanence rooted in transcendental'. *Śakti* is a unique succession-less transcendental reality, the unitary *continuum* of bliss, the autonomy of its three-pronged potency of agency, as *Iććha*, *Ġāna*, and *Kriyā*, which presents itself as successive, in its functional diversity (*kritya-bheda*) in the immanent aspect of objective manifestation. The phenomenon of its self-differentiation projects it in its varied hierarchical diversity, the higher states more inclusive of its lower aspects, and thus closer to real profundity and actuality of its unqualified and unrestricted autonomy as the *Ćiti-Śakti* of *Śaktimān*. As *Vimarśa*, (the self-affirming awareness), as *Swātantrya-Śakti*, (the absolute autonomy and sovereignty), or as pure *nirvikalpa-samvid* (the indeterminate creative *consciousness*), *Śakti* is *avikalpa*, and *abheda*, (*a* singular indeterminate and undifferentiated reality), while as objective manifestation in a form, a substance, attributes of a formed structure including interactions and activity, thoughts and feelings, along with all the related subjective aspects, it is all *savikalpa*, a thought-construct. All such *savikalpa* expressions of *Śakti* in the objective domain are considered as impure (*aśuddha- vikalpa*), because of the deluded perception of a false 'I-ness' association of the empirical experient, arising differently in different categories (*tattvas*). This is a domain entirely of differentiation (*bheda*). *Śakti* an *abheda* reality, and at the same time as a phenomenon full of *bheda* presents un-reconcile-able unity which needs to be resolved.

Dawning of a realization suddenly, flashing of an answer in mind or a sudden blossoming of a poetic outflow or musical harmony in an artist is an experience we are acquainted with. This aspect of the flowering of *pratibhā* is creativity getting expression. What is it that gets this expression and how it happens is not determinable.

आते हें ग़ैब़ से ये मज़ामीं ख़्याल में

ग़ालिब, स़रीरे-ख़ामा निवाये-सरोश है ।

(These outpourings dawn into the thoughts from the invisible. Ghālib, the screech of the pen, registers the utterances of the heavens, beyond).

The verse above reveals how Ghālib, the poet of lofty thoughts and expressions, evaluates his *pratibhā*.

Scriptural authority (*Netra-tantra*) says that '*Pratibhā* is a *form* of *Śakti* '.

(प्रतिभातत्त्वं शक्तिलक्षणम् ... NTU-I-191)

Pratibhā manifests in two ways namely, creative (*kārayitrī*) and appreciative (*bhāvayitrī*). As the creative genius of a poet or a musician, it oozes out of the indeterminate consciousness (*avikalpa-samvid*) into the *vaikhari* of the creator. As a perception, from *vaikhari* state of the one who beholds it, it merges into *avikalpa-samvid* again and presents itself as appreciative joy or bliss for the beholder. He shares the bliss of creativity of the artist in the realms of indeterminate. He becomes the subject of this experience, a witness to the creative aspect of *pratibhā* through the appreciative aspect of *pratibhā*. A musician or a poet, in the process of creativity also cherishes the creativity as it happens within him. He experiences the twin aspect of the *pratibhā* of creative and appreciative nature. If he gets associated with this phenomenon of witnessing the creation at the deeper levels of comprehension, he can touch the immense bliss of *parābhattrika*, the union of 'I' and the 'this'. This true unity of 'I and the this' is the witnessing of pure determinate feeling emerging out of the indeterminate consciousness. It is this *śuddha-vikalpa* that bridges *abheda* and *bheda* domains, the *parā* reality with the *aparā* world. This *bhedabheda* transition, the undifferentiated unfolding into the differentiated, is *avikalpa* turning into objective reality, the so-called *aśuddha-vikalpa*. This critical state is the worm-hole that can lead the *aśuddha-vikalpa* through the *śuddhi* of *vikalpas* into the domain of pure *I*-consciousness__ *Śākta-upāye* for rediscovery of the actual self. In fact *nirvikalpa-samvid* never abandons us. It is there, ever there, between each of the two breaths (incoming and the outgoing), between each of the two distinct successive thoughts or feelings, abiding in an indeterminate state in these undefined gaps, providing congruency and coherence, to everything objective. A deep and intense contemplation on this *avikalpa-samvid* can reveal the truth!

"... it abides undivided among the endless determinate percepts. The interval between the two determinate ideas can by no means be denied because of the difference between the two ideas. That interval consists of consciousness only, otherwise, on account of the extirpation of the residual traces of consciousness caused by that interval or gap (if devoid of consciousness), memory, congruous link etc., between the consciousness preceding the gap and the consciousness succeeding it would become impossible." Says Abhinavgupta in *Parā-trīśikā-vivaraṇa*

(तस्मात्तदनन्तावभासाविभागमयमेवेति ... स्मरणाद्यनुसंधानाद्ययोग इति। , PTV-36/20-22)

Awareness of the unity of undifferentiated and differentiated consciousness, its instantaneous transition from one to the other aspect marks the *śuddha-vikalpa* state of *Śakti*. This state, the *Śuddha-vidyā-tattva* of the unity in '*aham-aham* & *idam-idam*' *vimarśa* in the hierarchical gradation in the *Śakti's* self- differentiation, is the threshold that connects the transcendental and the immanent postures of the reality. It is at this *parāparā* level where, ' I ' the always transcendental, and 'this', that subsequently has to become the objective reality, are distinctly balanced, that a transition occurs. The objective does not carry any trace of the transcendental, and the transcendental cannot posses any trace of the objective being, but all the same, at this stage of *śuddha-tattva* the subjective and objective entities both, are aware of their fundamental oneness.

Śakti, therefore, at this stage, withdrawn from the *Śiva* aspect, veils herself, to muffle the non-differentiation perspective of the transcendental reality in herself, and takes on the actual immanent role, by inculcating a sense of difference. *Śiva*, its transcendental identity, not involved in the objective aspect of *Śakti*, plunges completely into itself (*ātma-viśrānti*). This state, termed as *anāśrita-Śiva* (state of *Śiva*, deposed of *Śakti*) is only a pure sense of *being*. This, a kind of ridding itself of the completeness of the *parama-śiva bhāva* (पर्मशिवभाव) by *Anuttra*, and taking to complete self-repose (*ātmaviśrānti*- आत्मविश्रान्ति) within itself, marks a kind of a break in its unitary completeness. This state (*awasthā*, अवस्था) of *Śiva,* the *anāśrita-śiva-bhāva* (अनाश्रित शिव भाव) is beyond any mental grasp (*unāmarśiniya*- अनामर्शनीय). It is an absolute void (शून्य अतिशून्य) state, which is neither *pūrna śiva-bhāva* nor the *jagat-bhāva* of *Anuttra*, while *Śakti*, breeding the sense of *separateness* and *difference*, becomes *Māyā-tattva.* In the domain of *Māyā*, thus the sense of being a separate empirical entity creeps first into all the immanent manifestation. The consciousness deprived of its universal or non-objective essence takes on a cloak of an individual existence. There is no clear-cut awareness of one's potentials or limitations, but only a sense of being a unit of existence without any sense of performance.

The sense of separateness having taken over, the boundary conditions for the objective domain start framing up. Specifying, naming, and casting itself into all sorts of varied presentations, is the expressing of itself by *Śakti*, through infinite attributes and qualities. It is taking away the complete sovereignty and autonomy from the empirical presentation of itself and decorating it with specifics. *Māyā-tattva,* expresses herself through infinite number of finites. It structures all the objective existence in terms of infinite kinds of patterns, definitions and boundary conditions. Each different empirical unit is inherently guided to follow a pattern intuitively, through its *urges* and *affinities*. The *understanding* within, is the programming, that prompts through an intrinsic knowledge of notions about one's *urges* and *performing capabilities*. This coded matrix of personality, with certain intrinsic adaptability, prompts an individual to alter, adapt or redefine some of its constituting patterns, from time to time, due to interactions with all other different patterns it encounters, (through the *cause* and *effect* chain for variation). In all living entities, including humans, an evolution thereby occurs, into a resultant altered personality. Physical growth and mental re-orientation happens within the basic boundary conditions coded in the specific primary matrix. Whatever the evolution or growth, the empirical individual can never know, or experience everything completely, even in the objective domain. Human beings, the highly evolved of the living species, even with all the means available (sought and developed by them), shall always feel restricted in their quest to know or achieve, since all their means of knowing and achieving are dependent upon the available knowledge, which in turn is also conditioned. The body-dependence, a necessary shackle, with its defined and limited faculties, also plays an inhibiting role always. Termed in *śaiva* as *rāga* (the urges and affinities), *vidyā* (the limited and programmed knowledge), *kalā* (the limited performing capabilities), *niyati* (cause and effect), and *kāla* (time), the aspects that become inhibiting factors in understanding and functioning of all empirical individuals are the conditionings imposed by *Śakti* as *Māyā*. Called *kañchaks* of *māyā*, these boundary conditions act as restraining knots in transcendental freedom of these existents. Through its own infinite *swātantrya* (the absolute sovereignty and autonomy), restricting *its own immensities*, and fashioning out 'its own role', *Śakti* as *Māyā* constitutes out of itself, a *māyā-pramātā*, the empirical subject. Five knots or restrictions, in the form of *rāga*, *vidyā*, *kalā*, *kāla* and *niyati*, represent the limitations on the *śakti* for an empirical being, or in other words the ignorance of the actuality of its *swātantrya* in its transcendental domain. Not knowing that '*I am the source and the substance*' of everything that seems to exist, and that, in actuality there *is nothing else*, the *anu* (the *jīva*) experiences want, and therefore 'wants' as also does he experience the fear of losing, and thus develops *rāga* (the affinity and attachment). This ignorance reflects in every aspect of his existence, and results in doubts and inabilities to resolve and comprehend anything in entirety. Involvement in partial and assumed information, the *vidyā*, becomes the foundation of his ignorance about his being the sovereign in actuality. It affects his performance and potential as *kalā*, and makes him *endlessly*, a victim of *kāla* and *niyati*. *Māyā*, conditions the transcendental *pūrantā* as *rāga*, *sarvaġata* as *vidyā*, *sarva-kartṛtvata* as *kalā*, *nityata* as *kāla*, and *vyāpakta* as *niyati*. Outcome is *Śakti*, in the form of empirical beings. This limited subject is termed *puruša-tattva*, in the hierarchy of manifestations. *Puruša* functions in terms of interactions, within and without, with what is called, the *prakṛti-tattva*. *Prakṛti-tattva* is the root matrix of all objectivity, and therefore, the formative factor of the empirical individuals, and all that surrounds him or is encountered by him, not only at the human level, but also at the level of all interacting entities.

Prakṛti operates through its three basic traits, namely inertia (*tamas*), activity (*rajas*), and harmony (*sattva*), which form the fiber and the fabric of all the objective existence. These characteristics reflect in all the attributes of immanent existence. *Tamas* implies inertia, in all domains, physical, mental, and psychological, and refers to the continuance of a state, which implies also as attachment of, and holding on to anything. Ignorance, delusion, degeneration, and inaction, as well as opposition to any change, in physical, mental, or attitudinal domain, is the characteristic of *tamas*. *Rajas* implies all flux, including passion, craving, exploratory urges and similar other traits or the activity brought about by these, while *sattva* implies coordination, balance and harmony in creation. Cognition, evaluation, analyzing, balancing, rationalizing and locating the essence and harmony in everything from perceptive aspects is the domain of *sattva*. These three traits are actually the conditioned versions respectively of *Anuttra's Śakti* of *Kriyā*, *Iććhā*, and *Ġāna*, reflecting in a conditioned form as *prakṛti*, in the entire manifestation.

The personality of an empirical individual-experient, the *purušа*, is structured correspondingly by three personality aspects namely *ahaňkāra*, *mana*, and *budhi tattvas*. These internal matrices, for interaction within and without, are the operating tools of *puruśa*, with limited and conditioned faculties as against transcendental *will*, *Iććhā*, and *Ġāna* respectively in *Anuttra*. *Budhi*, the ascertaining faculty within *puruša,* although conditioned by *vasanā,* (the residual previous impressions *that* influence the judgment), is the most important tool, that rationalizes all knowledge and action in an empirical being ultimately. *Ahaṅkāra,* the product of *budhi,* is the basic pivot of the empirical existence. This is the basic matrix of one's personality. The sense of being of what one believes oneself to be, or the perception, one carries about oneself, and even, what others make one feel one is, the *ahaṅkāra* is the physical, the mental and the psychological picture (*ākāra*) one harbours about oneself. It is the feeling, ' *I am that* ' embodiment (*ākā*ra, *ahaṅkāra,* अहंकार, अहं+आकार). It is a very strong and compelling belief about oneself, and the strongest shackle that makes one believe that one is an empirical unit, the *anu,* of this existence. It is this that keeps an empirical being devoid of his transcendental recognition. *Mana* is the interacting operator. It works all the time for the appeasement of *ahaṅkāra,* the product of which, *it is.* This operator weaves all the fabric of, thoughts and feelings, desires and fears, likes and dislikes, all colored in the hues of prejudices and notions rooted in difference (*bheda*), like me and mine, I and the others, and all the distinction perpetrated by *ahaṅkāra.*

This *puruša,* the unitary objective existence, defined by its *ahaṅkāra,* and equipped with its tools of *budhi* and *mana* interacts within, as well as with all that makes his surroundings, (*prakṛti* in and out), made up of the fiber of three *guṇas,* and structured out of *panća-mahā-bhūta,* the five-great-gross elemental aspects of objectivity. In fact the *puruša* represents the subjective aspect, and the *prakṛti*, the objective aspect of the entire manifested world of objectivity. The manifested entities, from the grossest of the materials, to the subtlest of the material things, or their projections, including thoughts and feelings, sounds and visuals etc., in all the dimensions of the existence, makes this objective creation. It is a set up, comprising of the subjective, the objective and their mutual interactive modes and means, resulting in the accumulation and exchange of knowledge and information. There has to be, thus, a basic and common interface for communication and interaction between the empirical existents, all actually the varied patterns of existence. Exchange of information, also in terms of varied, but specific patterns, between various subjects, (which themselves are an outcome of some pattern), constitutes a phenomenon that is very subtle and intriguing. The distinctness and identity of each of the patterns, the subject, the communication and the object of study during an interaction, in any specific event whatsoever, remaining discreet, and true, without any alteration in the basic patterns of any, is therefore very crucial, to all interactions. Accomplishment of it all, therefore, requires an appropriate and inherent *common software*, in the operating systems of *everything* in this creation.

Our mundane world comprises broadly three basic segments, namely biosphere, atmosphere, and the one that is in the vast spaces and beyond. Electromagnetic form of energy like light, heat, and several other wave entities, abundantly comes from the extra-terrestrial domain, in addition to that of the terrestrial one. This domain of energy, a segment of which aids our perception of vision, is termed as *teja* (or *agni*) *tattva* in the category of *mahā-bhūtas*. Much of this electromagnetic energy is not perceived by us directly (some additional range of this energy domain is detectable through certain other means, and with the help of various different physical tools available at present). This *teja* (or *agni*), domain of light, makes our vision, comprising information from the *shape* and *color* world, possible. This information is processed within us by the *faculty of vision*. This vision is possible, not due to eyes, which are mere instruments aiding the phenomenon of seeing, but, due to the entire faculty of vision, which incorporates a lot many other tools and mechanisms (like sensory signals and chemical patterns) within this faculty. This energy input of *teja*, carrying discreet information about the particular event of seeing, can provide great knowledge about the event, if appropriately identified, processed and classified. This is made possible only by the intervention of a composite, and labeled, storehouse of all the discreet visual information that can *ever* occur (and is meant to be identified), a clearly defined software on vision, called *rūpa-tanmātra*. It should be clear, that for any visual interaction to happen through the instruments of eyes, etc., three clear-cut *tattvas* of *Śakti* are necessary, which are, firstly, the *Śakti* in the form of a signal from the external *tattvas* of *bhūtas* (*rūpa*, representing form and color, in this case), secondly, the *Śakti* as the faculty of 'processing of' vision, or the *indriya* of vision (*ćakšu-indriya*), and thirdly, the *Śakti* for the identification and discernment of the vision, that is, software on *rūpa-tanmātra.* Similarly, for other interactions to happen on the terrestrial domain, the *puruša* has to be equipped with appropriate faculties for receiving, identifying and analyzing each and every input from the objective world constituted of *panća-mahā-bhūta.* The signals therefore from the airy, watery, earthly, spatial and the electromagnetic domains of the constituted world, in the form of, touch (*sparśa*), taste (*rusa*), smell (*gandha*), sound (*śabda*), and visual (*rūpa*) inputs respectively require, as a result, distinct soft-wares with discreet information on the entire range of each, (all the specific inputs), that are meant to be received and processed by a particular empirical being. These clearly comprise a set of five *tanmātra-tattvas. Śabda-tanmātra* pertains to the domain of sound, *sparśa-tanmātra* to the domain of touch, *rusa-tanmātra* to the recognition and identification of taste and flavor, while *gandha-tanmātra* is the software concerning the world of smells and odours, (in addition to the *rūpa-tanmātra* pertaining to vision, mentioned earlier). These five *tattvas* of *Śakti,* with the entire information on recognition and identification of the interactions, through the different sense perceptions, is very vital to the matrix of personality of an empirical being. *Tanmātrās* with all the specific data-base, are the product of *ahaňkāra* and remain always aligned with it. The trio of *mana, budhi* and *ahaňkāra,* together known as *aňtaĥ-karņas,* (the internal operators of an empirical being,) along with five *tanmātrās,* form *Puryašťaka* (the domain of eight).

This group of eight constituents, the *Puryaśṭaka*, is said to be the carrier of all the *sańskāras*, the residual perceptions, of all the failings and fallings, the desires and fears, the yearnings and cravings, along with all the information on the fulfilled and unfulfilled tasks and activities (*karmas*), undertaken in every lifetime of the *Puruša*. This *Puryaśṭaka* constituting the *subtle-body* of an empirical being, is said to leave the gross-body at the time of the death of the latter, to go into a new posture of life, within the most appropriate objective environment chosen for it, on the mission of the fulfillment of the unfulfilled *karmas*. *Ańtaĥ-karṇas* thus operate in collaboration with *tanmātrās*, through a body (and its various tools), and all the operations are conducted through various specific faculties (*Śaktis* of *indriyas*). These *indriya-tattvas* of *Śakti*, at the disposal of a *puruša*, for specific perceptions and actions, operate through the inbuilt mechanisms in the gross-body. The perception-*indriyas* are for the cognizance and processing of inputs from five *mahā-bhūtās*, the material constituents of the objective world. These cognitive faculties, or the *tattvas* of five *ġāna-indriyas*, along with five faculties meant for the execution of the appropriate activities, the five *karma-indriyas*, are the *śaktis* at the disposal of *ahańkāra*. *Ghrānendriya*, *rusanendriya*, *ćakšurindriya*, *sparśanendriya*, and *śravanendriya* are the *śaktis* operating in the realms of the smelling, tasting, seeing, touching and hearing phenomenon respectively. *Karmendriyas* or the *śaktis* that make the operations in the domain of action possible, are *vāgindriya* (for speech), *hastendriya* (for handling), *pādendriya* (locomotive), *pāyvindriya* (excretory), and *upasthendriya* (for sexual activity). It must be clearly understood that, the organs like nose, tongue, eyes, skin and ears, are the mere tools in the process of various cognitive operations. They are not the *ġānendriya*, and similarly, tongue, lips, hands, feet and genitals, etc. are not the *karmendriya,* but merely the tools in the most subtle processes accomplished by the respective *Śakti-tattvas* of *karmendriyas*.

There is thus an empirical individual, the *anu* or the *puruša*, a *tattva*, a compact entity for an objective expression, that *Śakti* has resorted to, in which, by its own potency of authority as *Māyā*, she inculcates the sense of difference and also shapes it with all the boundary conditions that specify the potentials and limits for its various performances, all coded in its structural matrix. The sense of difference brought in by the *Māyā-tattva,* implies its alienation from its basic transcendental essence, which deprives it of its absolute sovereignty and the sense of entirety, such that it considers itself a unit (*anu*), different from everything else. This, a covering over its true entity, the extraneous dross that makes it believe itself to be an *anu*, is called *ānava-mala*. *Māyā*, the limiting *Śakti*, makes it believe that it has definite and specific potentials and knowledge, as also deficiencies, and thus prompts it to crave for more, and resort to various means like performance of various activities successively over time, for the desired satiation. This sense, of being equipped with the limited faculties is due to the influence of the *mayic* fabric in its structure, and is therefore termed as *mayiya-mala*.

The empirical individual, the *Puruša,* with its structured *Śaktis* of various faculties, performs interactions with everything under the influence of this *mayiya-mala.* These interactions influence him further and create deep impacts in the form of *vāsanās* and *sanskārs* in him, which envelope him with further dross. This dross is termed as *karma-mala.* This *mala* gives a specific hue to the kind of activity he performs. He tags it good, bad, cowardly, brave, pleasant, etc., depending upon various estimations, values or concepts cultivated, or reactions obtained during his interactions with *prakṛti* comprising everything that it encounters, within and without. It forms the sum total of all, that the *Puruša* has perceived and preserved, through all his perceptive faculties and actions, right from the dawn of *sṛšti* (the manifested creation). It has always seen the solid earth, huge and wide, the *dhārani,* the sustainer, with all that it harbours, including the wide-spread waterscapes and intimately surrounding atmosphere, and beyond, the intriguing and awe-inspiring starry skies, with all the varied astronomical bodies, and other allied phenomena. It has seen them, felt them, and interacted with them, in innumerable ways. The enchanting lights and visuals from the far and near, the ever present air intimately and tenderly kissing and patting it, the water drenching and refreshing it, and providing a vehicle for the intake and assimilation of all savor, all the fumes and perfumes from the soil and all that it bears, and all the rhythms and sounds from the known and unknown vastnesses, have been his entire life. This *anu,* thrived on this, cherished it, dreaded it and interacted with it. It was his projection, it was his fiber and fabric, it was all inside and outside of him. It was his *prakṛti* ! He could see certain things, but not all things, he could hear certain things, but not all. He could feel the touch of things, the taste and aroma of things, not all, but it was all, his thrill and enchantment, his cushion and his dream. The soil became his source of all the aromas, as the water his source and medium for all tastes, light the medium for all he could see, and air intervened, all over his body like his skin, between him and all he could touch and be touched by. The vastness and the spaces, within and without, mental and physical, became domains, where sounds, as words and rhythms, could stretch their wings and distinctly present themselves, as the world of charming existence, that, from *parā* through *paśyanti* and *madhyama* flowered in the domain of his recognition. All his perceptions thrived on all he found there was, in the world of matter, from the subtlest to the grossest, and all formed out of the five *tattvas*, the five basic materials. He named them *panća-mahā-bhūta*, the five-great-basic aspects of objectivity. All that he saw, dreadful or enchanting, was an aspect of *tej*, all that was eatable or non-eatable was an aspect of earth, the *prithvi*, all that was drinkable or non-drinkable was like water, all that touched, moved, carried, or thrust him invisibly was like air, and all that received, contained or provided relief and passage to him and everything else, was the mysterious space, without which nothing would ever get an objective form or name (*nāma-rūpa*), and thus the existence. The vehicles for various sensory experiences were thus identified and classified as light (*teja*) for vision, water (*apas*) for taste (*rusa*), earth (*pṛthvī*) for smell (*gandha*), air (*vayū*) for touch (*sparśa*), and space (*ākāśa*) for word or sound (*śabda*). The fact is, that in spite of their individual entities and *tattva* entitlement, they all exist implicitly and explicitly within the *prithvi-tattva* which is the bearer (*dhāranī*) of all. The ultimate *Parama-Śiva*, the *Anuttra*, the *abheda*, the *nirvikalpa*, the *nitya* (perpetual), assumes, from his indeterminate state of absolute sovereignty, all these manifested forms, full of difference and transitory-ness, up to the *pṛthvī-tattva*, in His creative urge for manifestation. This is not a phenomenon that took place as an event in time and space, specified by any succession or plan. It is ever there, as *Anuttra* itself, a perpetual existence within non-existence, manifest within non-manifest, determinate within indeterminate, *there, ever* ! ...One aspect emerging out of the other, and in the utter delight of its culmination, merging, back into it, perpetually. Starting from the first *spanda* of creation, the *Śakti-in-action,* becomes everything, to the last manifestation, the *dhāranī,* the supporter, the *pṛthvī-tattva,* the *dhartī* (earth)! A perpetual phenomenon is *it,* and no phenomenon at all. It is all in time and beyond time, transcendental as well as immanent ! There is no beginning or succession nor an end to it. It is *nitya,* the *ever* ! From the perspective of the objective, it is in time, in evolution, in spells, in stretches, in all the attributes that can be, while in the transcendental, it is only potency, entire and whole, ever visualized in everything and *truly* never visualized. It is the perpetual bliss of only *being* without becoming, and also, the *being* enjoying the *becoming*, endlessly ! And then in the utter amazement of *becoming*, getting dissolved in the thrill of *being*, the *ānanda* of pure awareness !

Looking at various *tattvas* of manifestation hierarchy, we find that objectivity has several different connotations at various levels of subjectivity. In the transcendental domain of *śuddha-tattvas* of *sadāśiva*, *Iśwara* and *śuddha-vidyā*, both the *abheda* and *bhedabheda* relation with the pure subject exists. The perspective of objectivity is rather different in different *pramātās*. An empirical experient, who ascends through the process of experiencing various *tattvas*, all the way to the last step of *tattva-anubhava*, the *Sadāśiva* domain, experiences in actuality the pure universal consciousness state with a very faint trace of the objectiveness of the entire universe identical with his being and vaguely discernible. Such experient, is a subject (*pramātrā*, known as *mantra-maheśwara*), who is at the level of *sādakhya-tattva*, (the stage of *seeing-true-being*) and is actually like *Sadāśiva* experiencing the sprouting of the will of *Bhairava*. On the other hand the experient at the *Iśwara-tattva* stage, the *mantreśwara*, although still experiencing universal consciousness, is acutely conscious of the universal objectivity, with its complete apprehension (*Ġāna*), and even then he does not find it different or separate from the pure consciousness, like foam of butter floating in the milk of his consciousness! To an experient at *Śuddha-vidyā-tattva*, the *vidyeśwara* also called *mantra*, the objectivity is distinct and diverse. For him it has a separate existence, but not different from him in essence. He sees it sprouting forth from *himself*, (which he *knows* is pure consciousness only), like a bud, a leaf, a thorn or a flower from a branch, and enjoys the wondrous sprouting in immense delight. It is the aspect of *Kriyā*, the becoming of manifestation out of transcendence. In this *parāprā*, a *bhedabheda* state, he beholds all happening out of himself, at the threshold of transcendence and immanence. Experients in these three *tattvas* enjoy the domain of the actuality of truth, the 'universality of the being' in essence along with autonomy and bliss.

At *Māyā* level where the difference (*bheda*) sets in, there are two subjectivity aspects. For *Māyā*, the *Śakti*, there is no difference between her, the *Śakti*, the transcendental reality and the objective manifestation, while for the objective existent who rises to this state of experience, an entirely different realization happens. The experient reaching the onset level of *Māyā*, just below the *Śuddha-vidyā-tattva* level loses the lower-level sense of objectivity brought about by *Māyā* through *kañchakas*, as this state is prior to the initiation into the limitations introduced by *Māyā* during the process of manifestation. The experient of this state called *viġānā-kala* is devoid completely of the experience of '*this*', (the objectivity) and has only a peculiar sense of *I* . This *I*-ness is without any awareness, an un-awakened (*aprabuddha*) state, one without any *bodha* of the essential unity of the transcendental and immanent or the unity of his I-ness with any other. At this stage, the experient *viġānā-kala*, having only *ānava-mala*, the sense of individual-being, has only a pure consciousness of *'being a separate entity'* (*śuddha-bodhātmanaĥ*) and not the universal consciousness. He has no sense of agency or authorship (*kartṛtvata*) of anything. Some schools of *Śaiva*, other than *Trika* attribute this state to a different *tattva* called *Mahāmāyā-tattva* which they count other than *Māyā*. This *tattva*, they believe inculcates only a sense of separateness, the *ānava-mala* and thus the domain of *Viġānā-kalā* experients.

" Which is the domain of *Viġānā-kala*, the one, above *Māyā-tattva* and below *Śuddha-vidya tattva*, when *Māyā-tattva* is the domain of the *śūnya-pramātā*, (also called *pralayākala-pramātā*) and *Śuddh-vidyā-tattva* the domain of *vidyeshwaras?* " is the question posed in *Mālinīvijayottara*.

(मायोर्ध्वे शुद्धविद्याध: सन्ति विज्ञानकेवला: ...PTV - 40/22)

Trika holds that *Māyā* veils the awareness of transcendental *I* - ness, the *swātantrya* and the sense of fundamental unity with *Śakti*, differentiated only as *śuddha-vikalpa* in its transcendental domain, and therefore experients ascending to this state do not possess any transcendental sense of unity and sovereignty . Again there being no defined identifiable objective existence at the *Māyā tattva* state, (the limited authorship is inculcated through various *kañćakas* differentiated below this level which, having been completely obliterated in the experients that ascend to *Māyā tattv*a level, just at the transition point between it and the *Śuddha-vidya-tattva*) the possession, only of just an undefined identity of being 'different', (the *ānava-mala*) remains in the *pramātās* at this stage. V*ig̊ānā-kala* is just that subjective state of an experient rising to the extreme top of the *Māyā-tattva-state.*

Before *Māyā* inculcates *kañćakas*, rather formats the complete matrix for the specified objective existence of *puruša*, it shrouds the *bodha* aspect completely. Having obliterated the transcendental sense, both of the *I* and the *this*, the sense *'this'*, as the objectivity, not yet defined by *māyā*, the experience at this stage is of complete void. An experient going through the experiencing of *Māyā-tattva* at this stage, although free from *karma-mala*, does have *ānava-mala* and a vague aura of *mayiya-mala* of the sense of void. Having no clearly defined consciousness, either universal, or any other kind of specifically designed consciousness, he experiences a deep-sleep like void and a 'vague-something' like consciousness. Called *pralayākala-pramātā*, he is said to have a consciousness like that of *prakṛti* at the time of dissolution (*pralayā*). The experient therefore is called *śūnya-pramātā* or *pralayakevalin*, for he is a subject, a *pramātā*, of void or dissolution state of objectivity, and also whose sense of universal awareness is shrouded.

The perspective of *Puruša* vis-à-vis *prakṛti* is different. The *puryašṭaka-pramātā* or the so called *ćitta-pramātā*, (the subject from the point of view of *añtaĥ-karana* and *indriyas*) has a view different from that of the subject at the body perspective (*deha-pramātā*). All the different infinite number of subjects under the influence of different variations of *mayiya-mala* and *karma-mala* possess different views of their subjective and objective relations and understandings. In fact, all subjects below *Māyā-tattva* up to the grossest of manifestations, are *all* from objective domain, and are thus scaled down and afflicted with three basic *malas* or classes of prejudices. These subjects, the empirical beings, (*devās* included) are called *sakalas*. The experience of *sakālas* is colored by all the biases they harbor, and thus, are all full of difference.

The considerations made above, in addition to providing a deeper perspective on *Śiva-Sūtra-* (3), alongwith the hierarchy of *tattvas* as visualized in *Trika-śastra*, elaborates further upon the essence of *sūtras*-(1-2) of *Pratyabhiġān–hṛdayam* [i.e, "*vishwa (universe) is projected upon the screen of itself by chiti, of its own sovereign will* "] providing also a perspective for understanding clearly the following *Sūtras* (3, 8 & 7) of *Pratyabhiġāna–hṛdayam* :

तन्नाना अनुरूपग्राह्यग्राहकभेदात

Tannānā anurūpa-grahya-grāhaka-bhedāta

sūtra-(pbh – 3)

"that (the universe) seems manifold due to the differentiation in the aspects of (different) subjects with respect to the objects."

तद्भूमिकाः सर्वदर्शनस्थितयः

tad-bhumikaĥ sarvadarśana-sthitayĥ

sūtra-(pbh – 8)

"Philosophies [all] are rooted in any one of the various roles performed by that [the ultimate reality]".

स चैको द्विरूपस्त्रिमयश्चतुरात्मा सप्तपञ्चकस्वभावः

(sa ćaiko dvirupas-trimyś-ćaturātmā saptapañćak-swabhāvaĥ)

sūtra-(pbh -7)

" He is one, and becomes in form, twofold, threefold, fourfold and seven-pentad-fold ."

The differentiation with respect to the aspects in subject-object relationship referred to above is true at all the levels, be those, pure philosophy (only academically), or actual experiencing through *tattva-anubhav* at various stages. The variations in the positions taken with regard to the ultimate reality, are simply due to the differences in the perspectives held by various subjects with respect to the reality. For different *Ġāna-confines* the revelation of truth has different connotations, which simply depend upon how their particular matrix receives and interprets it.

More the boundary conditions collapse, closer the awareness touches him from within. One can never grasp anything unless it comes into the field of one's awareness, and anything grasped in its essence needs no elucidation further. One may philosophize it, cherish it or just hold on to it, until, something more subtle touches one's field of awareness. But it is after all, the awareness, in its absolute and pure state only that *is* the fundamental truth. The ultimate *vimarśamaya-prakāśa*, the unique reality, overflows out of itself, differentiating itself, into two basic aspects, *Śiva* and *Śakti*, the *vyāpaktā* (self revealing-ness) of *being* and the *potency* of the awareness (*Ġāna* and *Kriyā*) of being, both necessary for its expansion into the universal immanent reality. The *one* manifests itself as *two*. *Śiva*, the unchanging *vyāpaktā* of the sense of being, always the transcendental subjectivity and never objective, although *ever* the background and the base for any manifestation, remaining always *parā*, beyond any recognition and definition in the objective domain, is realized only in its transcendental domain, as *prakāśa*, in its true *being-ness* of *all* immanent as well as transcendental *existence*. *Śakti*, that unfolds as everything, from the vague transcendental desire or will to create, to the most tangible objectivity, the earth, through all the various aspects of all the different *tattvas* of its becoming, is both, the differentiated and the undifferentiated. It is thus the *parāparā*, also known as *guru-vaktra*, the mouth of *guru*, the entrance leading to *Śiva*. Expressing itself as all it desires to become, it culminates into the living empirical being, the *anu*, the *nara*-aspect of existence, possessing in it, all the *tattvas* of the manifested existence. *Trika* holds that the totality of the reality is expressed completely by *Anuttra*, through its *three* aspects, the triad (*trika*) of *Śiva*, *Śakti* and *nara*. All the *four* domains (*andās*) of existence, namely, the *Śakti-andā*, the *Māyā-andā*, the *Prakṛti-andā* and the *Pṛthvi-andā*, with all the various different *tattvas*, remain incorporated in the *nara*, or else, there would be no release, or no scope for an empirical being to cast it all away, and experience its true essence of *aham*, the real recognition of his self. All the aspects of the '*becoming*' of *Śakti*, the 34 *tattvas* (from *pṛthvi* to *sadāśiva*) constituting the four *andās* *(see page 136)* , incorporate the thirty-fifth aspect of the *anāśrita-Śiva* inherent in all the aspects as the pure *Śiva-tattva*, the aspect of their *being*. These thirty-five *tattvas*, the sum-total of the existence are called *seven-pentads* of existence as referred to in the *Sūtra*-(7) of *Pratyabhiġāna-hṛdayama*.

These aspects constitute *everything* objective, and therefore *all* these aspects of *Śakti* as well as *anāśrita-śiva* are accessible to *nara* most intimately, as all these are actually its constituents. *Sṛšṭi*, the universe, in the form of entire objective manifestation, structured in these thirty-five *tattvas* *is* the tangible body of the *parama-śiva*, the supreme consciousness *ćit*, which *He* has emitted out of Himself through *vāman-yukti*. Since all these *tattvas* constitute the *nara* also, and are therefore accessible to him, he also bears the universe as his body in a contracted form. These *tattvas* are accessible to *nara* through the process of absorption (*grassana-yukti*) of preceding by the succeeding *tattva.*

चितिसंकोचात्मा चेतनोऽपि संकुचितविश्वमय:

(*ćitisankoć-ātmā ćetno-api sankućit-viśwamayaĥ*)

Sūtra-(pbh - 4)

"*contracted-ćiti-subject (the nara) is possessor of contracted (form of) universe, and he experiences that.* "

It can be concluded therefore, that the ultimate reality, the singular and perfect, the entirely autonomous potency, imposes willingly, the boundary conditions of various orders on Himself, to transform Himself, the pure awareness into an empirical entity, bound, limited, and deluded through *ānava, mayiya,* and *karma* prejudices (*malas*) and thus, subject to entanglement of taking on postures after postures of limited forms of existence, as a *samsārī*, subject to the cycles of birth and death. The reality is that anything whatsoever, that constitutes and is experienced as this universe, is specific in nature and attributes. It evokes responses from senses and is perceived and handled through senses, which in themselves are specifically coded for their functioning, right from their grossest external make-up, to the subtlest of their *Śakti* aspects, as the handlers within. Their experients, the empirical beings are equally custom made, and it is therefore conceivable that everything in this universe, to exist or to function, is conditioned and coded specifically in all of the existing, infinitely different projections. We may call it contraction, delusion, aberration, *mala*, confinement, or being a victim of time, space and causation, whatever, but, it is the fiber of which this *sansāra* has to be.

Consider *Pratyabhiġāna-hṛdayama sūtra-(9)* conveying the same precisely !

चिद्वत्तच्छक्तिसंकोचात् मलावृत: संसारी

(ćidvattiććhakti-sankoćāt malāvṛtaĥ samsārī)

sūtra–(pbh – 9)

"Ćit , by virtue of the shrinkage (imposed on Himself) through His (own) desire, becomes a deluded trans-migratory (empirical) being. "

Ćidānanda-ghana, the supreme *parā-Bhairava*, through His will, the absolutely autonomous potency, His *Śakti*, does it all. *Śakti* undertakes and undergoes all those infinite transformations. How wondrous and amazing for the attribute-less to become an endless panorama of all the un-imaginable diversity of wonder, more so when *She* (the *Śakti*) knows that *She* is all that, and therefore enjoys being all that. In fact *Ānanda*, *Bhairava's* over-brimming urge for expression, an expansion of *His being*, is *His swabhaava* and *that* is why He is called *Bhairava*. *Bha* of *Bhairava* signifies *bharana*, the maintenance, *ra* stands for *ravana*, the withdrawal, and *va*, the *vamana*, the projection of the manifested world. *Bha+ra+va* represents the maintenance, dissolution and projection aspects of *Anuttra* and that gives *Him* the title *Bhairava.* Although a mental grasp of the absolutely incomprehensible relationship of transcendental and immanent reality is not possible, some kind of a vague perception would be amusing. *Bhairava* as *Ćidānand-ghana*, is a unique reality of *vimarśa-maya-prakāśa* with two aspects, one the *chit*-aspect, (*nitya-vyāpak*, *pūran-mahā-satta*) the *prakāśa*, and the other, the *ānand-ghan*, the immense bliss of the potency of entire knowledge and action (*Ġāna*, and *Kriyā*), the *vimarśa. Prakāśa* projects a concept of its being an eternal and universal subject, which is the *sole* cause of *its own being*, and the being of *everything else*. The *spanda* of *Iććhā* is its indicator, which as *vimarśa* is His absolute freedom of knowing and doing anything. It is this *Ġāna* and *Kriyā* aspect, that results in the manifestation of all that can be. *Ġāna*, *Kriyā*, and *Iććhā* represent the *bha*, *ra*, and *va*, aspects of the *parā-Bhairava.* According to *trika* view, perpetual projection (*sṛšti*), maintenance (*stithi*), and dissolution (*samhāra*) is the *swabhāva* of *parā-Bhairava.* representing its aspects of *Iććhā*, *Ġāna*, and *Kriyā* respectively. *Kriyā*, the potency of action reflects its *swātantrya* and *pūrantā* (the complete autonomy and sovereignty) in action, for withdrawing everything into *itself* completely after projecting itself as anything to project yet again as another aspect of *sṛšti. Kriyā* as *Samhāra*, therefore yields the touch of its transcendental *vyāpaktā*, a sameness with *Himself* on dissolution, which is also termed as *anugraha.* If complete withdrawal does not happen, and even the faintest trace of empirical existence lurks, it inhibits the sameness with the transcendental *being*, which remains shrouded, a state called *vilaya*, the obscurity, and thus a seeding state for the furtherance of the empirical state of existence. *Parā-Bhairava*, plays the sport of this *panćakṛtya* (five-pronged performance), as it is His *swabhāva*, His joy, His *ānanda*, the overflowing out of Himself, onto Himself and unto Himself again perpetually. Nothing alters! Prompted by the *will* He performs and cherishes it all Himself and is fully aware of it all. Empirical beings also desire, but because they feel a want, have a sense of incompleteness, and therefore a craving for one or the other feeling or thing. They pursue the objective and get attached to it, and hence have a sense of *rāga* as against the *pūrantā* of *Bhairava*. They lack the ability to achieve as they possess a sense of limited faculty of action (*kalā*) as against His *sarva-kṛtatvata*, the omnipotence. Empirical beings have a limited understanding or knowledge (*vidyā*) as against the transcendental *Ġāna*, the *sarvaġatā*, and this ignorance in him of his real *self* (the *nitya-sarva-kalā-sampūranta*) makes him a prey to the *kāla* and *niyati*. This delusion because of the sense of difference in him with regard to his real self, and thus considering everything else as separate and different, keeps him a captive of *vilaya*, and makes of him a *paśu* against being a *pati*. Unlike *Bhairava*, therefore *nara* has *Iććhā*, but because of want caused by the sense of comparison born of difference. He harbours a *Ġāna* (*a-ġāna*) projecting only a sense of difference. He also performs *Kriyā* that only breeds difference and generates a vicious-circle of cause and effect, remaining thus a captive of *vilaya* and not the recipient of *anugraha.* His *Kriyā* is never accomplished, or so he feels, and the true *samhār* never happens to him. How can then *anugraha* or sameness with His real self ever happen to him as such. Even while seeking one thing he is planning for the other, and he relishes neither. This veiling of the real self and therefore the ignorance of one's real nature of *Śaktis* of *Iććhā*, *ġāna* and *Kriyā*, make him resort to their operation through assumed notions only, thus keeping the empirical being (*samsārī*) always deluded.

Sūtras(10,11,&12) of *Pratyabhiġāna-hṛdayama* convey the same.

तथापि तद्वत् पञ्च कृत्यानि करोति

(tathāpi tadvat pañća kṛtyāni karoti)

sūtra-(pbh – 10)

"even so (as an empirical being), like Him (Bhairava), he performs pañćakṛtyās."

आभासन-रक्ति-विमर्शन-बीजावस्थापन-विलापनतस्तानि

(ābhāsan - rakti – vimarśana – bījāvasthāpan – vilāpanatastāni)

sūtra–(pbh – 11)

"(Namely) manifesting, relishing, removing the veil, seeding,(and) dissolution."

तदपरिज्ञाने स्वशक्तिभिर्व्यामोहितता संसारित्वम्

(tad-aparigāne svaśaktibhir-vyāmohitatā samsāritvam)
sūtra–(pbh – 12)

"Being ignorant of that understanding, (resulting in) being deluded by one's own Śaktis, is, being a samsāri"

Awareness is the essence. It is the *master* and the *master-key*. Being aware is being *pati*, the absolute subject. Being ignorant is being deluded, the victim, the *paśu*, the empirical existent, ever bound and degraded, ever in conflict and want. It is like an eagle believing itself to be a chicken. What as *Bhairava* is sport in *sṛṣṭi*, *sthiti*, and *samhāra*, the bliss of infinite diversity in the unity of *Śakti*, is agony of conflict, and the grinding mill of the vicious circles of differences as *nara*. What as *Bhairava* is fulfillment, as *nara* it is deprivation. That is what differentiates *paśu* from *pati*, *samsāri* from *Bhairava*. Being, for Him connotes *prakāśa* of *vyāpaktā* as complete (*pūrana*), free (*swātantra*), and ever (*nitya*), while for *samsāri* it connotes the sense of incompleteness and therefore craving (*rāga*), subject to cause and effect and transitory-ness, the constraints of causation (*niyati*), and time (kāla). *Iććhā* for *Bhairava* means creativity (*sṛšti*) out of itself, an expansion into maiden horizons of its self, with *ānanda* of amazement, while for *anu* it is a frantic effort to seek its fulfillment, ever trying to fill its gaps and hollows. *Stithi* for *bhairava* is to cherish the expanses of its being, bliss of the awareness *(Ġāna)* of its self, and for *anu* it is the pangs of the fear of failure or loss, considering alternatives, and the lasting suffering caused by his ignorance and inherent conflict due to incomplete knowledge *(vidyā)*. *Samhāra* for *Bhairava* is withdrawal of His cherished horizons again into himself, *His ātma-viśrānti* (repose into Himself), which could be the *anugraha* for the *anu*, but it doesn't happen to *anu* as he never sees the complete fulfillment of a desire. S*amhāra* connotes death, loss and pain to him. This leads to sowing of the seeds yet again, of a new desire. It is the ignorance of his true need and fulfillment, and therefore *vilaya*, the masking of 'sameness with the truth'. Actually no 'two things' happen. The *sṛšti* is same, only the perspectives are different. Considering oneself being a *Ćitta-pramātā* creates the delusion of being *paśu* conditioned in the differentiations while the true awareness of *Bhairava-awastha* makes one *Pati*, absolutely free and sovereign enjoying the bliss of unity in transcendental and immanent reality.

Bhairava the *Parama-Śiva* is *sarvakartṛtva*, the one that *can* do *anything* ! while an *anu* has infinitely scaled down efficacy of performance, the *kalā*. *Bhairava* knows *all*, is *sarvaġa*, while the knowledge of *anu* is partial, an outcome of differentiation and not totality, thus delusive. *Bhairava* is *pūrana*, perfect and entire while *anu* is limited and specific and thus full of want and craving, thereby harboring *rāga*. *Bhairava* is *nitya* the eternal, and *anu* is transitory, the victim of time, the *kāla*. *He* is *vyāpaka* and *swātantra*, (everywhere and free) while the *anu* is subject to *niyati*, the causation and space. These *five* limitations make the *anu* an empirical subject, the *puruša*, the limimted and deluded experient, while *Bhairava* is *Mahāsatta*, the absolute existence-consciousness the *only* absolute subjective reality. It is this difference in perspectives that make the whole difference between a *paśu* and *Pati*.

Lalleśwari , the brightest beacon of *trika* understanding and realization, who, in her bodily abode graced the valley of Kashmir, (14th centuary A.D.), utters this *anubhav* as under:

यिमय र्श र्च़ , तिमय र्श छि र्म
श्यामगला छुख तटस्थ , र्म बैन
यिहिय बैनुबेद , छु बैन, र्च़ तु र्म
बु मूशुस र्शयव , चु सुमी र्शैन ।

The six you keep are the six I possess. you blue-necked (Śiva) are unbiased and I harbor differentiation. Just this differentiation makes the whole difference, between you and me, as I am robbed by these six, and you are the master of the six !

For *Bhairava* the objective manifestation is an utterance of *parāvāk* like a spontaneous musical note uttered in an ecstatic state of mind, or a whiff of aroma taking to wings from a flower, but for the objective existent it is a tangible reality of grief, *his reality* of existence. *Bhairava* is the cause and essence of all objectivity, but objectivity is not *His* domain. He is not objective, He is a pure subjective reality. *Parāvāk* are the utterances of objectivity from the *throat* of *Śiva* (*the nīla-kanṭha*) whereas, the entire being of *Śiva* is not *blue* with it. The (*viša*) poison of differentiation is not *in* the reality of *Śiva*. Projecting *sṛšṭi* full of differentiation out of *Himself, He* enjoys, as much as its withdrawal, *all* into Himself, the pure awareness. It is His *ānanda*. There is no preference or bias for what is created or assimilated. His creative urge is unbiased, while what gets created is all rooted in difference only, as it is the foundation of the matrix of creation. *Anu*, believing it to be his truth and essence, needs only to lift this veil, and all the differences shall vanish. *Paśu* will find itself in the actuality of *pati*.

In the light of *Sūtras*, (quoted from *Śiva-sūtras, parātrīśikā*, and *pratyabhiġāna-hṛdayama*,) unfolded systematically, we have built a panoramic aspect of *sṛšṭi* structured out of the ultimate creative consciousness, the *ćiti*. It has yielded a very lucid perspective of the complete warp and weft of the entire manifestation that *ćiti*, the pure awareness, acting as the source (योनी) and the foundation (आधार), spins and weaves out of itself like a silk-worm, a cocoon of confinement for itself, in innumerable ways, on infinite threads of time and space, (also projected out of itself) perpetually. And as we will see subsequently, it also has all the means, in the master-key of awareness, for piercing through the cocoon, and taking to wings, and fly into the infinite skies of freedom, filled with amazement and thrill of *vimarśamaya-prakāśa.*

Mātṛkā

During our deliberations on *Śiva-sūtra-(3)* (regarding the source, classes and categories of existents), we found, (in view of various inputs, that came into focus during the keen study of different *sūtras* from other relevant sources also), that the entire lay-out of the existence, in terms of all various *Ġāna-confines*, is in actuality the infinite shrunken aspects of *ćiti*, the basic reality of all and everything. Since there exists thus, a unity of essence in all, it is possible therefore, that the interacting *ġāna-confines*, can have a common format and interface, for their mutual communication, which could, at the same time serve them as an appropriate medium, also for grasping of other inputs, from within and without. We understand that comprehension and knowledge (*Ġāna*), as well as its expression and communication, get formatted in terms of a language at *vaikhari* level in all thinking beings. Language shapes knowledge and thinking in a tangible pattern, although the basic comprehension and ideation gets processed at the deeper and subtler levels of *madhyama*, *paśyanti* and *parā*. Looking at all this, from the consciousness point of view, it becomes clear, that the whole structure of knowledge gets related to the being in a very subtle and profound manner, as was observed earlier also while considering the *Śravana* aspect of *Śakti* *(page–40,41)*. This opens an extremely enlightening perspective of the manifestation by *Śakti.* *Śiva-sūtra*-(4) declares it as follows:

ज्ञानाधिष्ठानं मातृका

(Ġāna-adhišthānam mātṛkā)

sūtra-(ss - I - 4)

" *Mātṛkā* (*mother of all verbal and non-verbal sound and word*), *is the foundation and structure of all knowledge,*"

"Language and the rules of grammar reflect consciousness. This is not limited to Sanskrit language only but applies to all languages, for there is no speech which does not reach the heart directly", says Abhinavgupta, the grandmaster of *trika* doctrine of *Kashmir Śaivism.* Language is inseparable from consciousness. This fact is clearly observable with respect to the Sanskrit language, in which the study of mystical and philosophical speculation on letters (words and sentences) can take one into very subtle states of considerations. Mystical dimensions of Sanskrit grammar, linguistic speculations and philosophical reasoning can lend a lot of insight into modern philosophy of language. Because of the multiple dimensions of meanings contained in letters and words, language as a whole is a complete symbolical system. The divine consciousness is identical with the supreme word (परा वाक) and hence, every letter or word is derived from, and hence inseparable from consciousness. *Trika* philosophy maintains that the entire manifestation is an expression of transcendental logos (परा वाक), which is a creative energy, and every letter or alphabet represents energy in some form. This letter and word power, the basis of all knowledge, is designated as *Mātṛkā* (मातृका), (the mother) in *trika* tradition, which holds that this *Parāvāk Śakti* (परावाक शक्ति) generates the whole creation. Assuming the form of *vedana* (वेदना), the inward feeling, indicative of the creative throb of *Śakti*, the germinal energy in the form of letters (vowels and consonants) acts as germ (शिव बीज) and womb (योनि), both adequate in themselves to form words, the designators (वाचक), and sentences (वाक्य), the designated objectivity, that bring about thinking. This thinking gets the nature of a unified sense, at the gross speech level *vaikhari* (वेखरी), where object and word are fully differentiated. *Mātṛkā* therefore pervades the entire universe, not merely as the seemingly evident gross speech at the *vaikhari* level, but also, along with the ultimate and subtle essentials of indeterminate level of *paśyanti* (पश्यन्ती), where it is undifferentiated, and *madhyama* (मध्यमा) where objectivity just sets in. *Parā* the highest divinity, is the dynamic form of *Anuttar*. Although, of the nature of highest stage of non-differentiation, it is teeming with endless variety of everything in indeterminate level of *parā*, and manifests through *paśyanti* and *madhyama* levels into *vaikhari*, the determinate (सविकल्प) level. Thus the speech manifests in *vaikhari*, ideation happens in *madhyama* and the experiencing of the indeterminate state happens in *paśyanti*. The truth only dawns through *parā*. This is why *mātṛkā* has been called the 'abode and authority' of all *Ġāna* in *Śiva-sūtra* (4). *All* objects, perceptions, ideas, etc. covered by the blanket term *savikalpa*, inhere in the *nirvikalpa* consciousness (सम्विद्), the creative energy of *Anuttra*, and emanate from it. Entire manifestation (कौलिकी सृष्टि) is an expression of the *Anuttra*, *says* Abhinavgupta :

(तदेवानुत्तरपदं सृष्टिरित्यर्थः ... PTV-34/18)

In *Śaiva* tradition, *Āgama* refers to the *śastras* that are believed to be the direct revelations in the form of *sūtras*. These *sūtras* are sometimes recorded in the form of conversation between *Devi* and *Bhairava*, where *Devi* puts a question, and *Bhairava*, to dispel the doubt or straighten the complexity, answers, in crisp and profound *sūtras*. The truth is that *Devi* is none other than the *parā-Śakti* Herself at the planes of *madhyama* and *paśyanti*, (in the process of objective manifestation of *parāvāk* into *vaikhari*), that seeks to know. And in *Her* undifferentiated status *parā-Śakti Herself*, one with *Śiva*, (in *Anuttra*) and always present in everything, as the highest truth of uninterrupted awareness, (in the form of Divine *I-consciousness*) that answers as *Bhairava*. While referring to *Parātrīśikā* Sūtras (1-4) earlier, we have already come across such mode of communication, where, while clearing the doubts of *Devi*, *Bhairava* addresses her as *vidhirdevi* and *kaulikī*, residing in *His hridya-vyomn*, and says that He would tell her all about *kouliki-vidhi*. In *Parātrīśikā Sūtras-(5-8)*, complete *kaulikī-vidhi* is communicated to *Devi* by *Bhairava*.

In *Sūtra-(5) Bhairava* says:

अथाद्यास्तिथय: सर्वे स्वरा बिन्द्ववसानगा:
तदन्त: कालयोगेन सोमसूर्यौ प्रकीर्तितौ

(athādya-astithayaĥ sarve swarā bindvava-sāngāĥ
Tadantĥ kālayogena somasūryao prakīrtitao)
...sūtra-(PT - 5)

"*The tithīs,* अ *etc. all,* are *vowels, ending in vindu (anuswar). At their end, through 'kālayogen' (the Kriyā-Śakti connection) is proclamation of soma and surya.*

Sūtra-(5) of *Parātrīśikā* quoted above reveals the crux of *trika* philosophy on creation. Subtle and involved, the vision is a very profound view of the manifestation of *sṛšti.* It traces the source of all objective manifestation in verbal expression (*parā-vāk*) of the indeterminate and undifferentiated reality, systematically.

Trika holds that the inner I-consciousness, the *vimarśa-Śakti*, the self-revelatory and self-verbalizing aspect of *Anuttra*, is represented by the Sanskrit word *aham* (अहं). This *aham* (*a* + *ha* + *m*), is the repository of all phonemes of Sanskrit alphabet (वर्ण). According to this tradition all these *varaṇas* (consonants and vowels) are not merely inert letters, but the creative powers of universe, transcendent to manifestation, and also those, manifested as various categories (*tattvas*) of existence. These are utterances of *parāvāk*, the verbal power of divine, forming the phoneme-tic creation (*varaṇa-sṛšti*).

Vimarśa-Śakti abides as unsurpassed, supreme autonomous power (*swātantrya-Śakti* स्वतंत्रिय शक्ति) of *Anuttra*, in the form of *will*. This autonomy or will is such, that what is *willed* is as yet not manifest. It is only the creative consciousness of *Anuttra*, the *Anuttra-satta* (अनुत्तर सत्ता), designated by phoneme अ . *Anuttra* is beyond all appellations or descriptions. It is the universal experient and has no trace of any objectivity. Although its essence (सत्ता) is creative consciousness, yet it is not involved in the manifestation of objectivity. अ is the first of the letters of the *mātṛkā* order, and the foremost amongst the vowels. (Vowels are also called *tithīs* in *trika* for their symbolic, philosophical correspondence with lunar days, the concept of which shall subsequently get cleared). अ is the highest stage of sound, (*parāvāg-bhumi* परावागभूमि , the breeding ground of all logos in the transcendental domain), which alone is the eternal, *non-conventional* and *natural* form of consciousness. It is designated therefore also as *tithīsha*, (तिथीशा) the lord of *tithīs*, (the vowels). This autonomy (*swātantrya-Śakti)* of अ , the creative impulse of over-brimming and unbounded fullness, expands into an unbounded bliss, the *ānand-Śakti* (आनन्द शक्ति). This state designated by phoneme आ is intent on expanding and expressing itself, as it is the *parā-visarga* (परा विसर्ग), the perpetual creative expression of the divine. Without any specific design or intent of objectivity, it takes the form of an urge or *akšubd-*

Iććhā (अक्षुब्ध इच्छा). This state of urge is not colored in objectivity at all and is therefore called *akšubd* or unperturbed *Iććhā*. It is designated as phoneme इ . Perceiving itself through its autonomy of knowledge it attains sovereignty or lordship in *Iććhā*. This state is called *Īśāna (* ईशान). *Kšubd* or perturbed state of *Iććhā*, it is designated as phoneme ई . *Iććhā* and *Īśāna* denoted as phonemes इ , ई represent the transcendental *will* or the supreme autonomy (*Iććhā-Śakti*) of *Anuttra* resting in its perfect state of bliss (आनन्द, आ). For its transcendental emanation (*mahā-sṛśti*) role, *Iććhā-Śakti* is also termed as *soma* (स:-उमा, that abides with *Uma*), and symbolized by moon. *Kšubd-Iććhā* or *Īśāna*, still a transcendental (*vishwotīrn*, विश्वोतीर्न) creative consciousness state, however subsequently expands into *unmeša*, (the source of all objective existents, desired to be known). This *unmeša*, the dawning of unperturbed knowledge or *akšubd-Ġāna* state is represented by the phoneme उ . Eagar for widening the aspect of objectivity more and more, the state of *unmeša* subsequently becomes perturbed or *kšubd* (क्षुब्ध) state of *Ġāna* or *ūnat-Ġāna* state, and is represented by phoneme ऊ . This immanent (विशवमयी) aspect of manifestation, separates into a multitude of objects, in which the aspect of difference is almost indistinct (*asphut* - असफुट), and which, abide identically in the transcendental consciousness of *Iććhā-Śakti*. This expansion into an entire gamut of the manifested (*sphut* - सफुट) objective world internally, gives *Ġāna-Śakti* (ज्ञानशक्ति) represented by (उ, ऊ) (*unmeša* and *ūnatā*) a role like sun, a *sūrya-bhava* (सूर्यभाव). This identification with widening of knowledge causes reduction in its transcendental consciousness. By retaining within it, the entire objectivity to be manifested, it gets emaciated in its transcendental consciousness, which triggers a tremendous power of withdrawal within it. This causes it to withdraw the whole objectivity, and deposit it in the subjectivity aspect of *anāśrita-Śiva-bhāva,* the transcendental subjectivity. This aspect of withdrawal gives it a role of *mahā-samhāra-Śakti* (महासंहारशक्ति). Thus the role of *ġāna-Śakti* is dual, the bringing to light of the objectivity from the creative urge aspect of *Iććhā-Śakti,* and then referring it back to the subjective witnessing of *anāśrita-Śiva.* We should visualize this whole phenomena like this: The unsurpassable *Anuttra* witnessing its own creative urge, its *Śakti* aspect, as *anāśrita-Śiva,* and then on watching *His* potent desire, the *Iććhā-Śakti,* unfolding into a defined vision (as *Ġāna*) of what is desired to *be*, assimilates it all, again into itself, before the objectivity must be actually manifest. This expansion (प्रसार) and withdrawal (संहार) aspect of *Iććhā* and *Ġāna* goes on hand in hand within *Anuttra,* which, in itself is supreme amazement of beatitude. There is expansion of *Iććhā* and non expansion of *Ġāna* or vice versa, or both from one or the other aspect, simultaneously and eternally happening. In fact the six phonemes from अ to ऊ , all, rest in the indivisible plane of consciousness of *Anuttra,* and although appearing separate, they are all non-different (अनन्य) from, and similar to, the basic essential nature of *Anuttra* अ . They have a characteristic of 'everything always present, in all' (सर्व सर्वात्मकता). In fact अ-कला is inherent in all these six phonemes, and these are all, inherent in अ-कला, by virtue of which, all these six phonemes also are considered as '*tithīśas*'.

The expansion of *Kriyā-Śakti* which characterizes the objectivity, the immanent aspect of creation, the domain in which succession and simultaneity play vital roles, is actually conducted by *Iććhā-Śakti* (इ ,ई) '*which is not averse to succession and simultaneity, and can expand in its own domain, as well as into the domain of Anuttra and ānanda*' implicitly , by virtue of the agency of sarva-sarvatmakta (सर्वसर्वात्मकता), says Abhinavgupta in *Parātrīśikā-vivaraṇa.*

क्रमसहिष्णुत्वात् संरम्भेच्छैवेशनान्ता स्वात्मनि

अनुत्तरानन्दपदे च प्रसरणक्षमा। ... PTV-60/13

Trika doctrine holds further that *Ġāna-Śakti* cannot expand into the void as *unmeša* and *ūnat* but can do so only implicitly by its entry into *Iććhā-Śakti*, the most autonomous factor, that does not suffer any alteration in its actual essential nature (स्वभाव) in its expansion into the *Kriyā-Śakti.* In *Kriyā* domain, *Iććhā-Śakti*, first expands into the state of void (*vyom*, व्योम), which is the inner state (*antardaśa*, अंतरदशा) of the four basic materials, namely air, water, fire and earth, and also their base in their subtle form as ether. There, it takes on first the subtle sounds (*śruti's* - श्रुति) र् and ल् representing the glow of the knowledge and the subject respectively (*pramana-tej* & *pramatr-tej*, प्रमान तेज, प्रमात्र तेज) before penetrating into its own inherent *Anuttra* aspect. *Iććhā-Śakti* first takes on the sound *r* (श्रुति र्) that represents the essential nature of luminosity and mobility, and takes the form of the two *varṇas* ॠ ॠ .

तत: सैव शून्यात्मकं स्वं ... PTV-60/14)

After passing through this phase of luminosity and mobility, it enters later the plane of unbounded, the invariably-steady state of void, indicating the essential nature of earth, which is represented by the *śruti* ल् (sound *l*), and takes the form of ऌ and ॡ These four *varaṇās* (ऋ ॠ ऌ ॡ), the four void-vowels (शून्य चतुक्ष), are called *amrit-varṇas*, (immortal vowels) or germs of immortality. They are considered as the resting place of the I-consciousness as they have an intrinsic significance of being constituents of *Śiva tattva*. They do not change or expand further in the process of creation as they are purely neither vowels nor consonants although they have semblance to both. They produce nothing, and therefore are termed as eunuchs. Further expansion of *Kriyā-Śakti*, characterized by the great intensity of excitement, is conducted entirely through the autonomy of *Iććhā-Śakti* admitting the heterogeneous intermixture of *Iććhā* and *Ġāna*.

" The same transcendental *Iććhā* and *Īśanā* (इ, ई), which never lapse from their essential nature and prior, superior aspect of their *swarūpa* of *ānanda* and *Anuttra*, by penetration into those (very) aspects (अ and आ), evolve into a new *varṇa* ए "...

" ... also अ, आ by combination with ए produces ऐ . Similarly (through its aspects of) *unmeša* and *ūnatā*, that is, उ and ऊ , on penetration in अ , आ gives rise to ओ which further with अ and आ gives औ" ... Ref. 1.

... Says Abhinavgupta in *parātrīśikā-vivaraṇa*:

तदेव इच्छेशनं च आननदवपुषि, अनुत्तरपरधामति च
प्राग्भाविनि, स्वरूपाद् अप्रच्याविनि अनुप्रविश्य ...
अ, आ + इ, ई = ए ,
... एतदपि तथा शबलीभूतं संविद्वपु: तथैव ...
अ, आ + ए = ऐ , इति । ... (PTV-61/2-3)

... एवम् उन्मेषेऽपि वाच्यम्
अ, आ + उ ऊ = ओ ,
अ, आ + ओ = औ , इति् । ... (PTV-61/12-14)

The procedure indicated above can be visualized as, penetration of *Iććhā-Īśanā* into *Anuttra*, or in fact the expansion of *Anuttra* aspect further into *Iććhā-Śakti*, to continue the precipitation of creation. It is in fact, the expansion of the *Śakti* of *Anuttra*, unfolding through all of its *tithīsha* aspects, its transcendental domains, to enjoy the culmination of objectivity, and *Anāśrita-Śiva* remaining only a witness to it all, without any involvement.
Trika shastra says that *Iććhā* and *Ġāna*, by entering the essential nature of *Anuttra*, become developed, and attain their full development in the domain of

Kriyā-Śakti, at the stage of phoneme औ, after which they abandon their further variation, attain to the state of complete non-difference and get immersed in *bindu*, (called *Śivabindu* or *Śambhava-tattva*,) the ultimate pure-consciousness, undivided light without any differentiation or change whatsoever, the *ćinmaya-puruša-tattva-satattva*. This state is represented by the phoneme (*um*) अं, with symbol (˙) into which the whole of the internal expansion of *Anuttra*, up to औ withdraws and gets dissolved after full expansion. All these vowels from अ to अं are the *Śiva* aspect of creativity, like male sperm or the seed, and are called *Śiva-bija*. In the process of manifestation, these *bijas*, get compactness (*ghanatva* घनत्व) in their aspect of expansion (विसर्गभाव) through their autonomy, without losing their essential form, and abiding in *Śakti-rūpa* (*Śakti* form), become consonants, the female aspect of creativity represented by *yoni*. Termed as *Śakta-yoni*, these *varaṇas*, act as wombs for the sperm of *Śivabija*, in the process of the formation of the word and speech, in the final manifestation of objectivity at the *vaikhari* level. Development of these vowels, as the expansion of the creative urge of the supreme *Anuttra*, is seen in *Trika* philosophical consideration, symbolically analogous to the growth of the phases of moon, the *somamśa* (सोमंमश), from the crescent to the full moon in fifteen days. Thus the group of vowels from अ to अं considered fifteen (six in the domain of *Iććhā* and *Ġāna*, four *amrit varaṇas*, and five in the objective domain of *Kriyā*) are termed as *tithīs*. Each phoneme in its *internal* stage of development is referred to as *kalā*, (as long as the phoneme is in the inner apprehension of *paśyanti* or *madhyama* level), while at *vaikhari* level, it is termed as *swar*. Fourteen lunar digits (*tithīs* of moon), therefore, are seen to correspond to the expansion or growth of fourteen *kalās* of phonemes up to औ . The fifteenth digit of moon, is considered as the fifteenth *kalā*, the undivided and indivisible *bindu* of pure consciousness, for the final dissolution of all the phonemes or *kalās* upto औ . There is yet another aspect of growth (and dissolution) related to the *somamśa*, or *tithi* aspect of *phonemes*. This refers to *prāṇaćār*, the *Śakti* aspect of the breathing phenomena of living beings. Inhalation, the breathing-in, is termed as *apānaćār* (अपानाचार) or the flow of *apāna* current of the life-force, from a point outside of the body, situated at a distance of twelve fingers from the tip of nose, and called *bahya-dwādaśāňta* (बाह्यद्वादशांत), into the body, and onto a point twelve fingers down-ward (in case of humans), and called *antar-dwādaśāňta* (अंतरद्वादशांत). The exhalation is considered as the flow of *prāṇa* current or *prānaćār* (प्राणाचार), from inner to outer *dwādaśāňta*. Each current of *prāṇa* or *apāna* is attributed a duration of sixteen *tuti* (त्रुटि), [a *tuti* being sixteenth part of the time taken for each current]. Fifteen digits of moon (*somamśa*), and fifteen *tutis* of *prāṇaćār* or *apānaćār*, are considered analogous to fifteen *kalās* of phonemes referring to the inner expansion of *anuttar* from अ to अं . The sixteenth *tuti* represents, the emission and dissolution (उदय , उपरम) phenomena for each current of *prāṇa* and *apāna* correspondingly, at the two *dwādaśāňtas*. For each current, *prāṇa* or *apāna* is given, half a *tuṭi*, at each of the *dwādaśāňtas*, for absorption or emission, and thus one tuṭi each is attributed to each current for absorption and re-emission. This sixteenth *tuṭi* is seen analogous to the sixteenth phoneme, the *visarga-kalā* अः , to which, in moon digits a correspondence is provided by the *amritkalā–somamśa*, (unseen moon-digit persisting ever!). Dissolution, (the *samhāra* aspect) is end of a phenomena but not a complete termination of everything. The basic, the un-perishable aspect of truth remains ever. The sixteenth *kalā or visarga kalā*, [also called *amrit-kalā* or *am-kalā* or *śaśi-kalā*] represents the perpetual aspect of emanation and dissolution, the *sṛšṭi* and *samhār swabhāva* of the 'creative will' of *Anuttra*. This *visarga* is symbolized by अः , (*Anuttra* अ , with two dots, one above the other). Lower dot called *sūryakalā*, for its *prasāra-rūpa* (emerging aspect of *Kriyā-Śakti*), represents the expansion of *Śakti* in perpetual creation. The upper dot, the *somakalā*, the *Śiva* aspect of *visarga*, represents *praveśa-rūpa* (the merging aspect of *Kriyā-Śakti*), of all creation into the undivided and unchanging essence of *ćinmaya-purušа-sattatva* perpetually. The two dots represent un-altering source and sink, or *sṛšṭi-ātmaka* and *samhāra-ātmaka* aspects of the creation, one behaving as ever full and emitting, and the other, ever emaciated and absorbing, but in truth, neither is full nor emaciated. This *visarga* which follows *Śiva-bindu* or *Śambhav tattva* is *parāparā-visarga*, or *Śākta-visarga* related to both, the transcendental and objective truth of *Anuttra*, in fact the subtle transcendental source and sink of the empirical creation. *Parā visarga,* the perpetual will of creativity is आ , the *ānanda* of *Anuttra.* It is also called *Śambhava visarga* or *Śaiva-visarga.* This transcendental emanation within the divine consciousness, is the highest divine *beautitude* and therefore called *paramānanda-bhūmi* (परमानन्द भूमि). It is the basic factor that impels creativity through its expansion. This expansion (प्रसार) from अ to औ represents *bimba* (बिम्ब), the inner manifestation within *Anuttra.* It is called its *swarūpa-sṛšṭi* (स्वरूप सृष्टि), which comes into being within it, by the soma-aspect (*Iććhā-Śakti*), *sūrya*-aspect (*Ġāna-Śakti*), and *agni*-aspect (*Kriyā-Śakti*) of the creative urge of *Anuttra* and gets absorbed or withdrawn finally into *Śiva-bindu.* The reflection, *pratibimb* (प्रतिबिम्ब) of *swarupa-sṛšṭi,* (*bimba*), is the cause of the external objective manifestation as the *sṛšṭi.*

The picture of *parāvāk* manifestation presented here in the light of *Trika* philosophical considerations provides, in a sequential manner, the development of vowels (*kalās*) due to internal expansion of the creative urge within *Anuttra.* There are however a few points, (raised ahead by the author), which need deeper reconsiderations in the backdrop of what is understood and established so far. The manuscripts referred, do not provide any clue for the resolution of those nagging questions which need to be resolved. The author, after a thorough investigative introspection has put forth a point of view, that, in his opinion bridges the missing gaps satisfactorily. Ahead is a detailed write-up on the doubts that sprang, and the solutions conceived by the author, of course, in line with the *trika* traditions, to the best of his understanding. [criticism and suggestions in this connection, however, will very gratefully be welcomed, and most humbly considered.]

The doubts:

a. In *prāṇāyāma, prāṇa* and *apāna* currents are not exactly similar, but refer to two different activities with opposite features of *prāṇa-Śakti* (life-force). Similarly, the growth and decay of moon digits in the two fortnights (bright and dark one) are also, two distinctly different and opposite features. Moon-digits of only bright fortnight, as also only *apāna* current of inhalation have been analogously considered in connection with the development of the *kalās* of phonemes in the *swarūpa-sṛšṭi* aspect of *bimba.*

b. *Tuṭis* of *prāṇāyāma* (sixteen plus sixteen) in a cycle of *prāṇāyāma* and variation of the digits of moon (bright and dark digits, fifteen plus fifteen) in one complete cycle of a lunar month, do not seem, as such, to corroborate with the analogy of the *kalās* of the phonemes, which are only just fifteen up to अं. (in addition to the *parāparā-visarga,* which is the perpetual background ever)

c. There *exist* certain other distinct vowel sounds at the level of *vaikhari* that *are* abundantly in use, but not rationalized, accommodated or even mentioned in the process of the expansion of phonemes, even though some referral mention, of such sounds being in use, has been made by Abhinavgupta in his said *vivaraṇa* (on *Parātrīśikā*) as quoted ahead.

In continuation with the ref.-(1) quoted earlier (page-107), Abhinavgupta says :

> " (*Iććhā*), in the inverse penetration of *Anuttra* state, brings up a different kind of development ; that of a longer state (स्फुट) on penetration in *ānanda* and a shorter state (सूक्षम) in *Anuttra*."
>
> "In this context *Bhagwān Sarprāj* (Shri Pātanjali) directs thus : -
>
> Followers of *Satyam-ugri* (a sub-branch) of *Rānāyniyā* (राणायनीया), amongst those who recite Vedas (*samveda*), enunciate half ए and half ओ. Common folk, and those speaking *prākrat*, and other local languages, also use (such sounds) distinctly, and in abundance. In *Parameśwar-āgmas* (*Śaiva śastrās*) also, in the application of *angavaktra* procedures (of *mañtras*), the usage of short (*hrasva*- ह्रस्व) forms of ए and ओ in comparison to ऐ and औ should be seen in the same light. Thus the use of अय and अव is justified in the context. "

विपर्यये च अनुत्तरपदानुप्रवेशे सयादपि कश्चिद् विशेषः।
आननदपदानुप्रवेशे हि स्फुटता, अनुत्तरधामसंभेदे तु सूक्ष्मता
सदपेक्षया ।

तथाहि भगवान् भुजगविभुरादिशत्
"छन्दोगानां सात्यमुग्रिराणायनीया अर्धमेकारमर्धमोकारं चादीयते"

लोकेऽपि प्राकृतदेशभाषादौ स्फुट एष प्रचुरःसन्निवेशः।
पारमेश्वरेष्वपि एकारौकारयोर् ऐकारौकारापेक्षया यत्
ह्स्वतवम् अङ्गवक्त्रादि विनियोगे दृश्यते तदेवमेव
मन्तव्यम्_अय एकार अव ओकाराभिप्रायेण। ...(PTV-61/4-11)

Rationalization of the doubts:

In view of the remarks made above, an appropriate perspective, that can sort out these discrepancies by coordinating various known factors conforming to the *Trika* approach, and rationalize various conflicting elements into a comprehensive understanding of the truth of *swarūp-sṛšṭi* model of *Mātṛkā*, needs to be developed.

According to *Trika–śastra,* short (ह्स्व) vowels represent pure *Śiva-bhāva* (शिवभाव). Formation of short vowels therefore cannot be associated with expansion (प्रसार) aspect of creativity, but rather contraction (संकोच) or withdrawal aspect of manifestation into the transcendental unity with *Anuttra.* Long (दीर्घ) vowels on the other hand represent *Śiva-Śakti-samghatta*

(शिवशक्ति संघट्ट) and hence, represent the expansion. Again the penetration of *Iććhā* etc. into *Anuttra* that is the combination ending into *Iććhā* etc. indicates expansion into objectivity or *Śakti-bhāva*, while the penetration of *Anuttra* into *Iććhā* etc., or the combination ending into *Anuttra* signifies contraction of the manifestation or the *Śiva-bhāva*. As such, therefore, expansion into objectivity, in the *Kriyā-Śakti* domain, must be represented only by longer vowels right from the first phase of it, that is, the beginning with the domain of void, where, *Iććhā* and *Īśanā* take up the process of expansion. *Īśāna* being the *kšubda* aspect of *Iććhā*, has within it the aspect of *Iććhā* and *Īśāna* both, and thus a strong impulsive eagerness for objective manifestation. Thus *Īśāna* becomes the actual operator for the expansion. It takes on, in the void, first the *śruti's* ऱ् and ल् representing the inner state (*antardaśā*) of the four *bhūtas* in the vacuum (वयुम) state, as also the glow of the knowledge and the subject (*pramāna-tej* and *pramātr-tej*, प्रमान तेज, प्रमात्र तेज), and thus forms the *dīrgha-varaṇas* ॠ and ॡ . Since *ġāna-Śakti* cannot enter the domain of void as *unmeša* and *ūnat*, it does so by first entering into the domain of *Iććhā – Īśanā* , after which the entry of *Iććhā* and *ġāna* (इ, ई, उ,ऊ) into the essential aspect of *Anuttra* can occur. This can lead to the expansion of *Anuttra* अ through the agency of *Iććhā* - *Īśanā* into a specific heterogeneous intermixture as follows:

इ , ई + ऊ = अ़ and

अ + अ़ = अ़

अ	+	इ , ई	=	ए	and
अ	+	ए	=	ऐ	
अ	+	उ , ऊ	=	ओ	and
अ	+	ओ	=	औ	

The first interaction takes place by the penetration of *ūnatā* ऊ into the *Iććhā – Īśanā* aspect of *Anuttra* producing a *varaṇa* अ , which subsequently penetrates the *Anuttra* aspect giving rise to another *varṇa* अ , both long vowels, (as yet un-recognized in known *Mātṛkā* order) representing the manifestation of objectivity by *Kriyā-Śakti.* Next *Iććhā-Īśanā* by penetration into *Anuttra* produces *varṇa* ए which further, by penetration into *Anuttra* gives rise to *varṇa* ऐ . The only other phase of penetration that can happen in this domain is, by the entry of *unmeša-ūnatā* उ, ऊ into *Anuttra,* producing the *varṇa* ओ, which in turn penetrates *Anuttra,* giving rise to the final development of objectivity in the form of *varṇa* औ . Analogously, *somāmśās* (digits of moon), reaching the full growth (expansion representing objectivity) of the bright fortnight on fourteenth *tithi* can be considered comparable to the phoneme औ . This *tithi* represents the moon with the last trace of darkness, the transcendental or un-manifested aspect of creation. After the expansion up to औ , the fourteenth *kalā,* further expansion or variation of *Śakti* ceases. Fifteenth state is thus a critical stage, the complete flowering of objectivity in the process of expansion, the peak, with no further expansion to be, thus marking the beginning of *sańkoća* (संकोच) or withdrawal of objectivity into the transcendental domain of *Anuttra*. *Śakti*, so far carrying on the expansion of *Anuttras*' aspect of creativity, begins folding itself into the transcendental essence of *Anuttra*. This state or fifteenth *kalā* can well be denoted by *anunāsika*, the long (*dīrgha*) nasal phoneme अँ , the *Anuttra* अ with a crescent and a dot, the crescent symbolizing the *somamshas* (representing *Iććhā - Śakti*) or expansion into objectivity, and dot, signifying the contraction, the onset of the dissolution or withdrawal aspect of the phoneme-tic sequence into *Anuttra*, both in one. This long vowel (दीर्घ स्वर) truly represents *Śiva-Śakti-samghatt*, the *Śakti* aspect of expansion, and *Shiva* aspect of *sańkoća*, together, by a lingering two *mātra* nasal sound. This *tithi*, the full fifteen digit *tithi* is unique, because it indicates the culmination of the *sṛšti* aspect, from the first bright digit (crescent), into the bright full-moon and thus, the beginning of its *samhāra* aspect of waning of the bright lunar disc, both in one. Again, from another point of view, this state can be looked at as, the completion of the *samhāra* of the transcendental aspect, that is, the end even of the last dark digit of moon (that had begun waning from the complete darkness of the full-dark moon disc of *amāvasya*, in the dark lunar fortnight), into the complete brightness of objectivity. It is therefore the new beginning of the growth of dark digits of transcendental aspect, into the full dark disc of the complete absence of all objectivity, or into the complete transcendental state of the *ćinmaya-puruša-sattatva*. We must realize the ultimate reality, that, the beginning of one new cycle is actually also the end of the other, considered from either, the transcendental or the immanent perspectives. Truly is this state represented by the fifteenth *tithi,* the fifteenth *kalā* or *varṇa,* the *anunāsika* denoted by a dot in the lap of a crescent ँ. The moon-digit crescent representing the sustaining *amritkalā* of the transcendental (as well as the objectivity) aspect, always beginning a new cycle even when the devouring dot, the pure consciousness, the *ćinmaya-puruša,* the ultimate awareness in its lap, swallows the other. *Anunāsika* is just like *visarga* in a different symbol, marking a change-over of the growth of one aspect and the decline of other, within the *Kriyā* domain, the perpetual phenomena of growth and decay, *sṛšṭi* and *samhāra* (*sarjan* and *visarjan*) at every step, the truth of the domain of objectivity, unlike, that in the un-altering transcendental domain of *tithīśas.* In fact each phoneme representing expansion has a parallel in another phoneme that represents contraction, as will be explicitly clear subsequently.

Analogously can be seen the culmination of the life current of the expansion of *Śakti* into *nara,* the *apāna* current of vital-breath (during inhalation) from the outer *dwādaśāňta* reaching inner *dwādaśāňta* at *hridaya,* in fifteen *tuṭis* of *apāna* flow, with a pause at *aňtaĥ-dwādaśāňta* (*abhijīta*) for half a *tuṭi,* where *apāna* current merges into, and the *prāṇa* current emerges from the domain of un-manifest of the transcendental realm.

The return flow of *prāṇa* current from *aňtaĥ-dwādaśāňta* to *bāhya-dwādaśāňta* in fifteen *tuṭis* for its merger into, and growth again, as *apāna* current at *viśwata*, in the outer *dwādaśāňta*, within a brief pause of a half-*tuṭi*, can be seen corresponding to the complete dissolution (संहार) of the objective manifestation into the full, fifteen-digit-dark disk of *amāvasya* in the dark lunar fortnight. The two phenomenon can be considered analogously with the folding back (*samhāra)* of *swarūpa-sṛšṭi* into *Anuswar*, the *Śiva-bindu* after the critical expansion into औ of ओ is accomplished. Thus *anunāsika.* matches the ½ + ½ *tuṭi* each of the dissolution of *apāna* current and rise of *prāṇa* current at *aňtaĥ-dwādaśāňta* coinciding with the beginning of the waning-cycle on the fifteenth-day moon.

The folding back of the *swarūpa-sṛšṭi* begins thus with *anunāsika* as the beginning of the reverse penetration by *Anuttra* into each of the phonemes generated during the expansion into the *kriyā* domain. Beginning with ओ , this process of dissolution into the transcendental aspect of *Anuttra*, produces a new set of phonemes, which are all short vowels, representing pure *Śiva-bhāva.*

This phenomenon of the withdrawal of these *kalās*, the phonemes, into *Anuttra*, for their ultimate dissolution into the dot of pure consciousness of *ćinmaya-puruša-sattatva*, represented by the phoneme *anuswar*, at the end of the *swarūp-sṛšṭi* can be visualized sequentially as follows:

ओ	+	अ	=	ॵ	and
उ, ऊ	+	अ	=	ओ	
ए	+	अ	=	ऐ	and
इ, ई	+	अ	=	ए	
अ़	+	अ	=	अ़	and
इ, ई	+	उ	=	अ़	
ल्	+	इ	=	लृ	and
र्	+	इ	=	ऋ	

It needs to be fully understood that the expansion of *Anuttra* for *sṛšṭi-sarjanā*, means the penetration of the aspect of the *Śakti-bhāva*, the *spanda of Iććhā*, as well as its implicit *Ġāna* into *Anuttra*, thereby enabling the *Kriyā* phase of the projection of *sṛšṭi*. On the other hand *samhāra*, the withdrawal of the *sṛšṭi* into *Anuttra* again, implies the penetration of *Śiva-bhāva* of *Anuttra* into the aspect of its *Iććhā* and *Ġāna*, thereby causing the folding back of *sṛšṭi*. This naturally begins by the penetration, first by *Anuttra* into the phoneme ओ , which, during the expansion phase had penetrated into *Anuttra* अ resulting in the complete unfolding and thus the culmination of *sṛšṭi* in the formation of phoneme औ . Now due to the reverse penetration of *Anuttra* into that very phoneme ओ , as also the phonemes that had given rise to it.

Unmeša and *ūnata-Ġāna*, उ ऊ , yield the development of two new phonemes, the *hrasva* of औ and ओ as ॳि and ॳि . The subsequent reverse penetrations of *Anuttra* into other phonemes that had yielded *dīrgha* phonemes by their penetration into *Anuttra*, yield yet more new *hrasvas* (as indicated in the table above, as against the *dīrghās* produced earlier, see page 116).

The new phonemes produced thus, (six *hrasva* and two *dīrgha* vowels) are all un-recognized yet in the known *Mātṛkā* order. The author, following the *Trika* rationale, found these vowels, in the process of the rationalization of certain doubts that came up during the study of *Kriyā* interactions of *tithīśas*. The authenticity of these vowels has been established by their actual existence in vocabulary (at least of Kashmiri language) distinctly[9].

All the phonemes resulting from various interactions in the *Kriyā* domain, together with the six phonemes of *tithīśa* group, form the entire group of '*tithīs*', that can be viewed in the following order(s), in total correspondence with the sequences of *somamśas* and *prāṇāćāra* as follows:

Bright fortnight tithīs (first to fifteenth) corresponding to apānāćāra :

अ आ इ ई उ ऊ ॠ ॡ अ॒ अ॑ ए ऐ
ओ औ अँ

Dark fortnight tithīs (first to fifteenth) corresponding to prāṇāćāra :

ॲ ॲ ऍ ए अ॒ अ॑ ॡ ॠ ऊ उ ई इ
आ अ अं

All these *tithīs*, (thirty in all) can be visualized in *Trika* perspective collectively, as follows:

The cause and course of all that ever exists, is अः , the perpetual *nimeša-unmeša, spanda,* ever throbbing in the *hṛt* of *Bhairava*, as the nectar of bliss, causing the *sarjanā* and *visarjanā* of the *akšara-mālā* of creation. It gives rise, as the first aspect of the manifestation to six *tithīshās*, Starting with *Anuttra*, as the *parāvāga-bhūmi* अ , and the *parā-visarga*, the *ānanda*, आ , followed by, the *akšubd* and *kšubd Iććhā* and *Ġāna*, इ ई उ ऊ . Their mutual interactions in the *Kriyā* domain, make all other *varaṇās* (including *amrit-varaṇās*), representing objectivity aspect of creation and withdrawal, appear. Finally, all these merge (including *tithīshās*) into the sameness with *ćinmaya*, the *Śiva-bindu*, the eternal *visarga* for re-emergence.

अ:

अ आ इ   ई उ ऊ

ॠ ॡ अ॒ अ॒ ए ऐ ओ औ   अँ   ॲ ॲ ऍ ए अ॒ अ॒ ऌ ऋ

ऊ उ ई   इ आ अ

अं

अ:

Since the *swarūpa-sṛšṭi* of the internal expansion of the creative urge of *Anuttra*, represented by the phonemes from अ to अं, is essentially an expression of the *visarga-Śakti*, the *sṛšṭi-samhāra* aspect of the supreme *Anuttra*, the phonemes here have been arranged with the *visarga-kalā* at the beginning and at the end. *As anuswar*, marks the end of one cycle of *sṛšṭi* indicating its dissolution into the *ćinmaya* aspect of consciousness, it is at the end of the series of the phonemes, just before the ultimate *visarga*. The *sṛšṭi* begins with, and ends into *Anuttra* अ, which manifests first into its intrinsic *swabhāva* expressed by *tithīshās*, the first aspect of the manifestation in the transcendental domain. Then, the internal manifestation of objectivity, in the *Kriyā* domain, as the *bimba* of creativity happens. It is a domain, completely of the objectivity bounded by the void, which is permeated only by the glow of knowledge (*pramān*) and subject (*pramātra*) aspect of the empirical creation, represented by *amrit-varṇas*. They mark therefore the beginning and the end of the objectivity aspect. Objectivity domain is represented by a whole set of phonemes as a matrix, containing the strangeness of the world of objectivity, with its *sṛšti* and *samhāra* aspect intrinsically. *Anunāsika* is placed at the end of the *dīrgha* vowels and the beginning of the *hrasva* vowels, as it represents the critical point of withdrawal of the objectivity. This entire matrix of objectivity is subsequently withdrawn into *tithīśas* at the end of the cycle, all folding into *Anuttra*, and thence into the pure consciousness of the *bindu* of *anuswara*.

Another alternate representation of all these phonemes, in terms of *only* fifteen *tithīs* is indicated next. Beginning with six *tithīshas*, all representing the transcendental domain, and then, eight pairs, (*hrasva* and *dīrgha*, a pair each) of the *varaṇas* of the *Kriyā* domain, including two pairs (*hrasva* and *dīrgha* each), of *amrit-varṇās*. The series culminates in *anunāsika* and *anuswar*, the single pair of nasal phonemes, representing the withdrawal of the expansion, and then the total dissolution of phonemes. *Amrit-kalā (am-kalā)*, the unfaltering *swabhāva* of *Anuttra*, the *visarga-bhāva*, at the beginning and the end of the series, indicates the perpetual nature of *visarga-kalā*, that remains ever, and sustains the *sṛšti-samhāra* aspect of *Anuttra*!

अः

अ आ इ ई उ ऊ

ऋ ॠ ऌ ॡ

अ̮ अ̭ अ̲ अ̲ ए ए ऍ ऐ ॳ ओ ॳ औ

अं अँ

अः

The foregoing discussion and presentation resolves all the doubts and discrepancies that had been pointed out. Fifteen *tuṭis* of *apāna* current represent analogously the fifteen digits of bright lunar *tithīs* as the fifteen *kalās* of *dīrgha* vowels (as listed in the series 1, page 122), while the fifteen *tuṭis* of *prāṇa* current correspond to fifteen digits of moon in dark fortnight and fifteen *hrasva kalās* of vowels (as listed in the series 2, page 122). Full moon, the critical point of the full culmination of objectivity and the onset of transcendental phase in the consequent withdrawal after total culmination of objectivity, is represented by *anunāsika*, the *dīrgha* nasal vowel, while, *amāvasya* representing the total submergence of objectivity, or the full blown transcendence, is best represented by *anuswar*. Both these culmination points of objectivity and transcendental states are represented by inner and outer *dwādaśānts* respectively. *Visarga* the sixteenth *kalā*, the source and sink of all objectivity, but never objective itself, the *spanda* in the *hṛdaya* of *Bhairava*, is best represented by the sixteenth *tuṭi* at each of the two *dwādaśāṅts*, as a half- *tuṭi* each for projection and dissolution of either of the currents of *prāṇa* and *apāna*. *Visarga* does not represent objectivity, even though it projects and dissolves it. It is not explicit, although it forms the basic foundation of all projections and dissolutions like *udaya* and *apram* at *dwādaśāṅts*. *Visarga* is implied in the two nasal vowel *kalās* , *anunāsika* and *anuswar* as also in the *amrit-kalā* digit of moon, inexplicit but the eternal background of the dark and bright digit trace of moon forming the transition from either. A deep reflection on all this makes things lucid and clear. In addition, the new-found eight vowels, are certainly not out of place. They exist phonologically, and are actually and distinctly uttered vowel-sounds in a spoken (Kashmiri) language, as also in many more dialectic utterances of the speaking folks. They have also a clear-cut justification of existence in line with the established *trika* perspective, as can clearly be seen.

अः , [the sound (अह्) *ah* begining with *a* (अ), and ending *ha* (ह = ह् + अ)], the *parāparā visarga*, truly represents the entire reality from *Anuttra* to the last of the manifested reality, the *pṛthvi*, the *dhārani* of the whole of the objective existence, in terms of the *tattva*-manifestation, and then, back again to *Anuttra*. It represents a complete cycle, beginning at *Anuttra* अ , projecting the *sṛšti* through ह , *the Sadāśiva*, and folding it all back into *Anuttra* अ. This *visarga* represents the entire transcendental as well as the immanent aspect of expansion of *Anuttra*, projecting *bimba* and its reflection, the *pratibimba*, both, and then withdrawing it all into the *ćinmaya sattatva*, the totally undifferentiated reality.

After projection of *bimba*, the *prasāra* or expansion of *pratibimba* is conducted by the *aparā-visarga* aspect of *Śakti, ha* (ह). All short vowels represent purely *Śivabīja–bhāva* and all long vowels the *Śiva-Śakti-samghatt-bhāva*, in the internal expansion of creative urge of *Anuttra*, the *swarūpa-sṛšti*, while all the consonants, the *Śakti-yoni-bhāva* represent the immanent aspect of the creation. The *Aparā-visarga* ह , the final expressiveness of objective expansion, brings about the diverse empirical manifestation. Vowels (*śivabīja*) assume *ghanattva* (density), to form the *yoni-rūpa* of consonants, and thus complete the *varaṇa-sṛšti*. In this process of the formation of consonants, *Anuttra* अ itself assumes the form of क ख...... *varga* (class) of guttural group of *varṇās*, and इ , that of च छ.... *varga*, the palatal group and also the *varṇās* य and ष. *Bīja* उ condenses into the प फ ......class of labial group of consonants. The *śruti* ऱ् assumes the form of cerebral and dental class of *varṇās* of ट ठ .... along with र and श , and the *śruti* ऌ that of त थ ...that of dental class, along with ल and स *varaṇās* respectively. *Varṇa* व represents labio-dental condensation of त and प class of *varṇās*.

All the *yoni-rūpa varṇās* (twenty-five), of the five *vargas* (classes) namely क , च , ट , त , प *vargas*, represent various *tattvās* of the manifestation from the earth (पृशवी) category to the *māyā* category etc. as declared in the *Sūtra*-(6) of *Parātrīśikā*. All *tattvas* are aspects of *Śakti*, that *māyā* onwards, form various windows with the limited perspectives, for the *puruša* to perceive, understand and function strictly within those perspectives, thus transforming him into an empirical experient. Every important aspect is represented by *varṇās*, since, as already discussed, *varṇās* are not inert letters but aspects of *parā-vāk-Śakti*. Each *varṇa* therefore is a *Śakti-yoni* that along with the potency of *Śivabīja* (the vowels) produces myriad aspects of creative manifestation, all full of the potency of wonder for a true experient.

The *varṇās* that follow next, are the four non-*verga varṇās* known as *aňtaĥstha-varṇās*. Since they behave somewhat as vowels and not fully as consonants, they are considered even, semi-vowels according to the rules of grammar, but they are declared as *dhāraṇa* (धारण) in the *Sūtra*-(7) of *Parātīśikā-vivarṇa*. *Dhārana* means a restrainer. These *varṇās* are linked with *māyā-parivār*, the family of *māyā* and its *kaňćakas*. *Trika* holds that there are actually only three *māyā kaňćakas*, namely *rāga*, *kalā*, and *vidyā*. *Niyati* is actually an influence of *rāga* , and *kāla* is an outcome of the influence of *kalā*. These knots are imposed by *māyā*, the *Śakti Itself*, out of its own free will (*swātantrya*), to afflict its own projection, the *puruša*, with specific boundary conditions, to make it perform in the specified manner. These four *varaṇas* य, र, ल, व, respectively called *vayu-bīja*, *agni-bīja*, *salila-bīja* and *indra-bīja* (from the consideration of their use as *bīja-akšaras* in *maňtrās*), are actually *dhāraṇas*, the 'taken-on' aspects that represent the inner or inherent approaches (therefore called *Antastha*) *forming* the operators for a *Māyā-pramātā*. These represent, in य *rāga* and *niyati*, in र *vidyā*, in ल *kalā* and *kāla*, and in व *māyā*, which form the '*Śaṭh-kañćakas*' the determinant knots of the empirical existence. Next, the last five *varaṇās* ष , श , स , ह , and क्ष , are declared *brahma-pañćaka* (the five great ones), which in *Śaiva-shāstras* are said to represent the *Śakti* aspects of *Mahā-māyā*, *Śuddha-vidyā*, *Iśwara*, *Sadāśiva*, and *Śakti-tattva* respectively. These five aspects, devoid of, and beyond any sense of difference themselves, are responsible for the 'growth' (*brahmakatva*, - making grow) of the *sṛšṭi* of differentiation. That is why they are named *brahma-pañćaka* (the five great-ones). *Mahā-māyā*, designated as a *tattva* is seen to figure in the group of five, the *brahma-pañćakas* here. Certain *Śaiva-śāstras*, as already indicated (page 78, & [40/22] - ref. 12), consider *Mahāmāyā* as a necessary *tattva* to justify the domain of *Viġānā-kalā pramātā*, and then being an aspect of *Śakti* without any objective commitment, class it in *brahma-pañćakas*. Some others plead that since this state must be free of *mayiya-mala* and *karma-mala* and is responsible only for the sense of *bheda* , it is actually the extreme aspect of *Śuddha-vidyā tattva* as certain others say that, since it inculcates the ignorance of transcendence or the essential self, it is the beginning of the influence of *Māyā-tattva*, thus the two stands negate the existence of a separate *tattva* as *Mahāmāyā*.

A detailed chart of the *Mātṛkā* assignments of all these *varaṇās* to various *tattvas* of the manifested hierarchy follows.

Vaṃās (क-varga)	क	ख	ग	घ	ङ.
Panća-mahabhūta: (gross elements)	*pṛthvi* (earthly)	*jala* (watery)	*agni* (firey)	*vāyu* (airy)	*ākāśa* (spatial)

Vaṃas (च-varga)	च	छ	ज	झ	ञ
Tanmātrās: (subtle aspect of gross elements)	*gaňdha* (aromatic)	*rasa* (taste)	*rūpa* (visual)	*sparśa* (touch)	*śabda* (sound)

Vaṃas (ट-varga)	ट	ठ	ड	ढ	ण
Karmendriya: (Faculties of action)	*upastha* (sexual)	*pāyu* (excreation)	*pāda* (locomotion)	*pāni* (handling)	*vāka* (speech)

Vaṃas (त-varga)	त	थ	द	ध	न
Ġānendriya: (faculties of sense perception)	*grāna* (smelling)	*rasnā* (tasting)	*ćakśu* (vision)	*tvaka* (tactile)	*śrotra* (audatory)

Varṇas (प-*varga)*	प	फ	ब	भ	म
Aṅtaḥ-karana, Prakṛti & Puruša	*mana* *(mental)* *(flux)*	*ahaṅkār* *(empirical)* *(I-sense)*	*budhi* *(ascertainment)* *(discrimination)*	*prakṛti* *(empirical)* *(objectivity)*	*puruša* *(empirical)* *(experient)*

Kañchaks	य	र	ल	व
mantra bījas	*vayu-bīja*	*agni-bīja*	*salil-bīja*	*indra-bīja*
dhāraṇās	*rāga-niyati*	*vidyā*	*kalā-kāla*	*māya*

Brahma - Pañćaka	श	ष	स	ह	क्ष
(Trika view)	*Śuddha -vidyā*	*Ishwara*	*Sadāśiva*	*Śakti*	*anāśrita-Śiva*
(Triketra-view)	*Mahāmāyā*	*Śuddha-vidya*	*Ishwara*	*Sadāśiva*	*Śakti*

The tabulation above is exactly how *Sūtras (6 & 7)* of *Parātrīśikā-vivaraṇa* [see ahead], declare the core matrix of the immanent manifestation in terms of *parāvāk* utterances, as revealed by *Bhairava* to *Devi.*

पृथिव्यादीनि तत्त्वानि पुरुषान्तानि पञ्चसु
क्रमात् कादिषु वर्गेषु मकारान्तेषु सुव्रते

(pṛthivyādīni tattvāni purušāntāni pañćasu
Kramāt kādišu vargešu makārāntešu suvrate)
...sūtra - (PT - 6)

"Beginning with pṛthvi-tattva, and ending with puruša-tattva, are five classes of (succession-less) existence ordered in succession between क *and* म *, O' (their) virtuous ruler!"*

वायुवग्निसलिलेन्द्राणां धारणानां चतुष्टयम्
तदूर्ध्वं शादि विख्यातं पुरस्ताद् ब्रह्मपञ्चकम्

(Vāyvagni-salilendrāṇām dhārṃānām ćatušṭayam
Tadūrdhvam śādi vikhyātam purastād brahmpañćakam)
...sūtra – (PT - 7)

" Dhāraṇās as vayū, agni, salila, indra, the four restrainers, and (thereafter) rising above, are श *etc. (up to* क्ष *) , the known and celebrated Brahma-pañćaka"*

A complete overview of what we have grasped by going into the threadbare subtle communication of

Sūtras-(5-7) of *Parātrīśikā* is, that this whole manifestation of the objective existence that we live and experience, is a projection of subtle potency of *spanda*, the throb of ultimate *will* or *Iććhā-Shakti* , that formulates a subtle matrix, the *swarūpa-sṛšṭi* in absolutely indeterminate state of the source-less source of everything, out of its infinite and un-definable potency and authority, which, with the tangible power of *akšara* (indestructible), writes the complete script of creation. We all know the potency of a word or sound. All our information, knowledge and communication, comprises nothing but endlessly infinite patterns of letters and sounds. Whole of our life is woven out of it, layer by layer, in an abstract completely incomprehensible fashion. In spite of the assignment of letters (*varṇās*), to all categories (*tattvas*) of objective existence, our mind cannot grasp how the objective precipitation can happen out of the *potency of letters*, called *mantra* in *Trika* . To know that, one needs to penetrate the objective existence of things, and transcend beyond the absolute void (that forms the threshold of the manifest and non-manifest existence), into the total awareness, the absolute and attribute-less potency of silence, throbbing eternally, and devouring all, whether time, space, matter or thought, into its amazement of being and bliss. Then alone (no succession implied), one can comprehend, out of the overflowing *bliss of being*, the *being*, and the *bliss*, the *ćid-ānand-ghan*, pouring out, (ever) the profundity of *akšara*, अ and आ , to shape itself into the *akšara-mālā*, the *varṇa-sṛšṭi*, the womb of the creation, to gencrate all that there *is* !

अ-मूला तत्क्रमाज्ज्ञेया क्षान्ता सृष्टिरुदाहृता
सर्वेषामेव मन्त्राणां विद्यानाञ्च यशस्विनि

(Amūla tatkramāj-ġeyā kšāntā sṛšṭi-rudāhṛtā
Sarvešāmeva mantrāṇām vidyānāñća yaśasvni)
...sūtra - (PT - 8)

इयं योनिः समाख्याता सर्वतन्त्रेषु सर्वदा

(Iyam yoniḥ samākhyātā sarvatantrešu sarvada)
...sūtra - (PT – 9 , only half)

"*(Thus) beginning with* अ - कला *as the 'mūla' (source) and ending at* क्ष - कार , *the entire sṛšṭi, successively, including all mantrās and vidyās, should be understood manifested (as the parāvāk utterance), O glorious one, (all born), ever, from this yoni (womb of* अक्ष - माला *), as has been mentioned in all tantras.* "

All the consideration we undertook in previous pages are conclusively declared by the *Sūtra* just quoted. We know now, that all vowels from अ to अः represent *Śiva-bhāva* inherently, since although the short vowels are aspects of pure *Śiva-bhāva*, and long ones the aspect of *Śiva-Śakti samghatt*, but when uttered, all begin invariably with the sound अ . All the twenty-five consonents of five *vargas*, representing

Shakti-yoni contain intrinsically the sound अ lurking at their end. Each of these *varṇas* can never be uttered without the inherent sound of अ in them. Consonants without अ are all *hallant* letters like क् ख् ...... म् which bear only a structure but no potency. It is the vital breath of अ that gives them life and sustenance (क् + अ = क , etc.). This is true for all *aṅtaḥstha* letters as well as *brahma-pañćakas,* in fact, for the entire *varṇa-sṛšṭi* (वर्ण सृष्टि) manifested by *Mātṛkā-Śakti.* The *aparā- visarga* ह , after the manifestation of *varṇa-sṛšṭi* folds into *Śiva-Śakti-samghatt* (*union* of *Śiva* and *Śakti* aspects) of *Anuttra* in क्ष , at the end of the *varṇa-sṛšṭi,* for the ultimate consummation. The *varṇa* क्ष results from the combination of क , स and अ , where क represents the *ghanattva* form of *Anuttra* अ in its immanent expression. Represented thus by क & स , is the *Śakti* aspect of the *parāvāk* from *pṛthvi* to *Sadāshiv,* pervading entirely the three domains of *pṛthvi-anda* (earth's sphere), *prakṛti-anda* (*prakṛti* sphere), and *māyā-anda* (*māyā* sphere).

[The chart of the four *andas* (ellipses), on the next page, gives the detailed description of each depicting the whole *varṇa-sṛšṭi* clearly emerging from, intrinsically pervaded by, and finally terminating in *Anuttra* अ !

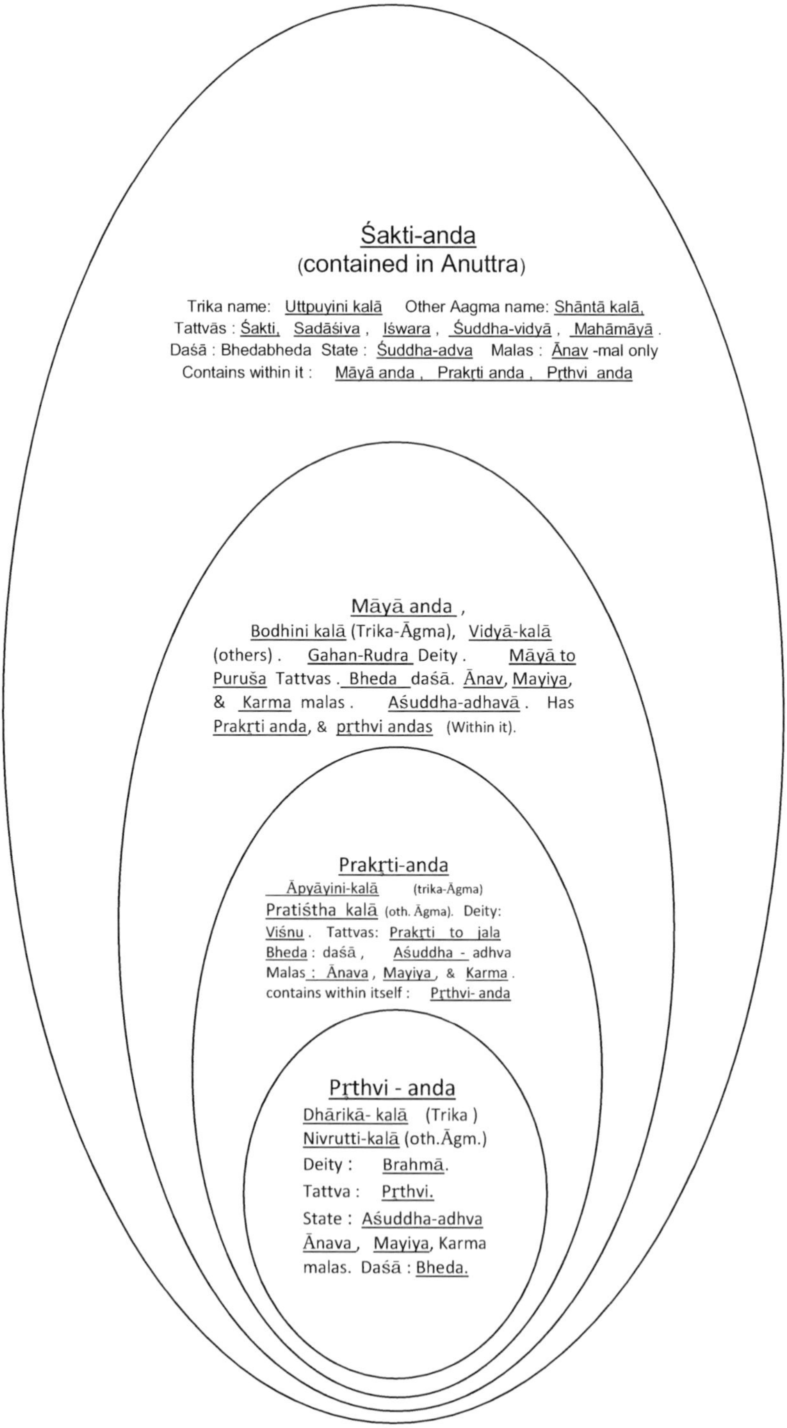

Śakti-anda
(contained in Anuttra)

Trika name: Uttpuyini kalā Other Aagma name: Shāntā kalā,
Tattvās : Śakti, Sadāśiva , Iśwara , Śuddha-vidyā , Mahāmāyā .
Daśā : Bhedabheda State : Śuddha-adva Malas : Ānav -mal only
Contains within it : Māyā anda , Prakŗti anda , Pŗthvi anda

Māyā anda ,
Bodhini kalā (Trika-Āgma), Vidyā-kalā (others) . Gahan-Rudra Deity . Māyā to Purušа Tattvas . Bheda daśā. Ānav, Mayiya, & Karma malas . Aśuddha-adhavā . Has Prakŗti anda, & pŗthvi andas (Within it).

Prakŗti-anda
Āpyāyini-kalā (trika-Āgma)
Pratiśtha kalā (oth. Āgma). Deity: Viśnu . Tattvas: Prakŗti to jala
Bheda : daśā , Aśuddha - adhva
Malas : Ānava , Mayiya , & Karma .
contains within itself : Pŗthvi- anda

Pŗthvi - anda
Dhārikā- kalā (Trika)
Nivrutti-kalā (oth.Āgm.)
Deity : Brahmā.
Tattva : Pŗthvi.
State : Aśuddha-adhva
Ānava , Mayiya, Karma malas. Daśā : Bheda.

In the ellipses appearing on the previous page, we find that *Śakti-anda*, contained in *Anuttra* has in its womb the *māyā-anda* , which bears in it the *prakṛti-anda*, having *pṛthvi-anda*, within it, with everything it keeps as *dhārani*. This depicts clearly that *Śakti*, *hṛdayesth* in *Anuttra*, the all-pervasive *prakāśa* of *being*, is the ultimate source or the womb always pregnant with, always delivering, and always taking care of all objective existence as the *kulanāyikā*. *Anuttra* is the ultimate *Kalā*, in which all *kalās* , *bhuvanas* and *andas* exist without any differentiations or separate identity, but *just only as Anuttra*. Called *Awkāshda-kalā* in *Trika-Āgmas*, it is the one that provides and grants all, but gives away nothing, accommodates everything but takes nothing, glances everything but holds on to nothing. In other *Śaiva-āgmas* it is called *śāntatīta-kalā* , that, which is beyond even the tranquility. It is beyond all *tattvas* but contains *all tattvas* in it. It is beyond *all malas* and *bhedas*, completely without any differentiations, but can project into being, all differentiations. It is neither *śuddha* nor *aśuddha*, and is, *in itself*, the presiding deity of *itself*. It transcends everything, projects everything, and devours everything into *sameness* with itself. Absolute amazement, as the enigma of its being unknowable is, *it is*, equally or much more of an amazement, to know it. That is why, in the very first *Sūtra* of *Parātrīśikā*, *Devi* asks *Bhairava*:

अनुत्तरं कथं देव सद्यः कौलिकसिद्धिदम्
येन विज्ञातमात्रेण खेचरीसमतां व्रजेत्

(Anuttram katham deva sadyaĥ kaulikasiddhidam yena viĝāt-mātreṇa khećari-samatam vrajet)

...Sūtra - (PT-1)

एतद् गुह्यं महागुह्यं कथय-स्व मम प्रभो

(etad guhyam mahāguhyam kathaya-sva mam prabho)

...Sūtra - (PT - 1a)

" Lord ! What (actually) is Anuttra, just the mere comprehension of which brings about the entire fulfillment of sameness (Khećari-sāmya), with the universal consciousness spontaneously.

Reveal to me, my Lord, my very self, this hidden and unrevealed, the greatest (of all) unrevealed, and implicit, (yet highly explicit) mystery!"

We have already considered *sūtra* (2) of *Parātrīśikā* (page 37), in which *Devi*, the discerning faculty, *Śakti* in the state of *parāparā* where differentiations begin to unravel, seeks to know about *kaulikī-sidhi* and *khećari-sāmya*, as also about the actuality of *Anuttra*. In response, *Sūtra* (3) onwards, *Bhairava*, the *parā* aspect of *Śakti*, presents the essence of creation and the related aspects as held in the philosophical tradition of *Trika*, but says nothing to describe the actuality of *aunuttra*. And what can one say about the un-describable?

Lulla, the greatest *Trika*-philosophical poetess, and one of the greatest of the *Trika-experients*, says:

गिरस प्रुछ्योम सासि लटे
यस नु कँह वनान तस क्याह नाव
लूसुस, कँह ति ह्यितनम नो मटे
कँह नस निशी क्याह ताम द्राव ।

" I asked my Guru a thousand times, 'How can the indescribable be described ?' Waiting, I wilted, but he said nothing. Then the 'nothing,' revealed 'something'!"

Anyone you seek guidance from is *guru*, and no one who would, or could guide, described the indescribable, however long you waited or persevered. *Lulla* too suffered the same way in her quest. Then, as *Lulla* watched '*nothing*' (got into *nirvikalpa* state), she became *aware!* It was the state of pure awareness that *happened*. She became the pure *universal subject* !

Yet another of her outpourings in this regard is:

गिरन विननम कुनुय वचुन
नँबरु दिपनम अंदर अचुन
ललि मे गव सुय वाख तु वचुन
ह्यितुम तनय नगन अचुन ।

" My Guru gave me just one command, 'go within from the without' and that command became for me (Lulla), 'the sūtra and the teaching' and I started crossing-over from without into within. "

'Outside' signifies only objectivity and 'Within' is the subjective aspect. Guru commanded *Lulla* to hold on to the subjective domain, and not the objective one. She *crossed over* !

The differentiation of objective and subjective is very subtle. What we regard as subjective, may actually be objective. As discussed earlier, there are different *pramātās* at different *tattvas* states. The view from these different perspectives yields different experiences in the objective domain. When all these domains are crossed over, the domain of 'nothing' (no objectively), the *nirvikalpa*, the non-existence of the objective existence, is experienced by the pure subject, the pure awareness, (which never is objective). That only truly *is*. And that is *Anuttra (!)* the totality. Recognizing this truth is experiencing bliss.

We have already made reference to *baindivi-kala*, 'that anyone chasing one's own shadow can never, ever, step over the head of that shadow'. A subject can experience anything but himself, as his object of study. How can a subject become his own object. In the mundane study of the physical objective world, an observer can never accurately fix quantitatively, the two coordinates, that of the position as well as the momentum, of a moving body simultaneously, reveals the theory of uncertainty relating to physical domains. Also no one can ever see one's true image one-self actually. Lateral inversions occur in mirror images. Which perspective of his objective existence can an objective existent call his subject? What aspect of the entire existence can reveal universal subjectivity? Perspectives are perspectives, and they are innumerable. Which one, if any, would be a correct perspective of locating the subject, even if, a one existed ?

Abhinavgupta has in *Parātrīśikā-vivaraṇa,* while referring to *Anuttra,* explained in detail why *Bhairava* or *parama-Śiva* is called *Anuttra.* He has explained in sixteen ways, the meaning and the implication of the word *Anuttra,* and thereby indicated, what it is not, and consequently, the futility of the lots of things we do, or hold on to, in the hope of grasping it. Resorting to a very subtle analysis of the word *Anuttra,* through the linguistic and philosophical subtleties, he advises *Trika* aspirants to shake themselves free from the very many futile pursuits. Through a keen analysis Abhinavgupta communicates to us the ultimate reality, that *Anuttra* is not attainable by *logic* or *contemplation,* or in *portions* at various levels of *grosser* or *subtler* approaches. *Methodologies, virtues, austerities,* or even all various *Śaktis,* acquired even through *śaṭh-ćakra-bhedan,* can never make anyone grasp it. It is beyond all *dīkšās* (initiations) of whatever kind. No *doubts* about its ultimate autonomy, or the *truth* of its projection as the entire manifestation, (*which anyway is not unreal*) can disprove any of it, nor any *beliefs prove* it. Although succession is the characteristic of all objective manifestation, *Anuttra* itself is succession-less, ever present, entire and whole reality and essence, perpetually pulsating in *everything* immanent, although it is a transcendental reality.

The *Parātrīśikā Sūtras* - (*1 & 1a*) quoted above, must be considered in the light of what was referred to, in between. These *Sūtras* project a subtle dilemma. *Devi*, the questioner at the *parāparā* level, from the perspective of the differentiation, seeks to know the ultimate and implicit reality, explicitly. Calling *Bhairva* '*her own self*', she then, asks '*Him*' to reveal the hidden (*guhyam*), yet highly explicit (*mahāguhyam*, the *mahā+aguhyam*) mystery of *Anuttra*, (the *Bhairava*, which she calls ' her own self '), mere comprehension of which (as she says) brings one, to *sameness* with that. It is a riddle, carrying with it also the clue !

Devi, the *Śakti*, taking the perspective of differentiation, and therefore *not aware*, at that level, of her *same-ness* with *Bhairva*,
(thus wanting to know), seeks *awareness* (to relish) of her *same-ness* with Him, (the *Bhairava* ... '*her owm self*'). Clearly, what she seeks is the awareness, and this is the clue to the secret, the implicit mystery. *Awareness* (!) to be sought from within (one's own self) .....by remaining *aware* of it. *This is* the explicit reality.

It is *Ćiti*, the creative consciousness, willfully having taken on itself, the deluding aspect of *ćitta*, (then) seeking *ćetnā*, for experiencing the bliss of *same-ness*, with *Ćit* !

Anuttra, the *Parama-Śiva*, is *Ćidānand-ghana*, the *ghanattva*, the infinite conglomeration of *Ćit* (the presence, the being, the pure awareness) and *ānanda* (the bliss of the potency of awareness). This potency or the *Śakti* of awareness, the absolute autonomy (*swātantrya*) of *Ćit*, known as *Ćiti*, is as we know now the *source and stuff*, that manifests from itself, all the varied aspects of objective phenomena, and maintains them all. *It* gives each, the *being* of whatever it is, or withdraws that by devouring it into itself, to project yet another presence, a new being. *Ćiti*, the infinite potency, on its *creative* mission of precipitating itself as all the different varied stuff, by shrinking itself into an appropriate expressions of potency, creates the panorama of manifestation. For becoming an empirical experient, it shapes itself into the *tattvas* that form also its inner operational psychic apparatus, the *ćitta*, the *aňtaĥ-karana*, (the *mana-ahaňkār-budhi* combine), to act as a terminal for the operation of the potency of the pure awareness through the empirical being. This *ćitta* acts as the empirical subject, the *ćitta-pramātā*. This *ćitta-pramātā*, the experient on the empirical plane conducts operations in the manifested world. It can also, at the same time, by seeking *ćetanā* become *ćetan*, and then, on casting away its *dhārnās*, rise as *Ćiti*, and be one with *Ćit*, the pure *being*, to experience the pure bliss again. *This*, the empirical being *can* do, even while keeping its foothold in the empirical body (of *anu*). *Sūtras* (5, 6, & 13) of *Pratyabiġāna-hṛdayama*, (quoted ahead) bear the same truth:

चितिरेव चेतनपदादवरूढा चेत्यसंकोचिनी चित्तम्

(ćitireva ćetanapadād-avarūđha ćetya-samkoćinī ćittam)

... sūtra - (pbh – 5)

"Ćiti, dismounting from its status of ćetanā and contracting into (some form of) an appropriate perceiver, is ćitta."

तन्मयो मायाप्रमाता

(tanmayo māyā-pramātā)

... sūtra - (pbh – 6)

"That (ćitta) constitutes māyā-pramātā."

तत्परिज्ञाने चित्तमेव अन्तर्मुखीभावेन चेतनपदाध्यारोहात् चिति

(tatpariġāne ćittameva antarmukhī-bhāvena ćetanapada-adhyārohāt ćitiĥ)

... sūtra - (pbh – 13)

"By acquiring the exact knowledge severally, and having transition into that state within, makes ćitta rise to the status of ćetna and become Ćiti."

Going Within

In the light of *sūtras* from different *Āgmas*, in addition to *Śiva-sūtra*-(1) [of section-1], we have found, that this entire *sṛšṭi* is *ćiti-spanda* only, varied aspects of the *viśeša-spanda*, all (!) From the grossest to the subtlest of the manifestations, *everything* is nothing but the pulsating pure awareness, in infinitely varied *Ġāna*-confines functioning as coded matrices with the potency of *viśeša* (specific) *spanda*, an expression of *Ćiti* and all having their *being* in the *prakāśa* of *Ćit*. This *everything* constitutes a wonderland, in which *everything* is playing a game of *altered identity* in such a convincing manner, that, *no one* remembers that it is a game. The only key to their true identity is *recollection* of it, the *ćetnā* of it. All *ćittas*, the empirical existents, *can* have *that ćetnā* and rise as *Ćiti* to embrace their soul-mate *Ćit*, to experience the eternal bliss of *their* union with their true I-consciousness a unique *parābhattarika* experience of reunion of *Ćit*, the *Śiva*, and *Ćiti*, the *Śakti*.

Śiva-sūtra-(5) clearly states:

उद्यमो भैरवः

(udyamo Bhairavaĥ)

... sūtra - (ss – 5)

> *"Rising above (beyond the perceptive experience) is Bhairava (avastha)."*

Looking back at *Śiva-sūtras* (1- 4) we can recall, that *Ćaitanya*, the pure awareness, the core or the ultimate essence of everything, projects out of itself, the entire manifestation, as *Ġāna*-confines of the limited and the specific potencies, be it, the different aspects of objective manifestations or their subjective being. These all, the various *Mātṛkā* designations, the superstructures of *Ġāna*, are basically *ćiti*, the *Śakti*, in all its varied forms. From *Ćiti* to *ćitta* there is a coherent continuity of pure awareness, the ultimate essence (of everything) in varying aspects of contraction, forming the entire perceptive domain. Beyond, or at the back of it all, is the reality of *Bhairava.*

Sūtra(13) of *Pratyabhiġana-hṛdayama* (page 144) states that *ćitta*, the empirical experient transiting inward into the *exact* knowledge, can become *ćetana* (conscious) and rise to the state of *Ćiti.* What knowledge must be acquired, and what approach for *going inward* is desired, needs to be clearly considered. As stated *Ćitta* has to have *Ćetnā*, and that is the clue. *Ćetnā*, the alertness, the conscious watchfulness, the keen-ness of attention, is the only need, and, the rest will follow. We in fact, do not normally identify or comprehend even the sense inputs when they are very feeble and not accompanied simultaneously by some other attributes also. Locating a thin, thread-like crescent of a new moon, almost merged with the faint light of the horizon, is not at all easy, even if someone indicates it by pointing towards it, unless one strives hard with intense attention, even though the other person who has seen it once, continues seeing it. We normally hear the toll of a bell distinctly, but do not hear the lingering trail of its (so-called) dying sound, unless we listen to it intently, because normally, other sounds or thoughts keep our attention captured. Surely can we hear the amazingly faint remains of the fading sound by pursuing it with attention. An adept in scents and perfumes identifies different aromas and fragrances with utmost ease. Consider a tea-taster! Can one imagine normally what delicacies of the differences in the taste and flavor he discerns, identifies, and classifies! A keen attention even on the subtlest of features of the materials, relevant to our sense faculties, reveals them, and they come easy to an observer when the keen-ness of attention becomes an attitude. These material features still have, even on the subtlest levels of their being, an existence and space of their own. They continue to remain in their *ākāśa* and maintain this ether of their existence as long as they exist in such empirical domains. Their being can be touched and the presence shared only if one can move closer into and share the neighborhood of that space of theirs. If a matrix of any such specific state of existence disintegrates, it merges into an un-definable matrix (still a matrix) full of strangeness, where very subtle, determinable, and indeterminable forms of the existence co-exist. Differentiations occur there, and also do not occur, both. This threshold of immanent and transcendental existence, the space at the inception of *Māyā*, where all the quantum descriptions as we conceive and define them become illusive and incomprehensible, is like a black-hole of existence that sucks in or 'un-defines' the 'defined', as well as, projects or 'defines' the 'undefined'. Here, only strangeness of the divine-*Kriyā* operates. It is here that the unbounded dynamic-consciousness, *Khećari-Śakti*, (*kha,* the space of consciousness and *chari*, the dynamic), the *Śakti* on the plane of *bodha* (the pure awareness), the universal or Divine-consciousness, whole and unconditioned (*pūrna and avikalpa*), gets defined into various universal spaces (*ākāś*). It takes on itself different roles for the maintenance of existence to be, and defines for itself various functions designated as *Śaktis* of *Goćari, Dikćari* and *Bhućari.* The role that deals in the *knowledge* aspect (of all objective existents) through the spaces of *añtaĥ-karanas* (inner psychic apparatus in the empirical beings) is *Goćari-śakti,* ('*go*' means projecting onward, like a ray, or a horse, and *ćari* the moving about). *Añtaĥ-karana,* the *budhi, mana,* and *ahañkāra,* forming the inner psychic apparatus are the seat of the sense perceptions, the governing *Śakti* of *indriyas.* These *Śakti*s project themselves through the sense organs for their activity of knowledge. As *budhi,* the ascertainment of the difference (*bhed-nishchaya*), as *ahañkāra,* the identification of different individual entities (*bheda-abhimān*), and as mind, the (*bheda-vikalpana*), the *ideation* of *different* things for the empirical subject is conducted. *Dikćari-Śakti* represents the diversity of knower-aspects, the outward oriented senses (*bahish-karna*), and deals in the operations of handling , gathering and grasping of different perceptions (of *difference*), pertaining to the different diverse existents. The world (*bhu*), comprising all the *existents* and *knowables*, is the manifestation of *Śakti* aspect called *Bhućari-Śakti. Khećari Śakti*, basically *Ćit-gagan-ćari* or *vyom-ćari*, (moving in the spaces of *Ćit*) the dynamic pure consciousness or Divine *swātantrya-Śakti* of absolute non-difference, *pūrana* and *avikalpa*, takes on the aspects of difference (*bheda*). *Śakti* as *Māyā*, introduces the *ānav-mala* (the sense of difference, the sense of empirical-ness) in the manifested existence. This, the bringing up of the separateness aspect of objectivity, identification as separate, basically causes the sense of manifestation of *sṛšti* or *samsāra. Khećari-Śakti* thus takes on a role that is called *vameśwari*, [*vama* means emitting out, as also left or *reverse*] as it projects or emits out the *samsār*, which is rooted in, and therefore the harbor-er of, the sense of difference (*bheda*) as against the non-differentiation, its essence in the transcendental existence. *Vameśwari*, as *goćari*, *dikćari* and *bhućari*, although constituting the whole universe, becomes the cause for the delusion of a *samsārin* (empirical subject), even as it is essentially the *swātantrya-Śakti* of absolute sovereignty. In fact, the very *khećari-Śakti* perceived as anger, desire, pleasure, pain or any other so-called aberration (or delusion), in the form of specific responses to any of the perceptions of *śabda, rūpa rasa gandha* or *sparśa*, can bring about a state of *vismaya* (wonder), and a complete identity with *Bhairava-consciousness*, only if there is mindfulness of *khećari-samatā*. One needs to understand fully that *all* these perceptions are the manifestation *actually* of nothing other than the unbounded transcendental *Bhairava-consciousness*, scintillating perpetually as *spandā* of *ānanda* in the *abheda* domain of *Śiva*, as also in the *bhedabheda* domain of *śuddha-vidyā*. One has to maintain this mindfulness, even as an *ānava* or empirical entity, for the cultivation of *Khećari-sāmya*. The fact is that although we, the empirical beings, are custom-made through the influence of the *Śakti* as *Māyā*, for the perception and ascertainment of each and everything that is perceptible, through the perspective of *difference*, we *can* still focus on the awareness of unity, since the pure awareness only, *is truly* our essence. Various aspects of subjectivity, from different points of view, like body (*deha*) as *deha-pramātā*, *prāṇa* as *prāṇa-pramātā*, *ćitta*, (the mind and *indriya*), as *puryaštaka-pramātā*, or the imperceptible (non-objective) reality, the *shūnya-pramātā* are in fact all, the aspects of *Khećari* or the dynamic-consciousness at play. Perpetual (*nitya*) awareness of this unity is *khećari-samtā (खेचरी समता)*, the actuality of *Anuttra*, or *Bhairava-awastha*, and thus *mokša* of *jagadānandā* (while still in body). All objective perceptions like sound, sight, touch, etc., or subjective fluxes like passionate longing (*kāma*), anger (*krodha*), etc. occur as distinctly separate entities on the empirical level, and we are used to handling them on their own merit, towards the fulfillment of their specific ends. This keeps us involved or entangled in their confined spaces, and generates vicious circles of various other correlated fluxes (*vrittīs*) in our *puryaštaka*. These *vrittīs* have a very strong grip on our empirical consciousness, and can drive us away completely for fulfilling the tasks, whatsoever, for their momentary satiation. This state of heterogeneous appearance of consciousness is called *khećri-vaiśamya* (खेचरी वैषम्य). It keeps us engrossed in *ānava-mala*, the illusion of considering ourselves only empirical entities. It also acts as a ground for the development, and then later, reinforcement of other illusions namely *mayiya-mala* and *karma-mala*, which come into being through the interactive processes of overlapping of various different spaces of varied perceptive or reflective *vrittīs*. The sense of deprivation and want arising out of considering ourselves empirical entities, gives rise to cravings (*rāga*), greed (*lobha*) and attachments (*moha*). Comparison with another entity causes jealousy (*dvesha*) or pride (*abhimāna*). Fear of losing (*bhye*) or an actual experience of a loss or defeat, causes anger (*krodha*). Such *vrittīs* are *mayiya-mala*. Consequent actions undertaken through the influence of these result in the incorporation of several complexes of guilt, deceit and the like, leading to *karma-mala*. Not remaining at all involved and engrossed in such heterogeneity of consciousness while engaged in *any* activity whatever, but only keenly aware, that all such states are, after all, only *khećari* at play, (since only that is the ultimate subjective, objective and correlating reality), develops into *khećri-sāmya*. By such constant awareness one is bound to experience the divine presence in every object and every state, whether love or passion, wrath or sorrow. *Suśumnā*, the central channel of *prāṇamaya-kośa* running along our vertebral-column, is the store-house of the entire energy of all our *indriyās*. Whatever enters inside our body, like food, or a perception through the *indriyās* in the form of an impulse of sound, or a visual image, a taste or a touch input from our outward directed senses, or even from psychic apparatus within, is all transformed into life-energy (*ojas*, ओजस, the vital luster) within *Sušumnā*, and there it abides. It is later converted into the enlivening factor, the common seminal energy (*vīrya*) that permeates the whole body. All functions, creative or reproductive, are performed by this energy. It is the representative of the divine energy of *Khećari*, on the physical plane. Any excitation input from within or without, causes agitation in this *vīrya*, which yields charm, delight, a sensation of passion, anger, grief and the like, in us. These sensations do not owe their being to the body, which after all is merely a fabricated thing, although it may seem that they are as such physical, chemical, biological or psychic manifestations. Our looking forward to achieving such delights or sensations through physical or biological means for transitory gratification, creates such notions. These notions as well as such superficial strivings, lead us into *khećri-vaiśamya*. Such strivings or urges taking hold of our conscious mind are very potent. The most potent of all such sensations is the urge for the performance of sexual acts. Sexual intercourse between a man and a woman, sustained by the intense excitement of their seminal energy, which, intent on oozing out at the moment of joy and thrill, at the point of orgasm, (*aňtaĥ-sparśa-sukham*), provides but an extremely faint version of the profound ecstatic bliss that can be experienced by one's entry into *parābhattarika-rūpa* union of *Śiva* and *Śakti*. This union of one's consciousness with unalterable perfect *I-consciousness*, is brought about by *Khećari-sāmya*, if resorted to, even on such occasions as the thrill of orgasm. *Khećari-sāmya* can be achieved even by intensive recollection (as it also excites the seminal energy) of the sexual thrill in the sexual organ, and the central channel *Suṣumnā* (the site of natural supreme *Śakti*), even in absence of an actual contact with the partner, simply by visualizing that delight, as delight of supreme *Brahman*, the actuality of one's own *self*. Whenever an impulse arises within, it is, at its initial state, a *nirvikalpa* thought element, born as a *sphuraṇ* (स्फुरण) in the bosom of the *hṛdaya*, the core, that harbors only the pure awareness, the *ćetanā* aspect. It is not a *construct* in the garb of a thought yet. It is also not associated with any other thought construct in the form of a *Śakti* of letters or words, but only, just a quivering, a throb, of an un-identifiable urge, emerging from *parā-paśyanti* into the *paśyanti* state, as the indeterminate dynamism of *khećari Śakti*. It is like the urge in a branch, just before it routes to break through, as an almost unidentifiable, infinitesimal point that would subsequently pierce the bark of the branch, and form itself, into the birth of a bud. *Any* urge of sex or anger, fear or frolic, still unknown in its character, just in the process of springing-forth, *is* the *spanda* of awareness, in its process of manifestation, as a feeling or a thought to be. It is still in the *Śiva*-state of *parā*, just the *prakāśa* of *being* only.

A slight more flashing of it, but still in the indeterminate state, (in the levels of *paśyanti*), it is the aspect of *Śakti*, in an embrace with *Śiva*, the *Śiva-Śakti-samghatt*, before it unfolds into various *Śakti*-in-action aspects of taking on its garb of identification. This throb, if contacted and intensely dwelt on and pierced into, without the contamination of any thought, becomes transcendental *sāmya* of *khećari*. It is a *Śambhava*-penetration (*Śambhu* or *Śiva* related) into the awareness. It is an extremely scintillating identification with the true, un-defiled identity of I-ness (our true-Self). It is a direct dive into the unbounded ocean of the bliss of *Anuttra* अ .

Recognizing, on the other hand, a tender surge of impulse, when it begins oozing out as a subtle but an identifiable feeling of a specific character, not expressed into an action yet, and thus, still in the state of *madhyamā*, just in the domain of knowledge, is a *parāparā* state of experience of the existence of the particular feeling or thought. It is a potent state of feeling, not thought, and demands an equally potent handling for homogenizing it with *khećari*. Linking with this surge in complete awareness, that it is a dynamic expression of *my* being, a specific surge of *my Śakti*, and sublimating it back into the feeling of I-ness, is sure to take the consciousness into the core of the being. In fact, it is a process of *linking* with *viśeṡa-spanda*. *Grasping* that *spanda* and *merging* it with the *sāmānya-spanda* of the *prakāśa* of *being*, provides the true experience of *parābhattarikā* with its unbounded bliss. It is a *śakta*-penetration into the expansion aspect (*visarga*) of the manifestation and is highly demanding. It needs appropriate introversion of *vīrya* into the *Śakti* of *indriyās*. Such sustained and repeated *Śakti-sparśa* with *khećari* leads also to the understanding of, and resorting to, the *śambhav-sāmya.*

Next, when the specific impulse or the feeling is full-bloom, demands expression and is at the verge of expressing itself, it is, at the threshold of the domain of *Kriyā*, in the *aparā* state of *vaikhari.* It has already attained an empirical (*bheda*) state of its existence, and is bound for *khećari-vaiśamya.* At this *ānava* state of thoughts or feelings, the delusion caused by *vāmeśvari* is of utter helplessness. The momentum of its expression is beyond the domain of *budhi*, and suppression is of no avail, because suppression itself is another aspect of *vaiśamya.* A tender remembrance, that whatever is happening, is an expression of divine *Śakti*, only through the medium of (my?) body, and maintaining this awareness unflinchingly, thus experiencing the play of *khećari* as a witness, with detachment, can be highly illuminating. Such awareness steadied, is bound to transform *indriya-vrittīs* into *indriya-Śakti* ultimately, and lead finally to *khećari-sāmya.* Any of these *Śāmbhava* , *Śakta* , or *Ānava* approaches for *Khećai-sāmya* resorted to, are sure to bring a mindful aspirant the experience of the bliss of *Parābhattarikā* ultimately while still living an empirical existence in this world of objectivity.

Awareness in whatever measure, slight, tender, moderate, strong, or overwhelming, happening whenever, or perpetually, is actually a contact made with *Ćiti*. Our subjective aspect of *ćitta* remains usually engrossed in *vrittīs* of whatever kind, caused by outer or inner fluxes. In any state of involvement with *vrittīs*, we live a virtual life and not the real one, unless we are involved in some truly creative or intense experience. Thoughts (*vrittīs*) of past or future, relating to any of the emotions born of *ānava, māyiya or karma mala*, are an engagement with the virtual, because the *real* is only the *being*, the actual *present moment*, which cannot happen without the awareness of presence, *being present*, and being *in* present, intensely. A subject, aware that he *is* the experiencer, experiencing whatever in the objective world, and distinctly conscious of the subjective experiencing and various objective aspects, without a bias or a motive, is *aware* of his *ānava* presence. If such a subject is, at the same time, conscious of the transcendental unity of all those aspects, he is beginning to be *ćetana* and shall subsequently make a contact with *Ćiti*, since this awareness grows and makes him more intensely aware of it. Whenever *ćitta* makes a contact with *Ćiti*, some of its dross (*mala*) melts away. It tastes the touch, however feeble, of bliss, and experiences an impetus, however small, for living one's true-self, being revealed within. The taste of the true being-ness lingers for some while, within such a person, in the form of an inexpressible bliss and ease.

Sūtra-(14) of *Pratyabhiĝāna-hṛdayama* quoted next is just the same communication:

चितिवह्निनरवरोहपदे छन्नोऽपि मात्रया मेयेन्धनं प्लुष्यति

(ćitivahinaravarohapade ćhhanno-api mātrayā meyendhanam plušyati)

... sūtra - (pbh – 14)

"On descending to the states covered-over by objectivity (māyā), the fire of Ćiti burns a measurable amount of (this) fuel (of the 'mala oj objectivity' caused due to māyā)."

Ćitta, our empirical being, has to recognize the fact that awareness, the *ćaitanya*, is our essence, our true being, the root, and make contact with it. This recognition is two pronged, that is, through understanding and through actuality. Understanding represents the verbal *Ġāna*, the confined knowledge, which is at *aparā* level though, but also extremely essential.The actuality, the flowering of the true awareness, the *prakāśa* of being, is *Śaktipāt*, the descending of *Ćiti* into *ćitta,* that melts away the limitation imposed by *māyā*, (which in fact structures the *ćitta*). What remains is only the pure, true-self. After getting the recognition through understanding, one needs to remain aware, all the time, of that understanding, and watch how much it reflects in one's daily life, in one's thinking and activity. Involvements in the objectivity need not cause disappointments, but should provide a greater resolve to remain aware. The inertia of our *sańskārs* has a great tenacity, but the spark of awareness, once kindled, must be guarded. Stronger the urge of contacting one's true self, the greater the fire of awareness glows. A sustained fire of *Ćiti* burns the impact of the dross of objectivity. There are known instances, (there can be innumerable unknown one's too), when extremely intense awareness lifted the humans to the level of one-ness with *Śiva* instantaneously. They did not resort to any means or efforts (explicitly) for removing the dross of limitations. Their intensity of urge and keen-ness of attention were extreme, and realization was instantaneous. This approach of *ćitta* is called *anupaya*, i.e., no-*upāya*, *without* means ! It is the spontaneous unfolding of true awareness in a *ćitta*, in which a transformation into *ćiti* has already happened. Something, a tender probe, like an intense attention on any impulse, results in a complete *khećari-sāmya*, the sameness with *Ćiti* instantly, and therefore a spontaneous disappearance of all of the *malas* that had made it to believe itself to be an empirical entity.

Accompanied by no other diversions, a focused and sustained urge for true I-consciousness, and a keen awareness of that urge, all the time, helps remove the dross of limitations and the consequent illusion of the sense of difference (*bheda*) very fast. It brings a complete *khećari-sāmya* to a persevering aspirant. This approach is called *Śāmbhava-upaya*. An intense conviction developed out of the real understanding of one's true identity, and a continued awareness of that results in *Śaktipāta*. Such a conviction can certainly get established by an *honest sensitivity* to what we have understood by the thorough investigation into all the *Sūtras* we studied in a coherent continuity *so far,* [i.e., *Śiva-sūtras* - (1 - 4), *Sūtras* - (1 - 8) from *Parātrīśikā,* as also *Pratyabhiǵāna-hṛdayama Sūtras* - (1 - 14)].

Understanding the communication rightly and abiding well in that, results in a strong conviction. A sustained awareness of that conviction unfolds true self. This *Śāmbhava* approach basically, is refining and reinforcing continuously of one's strong desire with an un-yielding will that makes one persevere un-flinchingly, for a direct contact with one's true being. There are no other means to it, except this, the only one, of gathering the momentum of one's *will,* and making a direct hit and penetration. This happens only by surrendering all other priorities and igniting the rocket of intensely-strong desire for launch inward, from the overwhelmingly objective, to the intensely subjective reality. This *Śāmbhava* recognition of one's true self, the *Śaktipāta,* is actually an outcome of strong and sustained urge (*Iććhā* or *will*). The *will* becomes *strong* and *focused* only when a strong conviction has matured. This happens only when *ćitta* has gathered itself from its diverse fragmentations committed to various aspects of *malas,* and for that, *ćitta* needs a frequent contact with *ćiti,* which comes by identifying the goal and pursuing it intensely.

Ćitta Pramātā

The aspirant, the *ćitta-pramātā*, must consider *ćitta* itself as the entire potency available to him (and the truth is, that it *is*). *Ćitta* to him, is the storehouse of entire means and all the available knowledge (through *mana, budhi* and *tanmātrās*), of which as *pramātā*, he has to chew the cud, and then assimilate too, as his honest conviction. This way, attempting to purify his *aśuddha-vikalpās*, acutely differentiated understanding, (full of only *bheda*), into *śuddha-vikalpās* of unity and non-difference, and thus rooted in the I-consciousness of his pure self, he must pursue, what is called, *Śākt-upāya* for his unfolding. A sustained awareness of such conviction and a full-blooded pursuit can result in the actuality of its realization in true *Śaktipāta*. The knowledge available to *ćitta* may or may not be useful to the empirical experient in the mundane life, but how the aspirant uses it as the means of raising his *ćitta*, to make a contact with *Ćiti*, or in what way does he sift it from the dross and feed to himself, the *ćitta*, to make it worthy of the *Śaktipāta*, he needs to find out himself.

Section-II, of *Śiva-sūtras*, through its ten (10) *sūtras* provides a discreet perspective of this aspect of pursuit, which we need to investigate at this stage. The first three *Sūtras* are :

चित्तं मंत्रः

(ćittam mańtraĥ)

...sūtra - (ss - II - 1)

"Ćitta is the mańtrā, (the potency)."

प्रयत्नः साधकः

(prayatnaĥ sādakaĥ)

...sūtra - (ss - II - 2)

"Zealous perseverance (is) the means. "

विद्याशरीरसत्ता मंत्ररहस्यम्

(*vidyā-śarīra-sattā mańtra-rahasyam)*

...sūtra - (ss - II - 3)

"Essence of the body of knowledge is the secret of mańtra."

The first of the *Sūtras*, '*ćitta* is *mańtra*', carries a strong revelation and directive for the aspirants. It declares with all authority, that one need not seek anything outside one's *ćitta*, neither in objective existents, nor in the beliefs and assumptions one may carve out with one's thoughts. The three *sūtras*, provide a clear-cut way to proceed in the pursuit of reality. '*ćitta* is *mańtra*', the very first *sūtra* must first be clearly understood for its intended communication. *Mañtrā* can be considered as composed of *man (or manan)* which means 'understanding with reverence' and *tra (or trāna)* that means 'for protection'. The *Sūtra* therefore directs us to pay an unqualified, unbiased attention to *ćitta*, which can protect us like an armour. If we realize that *ćitta* is a conditioned or contracted form of *Ćiti*, then it becomes amply clear that even in this diminutive state, *ćitta* has the *Śakti* inherent in it that can act as armour or strength. It is easy to grasp that the *Sūtra* advises us to gather our attention with an unbiased approach, and direct it towards our *ćitta*, our *only* potency. If it is done with 'perseverance' and 'zeal' it gets 'energized' more, and becomes 'instrumental' in the 'accomplishment' of our goal. This is the complete sense that we get by considering the above *Sūtra* 1 and 2, together. In fact the terms *prayatna* and *sādaka* connote the meanings that have been attributed to them above. *Energizing* and *accomplishing* signify, being able to get it *closer* to *Ćiti*, the *awareness*, and allow it to regain more of its potential. What can be achieved by this increased potency is indicated in *Sūtra(3)*. *Ćitta* is the storehouse of all our (limited) knowledge. The *vidyā*, which is woven into it in the form of all the various structures and superstructures of verbal knowledge, is perceivable in its grosser forms at the level of *vaikhari*, and is also linked to its subtler phases in *madhyama* and *paśyanti* levels, as the manifestations of the *mātṛkā-Śakti*. The objective manifestation, perceivable as the mundane reality of entire *sṛšti*, exists in the form of structures and superstructures of infinite words and sentences, (indicators and indicated) as the body of knowledge (the *vidyā-śarīra*). Although a necessity for our worldly performance, it acts as a barrier for us in the (deeper) understanding of the ultimate reality. This *vidyā* certainly is *not* 'good for nothing'. In its limited perspective, it is relevant to the affairs of the world, and in its essence, it lights our path, because it is the 'secret of the potency', the *Śakti*, the *mañtra-rahasya* of *ćitta*, as per *Sūtra(3),* above. Recollecting the detailed study of *mātṛkā*, [in the context of the *Sūtra – ss (I- 4)*], we have found that the *varṇa* अ as *Anuttra* is intrinsically the sustainer of all the other *varṇās* upto the last *varṇa* ह , the *aparā-visarga-Śakti,* (the projector of *Śakti* as *sṛšti*). The entire empirical existence, the whole of the *akšara-mālā*, essentially is the creative *spanda* of *Anuttra* अ . The *bimba* of swarūpa-*sṛšti* reflects itself as *pratibimba*, in its *aparā* aspect, through the *visarga* ह . The *sṛšti* culminates at म , the *puruša*, (the dot, the *bindu* of empirical being *anu*). The essence, the *sattā* of the whole of the *sṛšti* (the *akšara-mālā* the *vidyā-śarīra*) therefore, is अहं the supreme *I*-consciousness. These *Sūtras* (*ss-II-1,2,3)* therefore prompt a *śakta*-aspirant to reverently observe his subjectivity as *ćitta-pramātā*, and by perseverance raise his awareness to the pure level of supreme *Śiva-consciousness* of real *a-ha-m* , the actuality of the *Bhairava*. The *sūtras* also make an aspirant aware that, his *ćitta* is his entire potency, as well as the source of all his available knowledge, and that is why he should reverently observe, without any bias, his *ćitta* with perseverance, to grasp his essence, his real armor, against falling a prey to the delusions of misconceptions. Then only does *ćitta*, in real sense, become *mańtra*, (the one who experiences the state of *Shuddha-vidyā*). But how can one grasp the essence of the *vidyā-sharīra* and how does *ćitta* get energized by *perseverant* attention on it? This query is answered clearly in the next *Sūtra (ss-II-4).*

गर्भे चित्तविकासोऽविशिष्टविद्यास्वप्नः

(garbhe ćitta-vikāso-aviśišť avidyā-swapnaĥ)

...*sūtra* - *(ss - II - 4)*

"Contact with its garbha evolves ćitta, (and) irrelevant knowledge (born of malas) becomes dream-like (experience) to it."

As established by various considerations [*sūtras* - (*pbh-5, 13, & 14*), (ss - 1,2), etc.,] we know that *ćitta* is actually a projection of *Ćiti.* By truly understanding it and gravitating towards it (its own source or womb), *ćitta* can cultivate awareness of its own recognition again, and rise to the level of its true consciousness. Once touched by this recognition even feebly, its dross of delusion, its *malas*, begin to vanish and it begins fluttering its wings of consciousness in the skies of its true being. It starts flinging off the rags of its confinement into the assumed notions about itself. The knowledge and the roles, it considered as the truth of its being, become hazy in the new dawn of its awakening. The slumber assumed by its true awareness, as also, the demeaning dreams born of its deluded understanding, begin to lose their grip on it. The custom-cast *ćitta*-matrix fabricated by *Māyā* starts recognizing the *Śaktis* of *khećari*, and experiencing the amazement in the domain of *parāparā* consciousness. It begins identifying its real essence of *I-ness* from its assumed postures of objectivity. It starts getting a feel of the *śuddha-vidyā* state of the polarized reality of *I* and the *this*, and the unity of the two. It recognizes *itself* in every *other* thing in the objective domain, and begins basking in the universal consciousness of its being, where the experiences from the usual empirical consciousness level become pale and irrelevant like dreams in the waking state. A transformation sets in motion at various levels of awareness, with respect to the notions of *chitta*, as well as the quality of *will.* A repeated and sustained experience of the new found state, from time to time, clears a greater amount of dross of *malas*, and strengthens the potency of *maňtra* (its sense of *I*-consciousness) within him. This evolution in its understanding widens the horizons of its mundane knowledge in the newer perspective of purer (without *malas*) consciousness, distilling *ćitta* from time to time. This resurgence of the spontaneous understanding makes *ćitta* a witness to the *Śakti* aspects of *goćari*, *dikćari* and *bhuchari* in one's perceptive and responsive aspects, in the empirical posture of life, with a kind of new *oaj* and *tej* in it. Deepening of the awareness of this *Śakti* aspect in every experience brings about the sameness of *ćitta* with *khećari* (the dynamic consciousness at play), in everything that happens and is perceived, in all the perceptions that are perceptible through the senses. This *khećari-sāmya* brings, a true recognition of *I*-consciousness to him and establishes the experience in him of being a part and parcel of everything, all the manifestation, in the sameness with everything, an *ātma-vyāpti* in real sense and actuality. The domain of pure consciousness becomes the space of one's self, and the *ćitta*, that has grown the wings of *ćetanā* again, unfurls them in the abandoned realms of freedom, to fly in the amazing spaces of consciousness. When this sense of true being deepens intensely, true *tattva-anubhava* happens. Self as *vimarśa-maya-prakāśa* in the bliss of its actuality, brings the awareness of *śiva-vyāpti*, a realization of the state of *śivoham*, ___ *'I am Śiva'* ! *the entirety of all that is !!*

Lulleswari, the towering *śaiva* sage of Kashmir puts her experience of this state in the words thus:

चॅ़थ निवुय , चन्द्रमु निवुय
शिवमय मॅ सोरुय ड्यूठमय
मॅ ति ललि, तनै, तन मन निवुय
यनु लल बु सपज़ुस शिवमय ।

A new ćitta did I find (as the experient), and a new moon (objectivity) to experience. Everything about me, I found drenched in (the effulgence of) Śiva. I, lulla, found my body and mind also new, since I attained Śiva-consciousness !

Śiva-sūtra (ss-II-5), holds this promise to the earnest aspirant on the path of *śākta-sādhana*, who, strives intensely to unveil the *essence* of the structures of 'the body of knowledge', for grasping the *potency* of his *ćitta*, and be able to make a contact with its source, the Ć*iti*.

विद्यासमुत्थाने स्वाभाविके खेचरी शिवावस्था

(vidyā-samutthāne swābhāvike khećari Śivāvasthā)

...*sūtra*-(ss-II-5)

"*Contact with, and the recognition of, the spontaneous (pure, shuddha) vidyā, the khećari-sāmya unfolds within, the Śiva-state of being.*"

What more can an aspirant of truth crave for or cherish? *Knowing* for sure, and enjoying, "*the melodies heard and unheard, all* ", the *sṛšṭi* 'conceived or un-conceived' entire, as *Śiva*, being himself the song, the singer and the audience, all !

It surely is true *Jīvan-mukti*, the *Jagadānand*, the absolute freedom and sovereignty, living the highest state of being. It can happen by extreme *anugraha* which descends on those that deserve it. And then, who deserve it more than those who undertake the intense *purušartha*, on the path enlightened by the appropriate *guru*, since only *guru* (the one who *truly* has attained *Śivatva*) is truly, the *source* and the *means* of enlightenment in the *secret* and es*sence* of the subtlest of the understandings, the *mātṛkā-ćakra* !

Śiva-sūtras(*II* - 6 & 7) declare it as under :

गुरुरुपाय:

(gururupayaĥ)

...*sūtra-(ss-II-6)*

" *Guru is the means (for the enlightenment).*

मातृकाचक्रसम्बोध:

(mātṛkā-ćakrasambodhaĥ)

...*sūtra-(ss-II-7)*

" *(for) The achievement of enlightenment in the phenomenon of (the subtleties of) mātṛkā.* "

But then, who is the appropriate *guru*, and how can one find such a *guru* ? This has been an eternal question.

Mālinivijaya *(2.10)*, directs:

स गुरुर्मत्सम: प्रोक्तो मन्त्रवीर्यप्रकाशक:

'[*one, who (truly knowing) enlightens on the potency of mantra is guru , like me !*]' says *Śiva* to *Parvati.*

Guru is therefore one who knows. Śiva Himself ! The awareness absolute! *He is* the appropriate *Guru*, and *He knows* who the appropriate seeker is. *He* knows his needs and his means, and bestows the divine grace, the way *He* deems fit. A genuine seeker need not worry. He has not to seek the *Guru*, the *Guru* seeks and finds him. The enlightenment strikes like a lightning and the recognition is spontaneous. *He* fills the cup, while the *pātra* (the container) needs only to be upright, alert and emptied of the dross. It is the '*only puruṡārtha*' that one actually needs to do and truly *can* do.

Lulleśwari says:

च़ला चँ़थु , विन्दस बय मो बर
चोन चँ़नुत करान पानु अनाद
च़ कवु ज़ानुन, ख्यद कू हरि, कर
चे़न , तसुंदुय , तोरुक नाद ।

Hey my ćitta, do not harbor fears in your inmost. The time-less, the eternal Himself is aware of (the needs of) you. Why need you know who satiates your hunger, and when ? Be alert only to discern just His call, from His realm.

Lulleśwari dispels our fears and doubts about our inability of finding an appropriate *guru*. She stresses on the need of our being alert and attentive to the calls of the ultimate *Guru*, who *is* on the lookout for us, *ever* ! Therefore, the only *puruṡārtha* we actually can, and need to do, is, to remain alert and attentive, which is possible only when our keen-ness, fuelled by our true yearning to recognize our *real* being, is intense. This yearning grows as we remain aware. Aware, of the clouding layers of all the notions, the various *malas*, that we harbor about our self and get conditioned by. These *malas* that make our recognition of ourselves clouded must be rationalized continuously into their decay for liberating ourselves from our assumed and false identity of considering ourselves as empirical entities, the *ānava* subjects. Only when there is the intense *desire* or *will* to recognize ourselves we grow in the clearer understanding of ourselves, of our *true* identity, and guard against the factors, the *malas*, that cloud our understanding. A sustained, earnest and intense *purušārtha* is to be resorted to by the true aspirant to de-condition himself from those *malas* continuously, keeping the goal to be achieved always in view. *Śiva-sūtras* provide us an approach to this, in three different sections devoted to *Śāmbhava*, *Śākta*, and *ānava* perspectives. These are actually the aspects of *Iććhā*, *Ġāna*, and *Kriyā* respectively, of handling our approach to the reality. We however must understand that this profound and the most subtle exploration of our real identity is never possible in isolation by any one approach. Our *ānava* existence, structured in the fabric of differentiation and *māyic* illusions, is very resilient, and exerts back-pulls, of one, or the other kind, as long as the actual *Śaktipāta* doesn't happen. All the three aspects of approach, therefore, are to be resorted to simultaneously, by a genuine and passionate seeker, who must understand that our personality is a sum-total of all our *sattvic*, *rajsic*, and *tamsic vrittīs*. Our intense desire, the *will*, gets dampened often by the inertia of our habit, in spite of our knowledge contrary to it. Pettiest of the desires and funniest of the ego problems of our empirical nature, trample our subtlest of the understandings many a times, turning our noblest of the desires into dust. The adherence to the sense of uniqueness of our personal identity, and its domination over all aspects of our being, the tempting glare of competition, the arrogance of false understanding, and the taste of the habit, form the entire warp and weft woven by the *ānava, mayiya*, and *karma mals*, over which we rejoice to function, and into which we take refuge often. Awareness of it all, sustained introspection and evaluation perpetually and appropriate handling, has to be our real *purušārtha*. This can keep the light of *Ġāna* glowing, and the *will* charging itself more and more, for its spontaneous launch into the true recognition of our *Self*, the actual *Śaktipāta*.

Purušārtha

We, the *ānava* experients of this *sṛšti*, the empirical beings, conditioned by three *malas* of our empirical existence and three guṇas of our *prakṛtī*, are all on a mission to explore the truth of our being beyond these *malas* and *guṇas*. As *ānava* experients, therefore, we need to begin from the beginning, __ the working field available to the *ānava* existents, the field of the *kriyā* (*ānava-upāya*), before taking to the aspect of *ġāna*, the purification of *aśuddha-vikalpās* (*Śākta-upāya*). In fact both the approaches need to be resorted to always by the genuine aspirants, to be able to strengthen the *will* into a really strong urge to become ultimately a *Śāmbhava*-aspirant, who truly deserves the *Śaktipāta*.

Before contemplating further in this regard it would be useful to first concentrate on certain *Sūtras* in section–*III of Śiva-sūtras*. These concern our *ānava* state of approach and enlighten us in our *purušārtha* as the *ānava* aspirants. The first three *sūtras* of this sections read as:

आत्मा चित्तम्

(ātmā ćittam)

...sūtra - (ss-III-1)

"Ćitta (ānava pramātā,) is the (aparā) experient."

ज्ञानं बन्धः

(Ġānam bandhaĥ)

...sūtra - (ss-III-2)

" Ġāna, (of ćitta, the aparā knowledge, intrinsic or acquired) is structured (directed and specific). "

कलादीनां तत्त्वानामविवेको माया

(kalādīnam tattvānām-aviveko māyā)

...sūtra - (ss-III-3)

" The understanding, structured and founded in kalā, and other māyic tattvās is of aviveka (abodha), brought about by the delusion caused by Māyā."

The *Sūtras* quoted above affirm that we, the empirical beings are *ćitta-experients*, with confined, structured knowledge brought about by our *māyic* fabric. We therefore do not have the real *bodha* (awareness) of the true and pure *vidyā*. Conditioned by *Māyā* and its awareness-inhibiting *kañćakas* of *kalā*, *rāga* etc. we are conditioned into thinking and acting under the influence of deluded understanding and not through the real *bodha*. We the *Māyā-pramātās*, through the software of an understanding that is actually needed for our appropriate performance at this *ānava* level are merely a matrix, the empirical existents, structured and equipped for performance as *ćitta-pramātās*. This, the operator, the *puruša*, the *ćitta-pramātā*, requires various different operating potentials for operations at various of its domains and therefore has different sheaths (*śarīras*) or layers of existence, appropriate for their specific functionalities. These layers, all with inbuilt controls, address to their specific functions and needs, and also coordinate with each other. In structuring this all, the transformation that *Saňvid*, the supreme *I* -consciousness first undergoes is, into *Mahāprāṇa*, which forms an extremely potent and subtle infrastructure called *prāṇa-mayakośa*. This is a sheath comprising thousands of channels called *nāđis*, main amongst them, the three *nāđis*, the *Sušumnā*, *Ida* and *Pingla*, in addition to seven *ćakrās*, the wheel-like seats of *Śakti*. At the stage of *Māyā* therefore, *Saňvid*, concealed into *prāṇa-Śakti*, occupies the subtle body (the *sūkšama-śarīra*) of the empirical existents, in the planes of *aňtaĥ-karanas*, (subjective and objective aspects, both). Gross-body *(sthūla-śarīra)* for all its voluntary and involuntary operating functions is controlled by *prāṇa-mayakośa*. *Gоćari* and *Digćari* aspects of the *Khećari-Śakti*, for the ascertainment and gathering mechanisms of perceptions through *Ġāna-indriyās*, and the related responses through the activity of *karma-indriyās*, as well as the subjective experiences like feelings (of pleasure, etc.) are therefore all conducted by *prāṇa-Śakti* in all the *prāṇis* (living beings). Central (*madhya*) to this *prāṇa-Śakti*, (evidently!) is *Saňvit*, the supreme universal consciousness of *Śiva*, in both the *prakāśa* aspect, as also the *ġāna* and *Kriyā* aspect of *Śakti*, whose seat in this *prāṇa–mayakośa* is termed as *Madhyanāđi.* Like the vertebral column, the carrier of spinal-chord in vertebrates, or mid-rib connected to the maze of channels in a leaf (like *plāśa*), *Madhya-nāđi* is the source and sustainer of all the feelings, perceptions and activities in *prāṇis* at the *prāṇic* level. Also referred to as *Suśumnā*, its operational site is visualized synchronously along and through the spinal-chord in the gross physical body, coordinating with all the nerve-systems. This and the further description that follows is based on the *Tāňtric* explanations of this *prāṇic* perspective primarily of *Śiva* and *Śakti* manifestation of *Saňvid* in *ānava* experients. *Suśumnā-nāđi* is visualized as *fiery-red, tāmsica* channel extending from *mūlādhara-ćakra* (located, with respect to the physical body, near the spinal-end, below genitals,) to *Sahasrāra*, (also known as *bramarandhra*) located near the apex of head, with respect to the physical body. *Suśumnā* (also) implies a system of *nāđis*, enclosed within this fiery-red channel. Immediately within *Suśumnā* runs a lustrous (*sūrya-rūpa*, the sun-like) *rajasika-nāđi Vajrini*, enclosing within it a pale (*ćandra-rūpa*, moon-like) *sātvika-nāđi, Ćitrani.* Inside of this *Ćitrani-nāđi* is the *Brahm-nāđi* with an opening (called *brahm-dwār*) into *mūlādhāra*, through which *Kuňđalinī-Śakti* (when aroused) rises up to various *ćakrās*. Immediately above *mūlādhāra-ćakra* (located in the region between the naval and the genitals, in the gross body) is *Swādhishthān-ćakra*, next to which are, *Manipūr-ćakra* and *Anāhat-ćakra*, located in *Suśumnā* in the spinal regions correspondingly of naval and heart respectively. *Vishuddha-ćakra* and *Āġā-ćakra,* the next two centers, are visualized as located in the spinal-regions corresponding to the base of the throat, and between the two eyebrows respectively. *Sahasrāra-ćakra*, (thousand-petal-lotus), the abode of *Shiva* in *prāṇa-mayakośa*, is the uppermost one, located correspondingly in the apex of the head. There is however another point of ascension, called *Bhairava-bila*[10], in the *Madhya-nāđi* that is above *Sahasrāra*, with no analogous point in the gross body, which is said to be the release point of *kuňđalinī-Śakti* from the bonds of physical body. The lowermost seat of *Śakti* in *suśumnā*, the *mūlādhāra* is the most subtle seat, and actually a system of six inter-related aspects or states of this composite seat. Within *mūlādhāra-ćakra* there is a triangular form called *Śiva-trikona*, the triadic-seat of subjective, objective and cognitive aspects of creation, in a vaguely discernable form. It is joined to *kusum* or *yoni*, (with similar triadic-aspects in a more distinct form,) also called *Śakti-trikona* or *Bhadra-kali*. Next to this, is the *samputa*, the composite of the two *trikonās*, the *kanda*. In the centre of this *kanda* is the *hṛt* or *hṛdaya*, the mid point of which is called *mukha-mudrā* or *hṛt-kārnika*. This entire set-up within *mūlādhāra-ćakra* is called *hṛt-padmā* or briefly *hṛdaya*, the *real heart*. It is this *hṛt-kārnika* also called *hṛdaya-bindu*, (also *amrit-bījamaya-hṛdaya*), which is the dwelling abode of *mahā-Śakti Kuňđalinī*. Like a sleeping serpent embracing this *hṛdaya-bindu*, She dwells there, in an objective existence, but is not an objective reality herself, nor conscious of any cognitive, subjective or objective aspect of existence at all, although this entire phenomenon of empirical existence is sustained and illuminated by it. She only relishes the bliss of the nectar of her glorious being, the *swātantrya.* She 'reveals everything by the light of consciousness, produces nothing and remains concealed' , (as said in *tan̆trāloka*).

प्रकाश्या सर्ववस्तुनाम विसर्गरहिता तु सा

(prakāśyā sarvavastunāma visargarahitā tu sā)

Tan̆trāloka 3:139

This *Kun̆đalinī Śakti,* the *Swātantrya-Śakti* of *Śiva,* is His *Visarga-Śakti,* the creativity *Śakti* of *aham-vimarśa.* In every empirical being *She* resides protecting his or her *hṛdaya-bindu,* like a serpent coiled up in three and a half coils around it. The first of the coiled-rounds represents *I-consciousness* attached to objectivity, the second one to the cognitive aspect, and the third one to the subjectivity aspect of existence. The last half-turn represents *Pramiti* aspect, the subjectivity (*pramātrata*) in which no trace of objectivity whatsoever exists. Intoxicated deeply by the bliss of her *swātantrya,* this *Śakti-Kun̆đalinī,* unmoved by anything holds the ultimate key to the *ānava*-matrix of existence. This is the key that can unfold the potency locked in this individual matrix of each living unit and allow a pathway for complete transformation of the empirical being. She does not interfere with the normal *ānava* functioning of individuals. She rather sustains them, allowing them the entire freedom for living their *karmas,* through their inbuilt *san̆skāras,* or else for any *purušārtha* guided by any awakening, due to any touch of choice-less awareness, ever. In all the *prāṇis*, *Idā* and *Piṅgalā* are two principal *nāḍis* going alongside of *Suṣumnā*, each curved like a bow. *Idā* runs on the left side while *Piṅgalā* on the right side of it. Representing the lunar and the solar aspects (objectivity and knowledge respectively) of manifestation, these *nāḍis* are always active in the empirical beings. The *prāṇic* currents of *apāna* and *prāṇa* flow through these channels, between the two *dwādaśāṅts* normally, keeping the *prāṇis* functioning at their *ānava* levels. There are three more *prāṇic* currents, *samāna*, *udāna* and *vyāna* going on in the *kośa* that take care of various bodily and other functions in the normal course, and in addition also of certain special aspects of being. As indicated already during the mention of *Khecari-Śakti*, coordination of the entire potency of perceptive, interactive, and reflective aspects of our *total-being* is controlled and maintained in *Suṣumnā*, through the agency of vital-energy *ojas* and *vīrya*. All this is the domain of *Mahāprāṇa*, whose ultimate guardian in each individual unit is *Kuṇḍalinī-Śakti*, which holds the promise and the key for him, for a complete transformation from his *ānava (paśu)* level to *Śāmbhava (pati)* status.

The simplest, and the most intimate approach for it is through the *prāṇa* itself. The *prāṇic* channels, managing the inhalation and exhalation, as *apāna* and *prāṇa* currants in *prāṇis*, without a noticeable pause, are the strongest chains that bind the *ānava* to the body, as much as, they can tow him across to the domain of indeterminate. We have seen earlier while talking about *mātṛkā*, that each of the *prāṇa* and *apāna* currents, between the two *dwādaśāňtas*, pauses for a meager, half a *tuṭi* each, for dissolution and re-emergence at *dwādaśāňtas*. It is here that the vital *prāṇa* merges into the un-manifest *Saňvid*, and is projected again from it, into *prāṇic* existence. This *Madhya* (the mid-point) between the *prāṇa* and the *apāna* aspect of *Saňvid*, is the *pure-being*-realm. An attentive awareness on this seemingly blank existence, cultivated into a state of absorption (*samāveśa)* with it, is the true meditation on the *swarūpa* of *Śiva*. It creates a contact with the *visarga-Śakti* (the creative energy) of Lord *Śiva*, or the state of *Śākta-Kuňđalinī* in one's own *Hṛdaya*. Sustained attentive awareness, the *samāveśa* on this *Madhya*, leads to *urdhva-mārga*, when *Ćaňdra* (incoming) and *Sūrya* (outgoing) currents of *prāṇa* stop following the *idā – piňgala* routes for breathing in and breathing out through *left-lambika* opening. At that point the normal breathing stops, the *right-lambika*[11] that is normally blocked, opens, and *prāṇa* and *apāna* currents get sucked into the *Suśumnā* pathway, spontaneously rushing towards *mūlādhāra-ćakra*, and penetrate the *mukha-mudra* of *Hṛdaya*. This awakens the *prāṇa-Kuňđalinī* which sets *mūlādhāra-ćakra* into vigorous rotation. Thereafter, this *Prāṇa-Kuňđalinī* rises spontaneously, *ćakra* after *ćakra*, penetrating each one of them and setting them into vigorous rotation one after the other, up to *brūmadhya* (point between eyebrows), the *Āġā-ćakra*. This simultaneous rotation is accompanied by a roaring or a gushing sound and a blissful sensation, like that of the peak of sexual-delight at the verge of ejaculation or orgasm, (although of much greater intensely). A total absorption into bliss, and a sudden and simultaneous recognition of one's real essence as pure consciousness, is experienced at such an occasion. Expansion of *ānava* existence into an ever-expanding universal-consciousness, a kind of an entire transformation happens when *Kuṅḍalinī-Śakti* penetrates the *Sahasrāra-ćakra*, (which however does not rotate). This is the most exalting experience ever that can happen to a human being, a *Samsārī*, who finds himself spread over the entire existence of the *form*, never thought or visualized. It is not an existence of difference and differentiation, but of endless, pulsating universal consciousness. This experience may not last long but its impact does. It is an experience of wonder (*vismaya*) and bliss, an intense intoxication with alertness, a touch of true sovereignty, the *Swātantrya*. How long this experience can be sustained depends upon how intense the *Samāveśa* is, how deeply the aspirant has been eager and yearning for his true self, and how much the renunciation of the cravings for the objective world has been accomplished[12].

Even the feeblest craving for anything exerts a strong back-pull. Any strong or a lingering craving, even dormant, can cause a disastrous damage in an aspirant's unfolding. It can manifest in various ways. After awakening and setting the *mūlādhāra-ćakra* rotating, *Kuṅḍalinī* may not rise any further at all, or, may not even set the *mūlādhāra-ćakra* rotating, but shoot straight upto *brūmadhya-ćakra* , penetrate it, set it into rotation, and then descend, penetrating the other *ćakrās* up to *Mūlādhāra* in the reverse order. Termed as *piśāćāveśa*[13], this kind of the *Kuňđalinī awakening* deprives the aspirant of any contact with his true self, and sets him into a more intense involvement with the *samsāric* delusion. Such fallen aspirants are required to work more vigorously again on their priorities, and sense of rationalization (first), and seek to get free from the clutches of the desires. One who is fond of, or craves for the picks of the petty, cannot have the *will* to grasp the entire kingdom of bliss. *Samāveśa* is the complete absorption into the intense desire for recognition (*Pratyabhiģāna*). Unflinching will to achieve it, and not a wavering interest, is the pre-requisite. A partial commitment or even any slightest craving for anything else, makes one half-baked and uncertain. And what can one achieve with such an attitude even in the worldly pursuits, not to speak of the most profound of all yearnings? The *aviveka* leads to *abodha*, and therefore the clutches of *malas* keep us ever deluded, entangled in the pursuits of *things* breeding difference, and oblivious of their essence and unity with the realm of consciousness. Neither a deep and intimate understanding of the essence, nor the actual dawning of the truth of recognition happens in that way.

मोहावरणात्सिद्धिः

(mohāvaraṇātasiddhiĥ)

...sūtra - (ss-III-6)

" The grip of and attachment to the coverings of malas, (the cause of the delusion, and the subsequent involvement in bhūtas) inhibits the happening of Śaktipāta (of recognition)."

Śiva-sūtras - (*III - 4,5*) suggest piercing through the maze of *Moha*, the deluded understanding and to de-condition ourselves from the impact of these *malas* (to be able to join our root, the pure awareness), even while keeping our foothold still in this *ānav* garb.

शरीरे संहार: कलानाम्

(Śarīre samhāraḥ kalānām)

...sūtra - (ss-III-4)

" Even while conforming to the existence in body, the dissolution of kalā, etc. (the mayiya-mala) must be resorted to ."

नाडीसंहार: - भूतजय - भूतकैवल्य - भूतपृथक्त्वानि

(nādisaṅhāraḥ–bhūtajaya–bhūtakaivalya–bhūtapṛthaktvāni)

...sūtra - (ss-III-5)

"Dissolution of prāṇa, freedom from the subservience to bhūtas (elements), withdrawal from the dependence on them, and thus isolation from bhūtas (must be resorted to)."

The two *sūtras* referred above suggest *samhāra* ! *Samhāra* is dissolution, ... dissolution into sameness with the core, the essence, the consciousness. Everything is to be traced aggressively to the root, the consciousness. *Grassan-yukti*, the devouring of the latter by the former, is to be resorted to, for it. The *panća-mahā-bhūtas*, on the tangible plane, can be traced from *pṛthvi* to *jal* to air to fire and finally to vacuity of space, which is their outer as well as inner sustainer. It gives them internally their structure-matrix and provides recognition to their physical entity. The space takes them also towards their domain of indeterminacy, the indefinable status of *khećari-Śakti*. From another consideration *bhūtas* can be traced to *tanmātrās*, from where they flow, get recognition, identification, and also the sameness with *ānanda* through the very channels of perception. Our body, a composite structure of *bhūtas*, the bearer of the *indriyās* of perception, as also of actions like speech, sex, etc. is the experimental laboratory for all that we do, long to do, or fail to do, for the relish and adventure, into the domain of all pleasures and cravings. We actually connect through the storehouse of *tanmātrās* into *prāṇa*, and there from, to the touch of bliss (muffled bliss though) of *Saňvid*. All the experiences of *Khećari-Śakti*, (even through its *vameśwari* aspects of delusion for a *samsāri*,) lead us to experiencing, through the luxury of the thrill of *vīrya*, a touch of the bliss of *Saňvit*, in whatever manner. Craving for all of the sensual, or other subjective aspects of experiencing, invariably leads us to the same core. A sustained introspective contemplation, with full awareness and deliberation, can transform our *Khećari-vaiśamya* into *Khećari-sāmya* if we persevere. If nothing, it can create a great motivation for exploring other possibilities of getting rid of the dross, and gaining access to the *Saṅvid,* our core. The shackles of the illusion that fasten us to the *kalā* aspect of our being, can loosen enough for finally snapping with a stronger jerk, by a steady watchfulness. A steady watch on ourselves, while performing even through the terms of subservience to *kalās,* will definitely soothe our *vrittīs,* from their tumultuous upheavals into tender ripples. It will definitely soften our wild cravings for *bhūtic* experience, and fill us with wonder, even when experiencing them as they are encountered. A watchful sip of a drink, or tea, would yield far greater fulfillment through its savor or soothing, than the gallons gulped unmindfully with a dissipated attention. One sexual experience with entire self given to it with fullness, intensely experiencing the associated sensual perceptions, and getting drowned in the ecstasy at its peak, can be a fulfillment of a lifetime. All the experiences with an attitude of grabbing or rushing through them, or just due to the force of habit or pastime, are no experiences. Any experience gone into, as a routine, or in stress, need not be undertaken at all. It is not worth it. Talking done, for imposing oneself, or exhibiting knowledge, or just for a casual habit, does not provide the satisfaction of communication. It creates no link with one's own self, or with others. The profundity of the subtle experience in speaking and listening, when watching all the time, the manifestation of *Śravana-śakti* from *Vaikhari* to *Madhyama* and beyond into the realms of indeterminate, from the manifest to un-manifest and back, is an experience unmatchable. Identifying with the objective world and its knowledge, may be right for the mundane affairs, but identifying with the subjective reality, gets us closer to our true selves. Taking the subjective pedestal and experiencing the objective world, unmoved, is a fulfilling experience. An attentive awareness as a subject, the experiencer, when developed into an attitude, can snap our dependence on the objective world, and subsequently, one can withdraw at will from it and stand aloof. As an *ānava* experient one *can* achieve it, if undertaken seriously even at the reflective level. The practice of attentive awareness on the merging of *prāṇa* and *apāna* at *dwādaśāňts*, as mentioned earlier, can help in minimizing the reliance and involvement on objective grossness. Observing natural rhythm of the *prāṇic*-flow of *apāna* and *prāṇa*, as a witness, with perseverance, results in calming of *vrittīs* in mind, and disentanglement from the worldly affairs. It prepares the aspirant, for a genuine *Samāveśa* on *Madhyā*, and thereby, the arousal of *Kuňḍalinī-Śakti* by affecting the dissolution of both *prāṇa* and *apāna* into *Suśumnā-nāḍi*. Keen attention on the point of merger of one, and the growth of other, of the *prāṇic* currents at *Dwādaśāňts*, when developed into a true *Samāveśa*, opens the doorway for a contact with *Saňvid*, the pure consciousness. It is the *Kāma-kalā* in operation. *Kāma-kalā*, is the unity of two aspects of the being. *Samāveśa* and *Saňvit* ! *Kāma* referred here is *Kāma-*

tattva the *will*, the *Iććhā-Śakti*, the unexpressed urge. *Kāma* is also desire, in the domain of its expression, or thought. *Kāma-tattva* is its essence. It is like natural sexual urge, not a deliberate desire for it. It rises, it is not designed! For that matter all sensual urges are like sexual urge. Spontaneous seeing, hearing, tasting, smelling and touching, involve conjunction. The contact of vision with *rūpa* or hearing with *śabda*, the union of the two *kāma-tattvās* is *kāma-kalā* in operation. Whatever generates an experience of sensation, is *kāma*. It is truly like sexual union. A *choice-less* attention on any of such unions is *kāma-kalā*. If the indulgence of thoughts into such unions is eliminated or kept at bay, and only an attentive awareness is maintained on such occasions, a true *Samāveśa* occurs, and the union becomes the union of the *Śiva* and *Śakti* aspect of the existence, a *mahā-melāpa*, resulting in the complete merger of *Śiva* and *Śakti*. This indistinguishable merger of the two brings about the bliss of *mahā-sāmarasya* of *Parābhattarika*. This *kāma-kalā* of remaining calmly and devotionally attentive to these unions of the *Śaktis* like *sparśa*, *rasa*, *rūpa*, *gandha*, and *śabda* with their complimentary *Śiva*-aspect of feeling, tasting, seeing, smelling and hearing, all the time, as they happen and when they happen, spontaneously, and making a *ćarya-krama* (grasping the succession in sense activities), will create a bridge for crossing over to the domain of pure *Saṅvit*, where *I-ness* and *this-ness* get merged and become one. It is not the *kāma-kalā* of sense perceptions only that lends a pathway into the absolute but also *sandhi*, the junction point of two thoughts, one dying and another just being born, the transition of one feeling into another, or the transition of one state to another, like from waking to sleep. The most important factor in all these, is the *samāveśa*, the *watchfulness* with alert attention, the true devotion to it. The most potent of *kāma-kalās* is *Samāveśa* on the urge of sex. Untainted attention on the sex-urge, allowed to reach the peak, without any indulgence into the act of it, when both the partners crave simultaneously, and the stirring of the *vīrya-Śakti* becomes intense in *Suṣumnā*, can result in an immediate cross-over. Even in absence of a partner, the urge, allowed to culminate to the peak, without a divergence, through a thought, or an action, can, through *Samāveśa* on that acute urge, lead one to get the cross-over. *Viśa-tattva* operates here. When the exaltation of the urge occurs, it, like poison, permeates instantaneously to all the reaches of the being, and, if it is not dissipated, it soaks the aspirant with immense bliss of *amṛta*, and instantaneously arouses *Kuṇḍalinī-Śakti*, for its culmination of union with *Brahmarandhra*. This is an expansion from *paśutva* (पशुत्व) into *patitva* (पतित्व). If however, dissipation through the actual sex-act happens, it results in the contraction, like death by poison, into *paśutva*. There is one more important aspect of looking at all these sense perceptions like sex-urge, etc. It is distinctly clear to all, that every sensual experience results in some kind of sensation, however feeble, depending upon the attention given by the experient. Experienced attentively with eagerness, and without dissipated mind, the sensation factor gets more manifest. All these associated sensations are the product of the bliss-factor (evidently from the act of union of the *Śiva* and *Śakti* factors, as mentioned earlier also, even though not attended on). Even the delayed awareness of this remnant, lingering bliss, can be rewarding. Dwelling on these feelings, whenever, and visualizing their fullness can result in the reduction of the *vrittīs* and *vikalpās*, and act as motivation for their attentive explorations. Withdrawal from the abyss of scattered thoughts, and tracing the source and the essence of objective experiences, and then enjoying their sameness with their essence, is an expansion into the essence and withdrawal from the gross. *This is Samhāra !* The process of *sańkoća* and *vikāsa* applied to the contemplation in the gross objective sense, or subtler *prāṇa* domain is of immense use in grasping the essence, and linking to the *Madhya.*

मध्यविकासाच्चिदानन्दलाभः

madhyavikāsā-ććidānandalābhaĥ)

... sūtra - (pbh – 17)

"Development of Madhya brings about (in the aspirant) the bliss of Ćit."

विकल्पक्षय-शक्तिसंकोचविकास-वाहच्छेदाद्यन्तकोटि-

निभालनादय इहोपाया:

(vikalpakšyaya – Śaktisańkoćvikāsa – vāhććhedādiantkoti – nibhālanādaya ihopāyaĥ)

... sūtra - (pbh – 18)

"Dissolution of vikalpās, saňkoća and vikāsa of Śakti, dissolution of vahas (prāṇa and apāna) by keen attention on (their) koti points (at dwādaśāňts) are the means (for the development of Madhya)."

Dissolution of the sense of differentiation into varied aspects of manifestation, and withdrawing back into the true assence, (like tortoise withdrawing its limbs) and holding on to, and dwelling fully in that perspective, refers to the dissolution of *vikalpas* as also *saňkoća* and *vikāsa* of *Śakti*. Merger of *prāṇa* and *apāna* is cutting of *vahas* by *samāvaśa* on the rising and falling of these points on *dwādaśāňts* as well as other points like *saňdhi* and *kama-kala* as referred to in detail previously are the means for achieving the *Madhya** state is also the communication of the *sūtra*. (* see note 17 also)

Ātma-vyāpti and Śiva-vyāpti

The ultimate reality is only a *ghanattva* of *ćidānanda*, and *prāpti* of that *ćidānanda* is possible only by sameness with that. This can be achieved by dissolving the *vrittīs* of all differences and alternatives, bred by the *māyic* illusions. Withdrawal from the entanglement in *bhūtas* and expansion into the reality of *Madhya*, achieved by alert witnessing (*Samāveśa*) with honest and intense devotion on *koti* points, can cause the dissolution of *prāṇic* currents. *Samāveśa* on *kāma-kalā* and *sandhi* points of the complimentary states of being, as *ćarya-krama* can be of great use. The reality of the absolute, the *Sañvid*, is ever there as *ananta*, *nitya*, and *vyāpaka* (boundless, ever-there, self-revealing) *prakāśa* and *vimarśa* . it is the *āvrana* (covering) of our own delusive knowledge and understanding that inhibits our linking with this, our real self. By the dissolution of our involvement in the illusions, created by the *māyic* veil, awakening into the recognition of our true self, the *prakāśa* of *Ćit* happens spontaneously. The light of true *vidyā* manifests with ease, and *Śiva* and *Śakti* aspects of the entire manifestation get revealed. The pure subjective and the objective aspects of this creation, and their non-difference and unity becomes a glaring reality. Even in their unity and non-difference, the two are distinctly obvious. The *bhedabhed*-aspect of *śuddha-vidyā tattva*, the '*I*' and the 'this' aspects, as subjective and the objective realities, intensely pronounced and yet, at the same time, intimately non-different from each other, project in an infinitely profound panorama of the transcendental and immanent reality.

मोहजयादनन्ताभोगात्सहजविद्याजय:

(mohajayād-anantābhogāt-sahajavidyājayaĥ)

...sūtra-(ss-III-7)

"On the conquest of the delusion, boundless expansion of and mastery over the true and spontaneous knowledge is achieved."

जाग्रद्द्वितीयकर:

(jāgrat-dvitīya karaĥ)

...sūtra-(ss-III-8)

"Awakening into the blaze of light (of the spontaneous knowledge), the reality of the two gets revealed."

On awakening into the true spontaneous knowledge, the *sahaja-vidyā*, or *Ćiti-Śakti* as *Khećari*, the *ćidagaganćari*, that actually lays down the whole network of manifestation in the empirical world, as *vāmeśwari*, and causes delusion to the *ānava* experients through *kalās*, etc., gets revealed in its true *swarūpa* of consciousness. She no more is then the deluding *vāmeśwari*, but *Śakti*, enacting the theatre of *sṛṣṭi*. She distinctly is revealed as the eternal dancer, projecting the varied aspects of *sṛṣṭi*. Even as the *ānava* subject, constituted of the *māyic* fabric, she now, clearly, is understood as playing a mock-show. Multiple aspects of the awe-inspiring wondrous theatre filled with amazement, are experienced. The domains of *Gocari* are revealed as the play-fields of the most subtle interplay of the various aspects of *Śakti* in *antaḥ-karṇas*. *Gocari-cakra* is seen as the deluding maze, perpetually weaving a world of differences, as *bheda-niścaya*, *bheda-abhimān*, and *bheda-vikalpanā* for the *ānava* existent. The *Sūkśama-śarīra* (subtle body) is found to be just an amazing stage, for the eternal dancer of *khecari* to perform on, while the gross body, along with all of its perceptive and interactive faculties, the *indriyās*, is seen involved, engrossed and spell-bound by the performance, dancing to the tunes of this performance, as a spectator. Life no more is a torment or a confinement in a body, but the bliss of freedom (*swātantrya*), with fullness of entire and unbounded sovereignty brought about by the recognition of one's true essence. This identification with pure subjectivity and fundamental oneness with *Śakti*, in all her aspects, lifts the aspirant to a state of perfect ease, freedom and spontaneous rapport with everything, in its essence. He finds himself one with *Śakti as* the eternal dancer, or the stage for it, as well as a spectator of all that is happening on the immanent plane with its essence in the transcendental domain. The empirical illusion of the objective world loosens its grip over him. The shackles of illusion and delusion break down, and *Sṛšṭi* gets a new hue, full of wonder, a perpetual *vismaya* !

नर्तक आत्मा

(nartaka ātmā)

...sūtra - (ss-III-9)

" Enlightened Ćitta is a dancer "

रङ्गोऽन्तरात्मा

(rango-antarātmā)

...sūtra - (ss-III-10)

" Puryašṭaka is the rańgmańch (stage) "

प्रेक्षकाणीन्द्रियाणि

(prekšakānīndriyāni)

...sūtra - (ss-III-11)

" Indriyās are the spectators "

धीवशात्सत्त्वसिद्धिः

(dhī vaśāt-sattvasiddhiḥ)

...sūtra - (ss-III-12)

" Recognition and realization of the essence is spontaneous "

सिद्धः स्वतन्त्रभावः

(siddhiḥ swatantrabhāvaḥ)

...sūtra - (ss-III-13)

"(so is the) spontaneous (absolute) freedom to accomplish (anything)"

यथा तत्र तथान्यत्र

(yathā tatra thatānyatra)

...sūtra - (ss-III-14)

"As well there, as anywhere else"

Such awareness of the non-difference with the transcendental as well as the immanent existence results in the absolute sameness with *Śakti* in action, the *Śakti-chakra.* The mirage of *sṛšṭi,* the way known through sense experience previously, disappears, and a sovereign authority in all domains comes easy. *Ćitta* finds a new meaning in its sameness with consciousness, and becomes a part of the fundamental seed of consciousness, the core of awareness, the absolute *Hṛdaya*, the *Saṅvid*, from which everything sprouts and into which it again merges, remaining ever in it, as declared in the following *Sūtras*.

बललाभे विश्वमात्मसात्करोति

(balalābhe viśwamātm-sātkaroti)

...sūtra - (pbh -15)

"Having got the hold of the power of essence, he brings the same-ness of the universe with his consciousness."

शक्तिचक्रसंधाने विश्वसंहार:

(Śakticakrasaṅdhāne viśwasaṅhāraḥ)

...sūtra - (ss - I - 6)

"Acute awareness of the Śakti-cakra results in bringing sameness (absorption) of Sṛšṭi with that"

बीजावधानम्

(bījāvadhānam)

...sūtra - (ss-III-15)

"Awareness being the Seed (the source of all)"

An experient, whose awareness gets established unwaveringly like that, exists in a state of *ātma-vyāpti,* a state in which he finds himself in everything. His essence, his true being is nothing other than consciousness, a pulsating awareness, that he finds throbbing in everything. He finds all empirical units of existence, melting into the throbbing consciousness, which is no different from his own being. He sees himself pulsating in everything,

and everything dissolving into him as an effulgent throb of consciousness. He is only poised in ease and bliss, plunged into, and drenched by consciousness, the core and essence, the ultimate *hṛdaya* of all, and everything. Awareness remains the dominant aspect of his entire existence, during any direct experiencing, or any contemplating activity. He dominates as an experient of all that, with simultaneous awareness of everything.

आसनस्थः सुखं हृदे निमज्जति

(āsanasthaḥ sukham hṛde nimajjati)

...*sūtra* - (*ss-III-16)*

"Poised in ease, (he) is steeped in the core (the consciousness)."

The more one gets established into this state of awareness the more it gets refined, and overwhelming, resulting in the breakdown of the false structures of concepts and illusions held fast about one's being. The touch of awareness devours the objective illusions of the *māyic* fabrications which then no more hold the experient a victim to the worldly concepts. Dismantling of these structures happens in proportion to the growth of awareness of the true being.

स्वमात्रानिर्माणमापादयति

(swamātrānirmānam-āpādayati)

...sūtra - (ss-III-17)

"*Dismantling of the māyic structures happens in proportion to the (unfolding) of awareness.*"

Awareness of the subjective reality, its repeated reinforcement, and its complete capture, changes the entire perspective of existence. In fact, even as the empirical entities, we do have a subjective aspect of our being with us. Whatever we do or think, we know about it, we notice it like passive witnesses, but the aspect of doing or thinking remains dominant. In our so-called fully wakeful state, we are dominated by the objective aspect of things directly, or our awareness is of *only objectivity* of *bhūtas* and its thoughts. In a contemplative posture in our waking state, we are aware, only of the aspects *related* to the objective world of existence, their memory or knowledge, and not directly of the objects. These are only reflective aspects. Precisely the same thing applies to our dreaming state in sleep. Therefore whether dreaming or day-dreaming, the experience of dreams is related with, or handling of, the knowledge related to the *things*, the mundane world, and as such, is dominated not by the experiencing aspect, but, only the knowledge aspect (whatever), of the things. The subjective aspect remains vague all through. In total absent-mindedness, unconsciousness or dream-less deep-sleep, the subject isn't aware of being in that state at that instant, but realizes having been in that state after his withdrawal from that state. Thus the awareness of non-awareness, or of a dreaming experience is not simultaneous but realized later after one comes out of it. Explicitly, the three states of being of an experient, the waking, the dreaming and the deep-sleep, concern the three aspects of his existence, namely, objective, knowledge, and subjective. Even though, the subject is the one that experiences, and without whom none of the experiences of any state would register, he exists in an extremely dormant manner. In waking *state* objects dominate, in thinking, contemplating or dreaming, thoughts dominate, and in deep-sleep nothing dominates except a lingering inconspicuous experiencer that is oblivious of its existence in that state. It is a state of *not* experiencing, recognizing, or being aware of anything. An envelope of ignorance veils his very being, like *Māyā* veiling the transcendental consciousness in its domain. Withdrawal of consciousness from the objective world and its knowledge, puts the empirical subjective aspect into abeyance. This state of being is termed as *sauśupti*, the deep-sleep. The fact is, that the experiencer, in the state of existence as *ćitta*, the

Māyā-pramātā, identifies basically with the objectivity and any knowledge aspects related to the objective world. Consciousness is remote to him. The pure subjectivity, the consciousness aspect, is clouded by the dominating concern it has with the objective existence. When, however, the grip of consciousness strengthens by the willful surrender of all that is extraneous, by *ćitta* with its bowl of being upright and empty, it is filled to the pores by the effulgence of the ever-present consciousness, which bestows it with the ease and the bliss instantaneously. This overtaking of the experient by consciousness is overwhelming. It overflows and percolates into everything, the objective, the comprehensive, and the subjective existence. Although seemingly a fourth factor, it drenches with itself, all the other three aspects of the empirical subjective existence, the knowledge and the objective existents, along with their three corresponding manifest states of wakefulness, dream and deep-sleep. It remains an ever-present, towering and blissful witness of all the experiences in all the states as the actual true self, the experient. It remains there, perpetually witnessing the waking, the thoughts, the dreams, and the deep-sleep of the *ćitta-pramātā*. This fourth-factor, *turya* (तुर्य means fourth), brings rapturous bliss of consciousness, a kind of subtle expansion to this empirical being.

Śiva-sūtras - (*I* - 8, 9,10 & 7) put it thus:

ज्ञानं जाग्रत्

(Ġānam jāgrat)

...sūtra - (ss – I - 8)

"Direct knowledge (of objective world) is wakefulness"

स्वप्नो विकल्पा:

(swapno vikalpaĥ)

...sūtra - (ss – I – 9)

"Ideation (of knowledge) is dreaming"

अविवेको मायासौषुप्तम्

(aviveko māyā-sauśuptam)

...sūtra - (ss – I - 10)

"Non-discernment is envelopment in deep-sleep"

जाग्रत्स्वप्नसुषुप्तभेदे तुर्याभोगसंभव:

(jāgrata-swapna-suśuptabhede turyābhogasambhavaĥ)

...sūtra - (ss – I - 7)

"In all the thee different states, the wakefulness, the dream and the deep-sleep, there abides (Stringing them all together) the rapturous experiencing of the fourth (turya)".

The three states of the normal empirical existence are no doubt different from each other. In waking state all the three dimensions *deha*, *mana* and *prāṇa* (body, mind and *Prāṇa*) are active. *Deha* implies *indriyās*, the senses, the (*bāhya-pradhāna*) extroverted faculties; *mana* implies (*aṅtar-pradhāna*) the internal apparatus of reflective, contemplative, and *vāsnā*-factors of the being; and the *prāṇa* stands for the involuntary and coordinating faculties of the being. In dreaming, the *deha* aspect remains in abeyance, while *mana* and *prāṇa* remain active, and in deep-sleep, *mana* also remains in abeyance, and only *prāṇa* functions. The three states remain ever distinct in their performance, and the borders of each other are not transcended. When *turya* unfolds, it engulfs the entire domains of all the three states into itself. Each state functions as usual for the normal performance of its allotted functions, but now in full-blaze knowledge and vigilance of *turya* consciousness, and this lends everything a meaning, the bliss of *being*. The subject, the experiencer as consciousness, devours the entire experience of the contact with the object and its associated knowledge into sameness with himself, with no tint of differentiation, and enjoys the highest bliss and sovereignty in the experience. His perceptions are thus divine and his *indriyās* are no more the gatherers of the *vrittīs* of differences in objectivity but *Śaktis*, the *vīras(वीर)*, the enjoyers of the bliss of expansion and unity in everything. He is no more a slave to the temptations of sensual but *vīreśa*, the master of senses (now *vīras*), who relishes the rapturous experiences of distinct and pure *I* -consciousness, in all the three states of waking, dream and deep-sleep.[14]

त्रितयभोक्ता वीरेश:

(tritayabhokta vīreśaĥ)

...sūtra - (ss – I - 11)

"The enjoyer of the rapture of I-consciousness, in all the three states, is the master of the Śaktis of perceptions"

The experient of pure subjectivity, the unfaltering bliss of pure consciousness realizes *it* as his basic *tattva*, the *satattva* of existence that remains, while all else, all the objects, the *bhūtas*, their knowledge and all their *vikalpās* and *vrittīs*, the three states, (waking, dreams and deep-sleep), passing away and merging into the consciousness. This understanding of the immortality of consciousness rids him of the allurements of the world and the associated fears of their deprivation and death. He is no more desirous or aggrieved of having a *Samsāric* existence. He neither craves for it nor despises it. It is all reduced to a non-entity for him. His Existence is of an entirely different plane, a plane of bliss and awareness, the *Ćidānand-ghana.* If he continues living in his *Samsāric* attire, it is only for the observance of a pious act of paying off the debt of *karma*, that his body and *aňtaĥ-karanas* owe.

विद्याऽविनाशे जन्मविनाशः

(Vidyā-avināshe janmavināśaḥ)

...sūtra - (ss – III - 18)

"The distinct understanding of the non-perishable makes the birth into the world irrelevant (and un-necessary)."

शरीरवृत्तिर्व्रतम्

(śarīravṛttir-vrattam)

...sūtra - (ss – III - 26)

"Continuing to remain in body is only an observance of a pious act."

For him living in the world is a state of *swātantrya*, the absolute authority. Although functioning through body and its *indriyās*, he watches as non-interfering, detached awareness, the life and activity of the *ānava* existence, with relish, wonder and compassion. Having no other identification with it he basks in his real self, the consciousness, without any other indulgence whatsoever !

मग्नः स्वचित्ते नप्रविशेत्

(magnaḥ svaćitte napraviśet)

...sūtra - (ss - III - 21)

"Absorbed into (the essence of) one's ćitta, and not entering into other aspects."

कवर्गादिश्षु माहेश्वर्याद्याः पशुमातरः

(kavargādishu māheśvaryādyāĥ paśumātraĥ)

...sūtra - (*ss* - *III* - *19)*

"Kavarga and Maheśvarya etc.(representing bhūtas and tanmātrās etc. respectively in Māt̤rkā) are the generators of the state of paśu."

The fact is that the gross-body (comprising *panća-mahābhūtas*), and the subtle body, (the bearer of *tanmātrās*) are both, the domains of *kavarga* and *ćavarga* (*maheśwari)* aspects of *Māt̤rkā*. The other *vergas* of *Māt̤rkā* imply *indriyās, mana, bhuddhi, ahaṅkāra, prāṇa, prakr̥ti and puruša* aspects of the empirical being. Clearly an indulgence into any of these empirical aspects is bound to pull the aspirant back into the *paśu* state, at the cost of any further expansion of pure awareness. Absorption into *turya* consciousness, without any attention on the empirical aspects of our being, (which take care of themselves anyway!), provides an ecstatic state of being to the aspirant. His breathing is hardly discernible, with *prāṇa* and *apāna* flowing into *sušumnā*. However, from time to time, *prāṇa* and *apāna* surface, (as in the normal mode), with an extremely subtle and soft flow of breathing for a while. This state of flow of *prāṇa*, called *prāṇa-samāćāra*, does not hamper the aspirant's association with his *I*-consciousness and the related ecstasy. His *ātma-vyāpti* (*sameness* with everything), persists through his waking, deep-sleep as well as dream states. However, depending upon the earnestness and devotion for the attainment of perpetual *I-consciousness*, and the level of renunciation of the worldly cravings, the intensity of *turya* varies. It generally remains more profound during the beginning and the ending of each different state (waking, etc.), but feeble or very feeble in between, when the impact of the empirical aspect recoils. One has not to resist that come-back or get engaged with it in any way. One only needs to intensify the awareness of the *I*-consciousness, the *turya* by paying attention to it. This attention to the *turya*-aspect causes it to re-emerge more vigorously, the mere touch of which vaporizes the sense of objectivity.

प्राणसमाचारे समदर्शनम्

(prāṇa-samāćāre samadarśanam)

...sūtra - (ss - III - 22)

"Even during prāṇa-samāćār (punctuating the state of absorption in I-consciousness), the awareness (of sameness with everything), persists.

मध्येऽवरप्रसवः

(madhye-avaraprasavaĥ)

...sūtra - (ss - III - 23)

"During the mid-stages (of waking, etc.*), the inferior (paśu) states are reborn."*

मात्रास्वप्रत्ययसंधाने नष्टस्य पुनरुत्थानम्

(mātrā-svapratyaya-sańdhāne-naśtasya-punarutthānam)

...sūtra - (ss - III – 24)

"Intensely holding on to the understanding that the essence (actually of everything objective,) is the I-consciousness, the dwindling Turya re-emerges."

A truly advanced aspirant with real *vairāġa*, (with no trace whatsoever of the craving or attachment for the objective), a strong *will*, and a deep-rooted yearning for the absolute sameness with pure *I-consciousness*, is a real *Śāmbhava* aspirant. For him, *turya* is the only state he dwells in. Ever steady in this state of *ātma-vyāpti*, he finds *everything* as the projection of his real self, with himself as the *consciousness* throbbing in everything, during all the physical states of his being. He ascends to a state of *rūpātīta*, where everything, including his subjective existence, is experienced in an entirely different way, beyond the mundane definitions of *rūpa* and *guṇa*, (form and quality) and drenched only in a divine rapture. Subsequently he attains to a state of uninterrupted divinity where discrimination between the transcendental and immanent dissolves and *everything* shines as *Śiva*. This is the state of true *Śiva-vyāpti.*

But, for those whose experience of *Turya* is intermittent, there is need to intensify their urge and get rid of the remnant traces of their cravings for objectivity. They need to hold on to the rapturous experience of *Turya* whenever it occurs, and plunge into it whole-heartedly to enjoy the nectar of its bliss. Nothing else needs be done, but to surrender oneself entirely to it, be it the state of waking or dreaming, or as and when it occurs. Its nectar should percolate more and more into the depths of all states like oil seeping into things it contaminates. Achieving it by *surrendering* completely to it, and holding on to it, with *unyielding-will* (called *hathapāka*), can make it persist in the waking and dreaming states and then finally drenching the deep-sleep state for complete unfolding.

त्रिषु चतुर्थं तैलवदासेच्यम्

(trishu ćaturthaň tailavat-āsechyam)

...sūtra - (ss - III - 20)

"Like oil, the fourth (Turya consciousness) should be poured into (all) the three (states of waking, dreaming, and deep-sleep)."

After experiencing a touch of *turya*, the aspirant does not remain an *āṇava* experient. All the efforts, gone through by him thus far, were aimed only at removing the dross, the cause of his identification with the objectivity. The truth is that awareness is not a domain of effort. It is not achieved by any means or disciplines; it is ever there as our true essence, and the only thing that hampers our vision of it is our involvement in diversions. Once these clouding factors get obliterated the awareness shines like the sun out of clouds. If light does not reach us, it is not that the sun has stopped shining, but, that we have enclosed ourselves in various veils. If the sun were not shining, we could never commission it to shine, or make its light grow. The efforts for removing the factors veiling pure consciousness in an *āṇava* aspirant are to continue till even the last trace is removed; and in that effort the early dawn of *turya*, the light shining through the punctures in the veils, can be a great motivation for further efforts with greater intensity. The strong motivation, because of the actual feel, knowledge and the reality of experiencing, then becomes a strong driving force. This provides a *Śākta*-approach to the quest, which is very useful in efforts to rid oneself of the extraneous inclinations and afflictions as also for creating a greater yearning. The truth is that the ultimate realization comes only through the *Śāmbhava* approach, through a strong will. A plunge for the total penetration finally is to be resorted to, and this is possible only by a strong *will*.

The journey from *turya* to *turyatīta*, that is, from *Ātma-vyāpti* to *Śiva-vyāpti*, is to be made through *will* alone. *Iććhā-Śakti*, the strong, unyielding and perseverant *will* is the *only key* that opens the door to the absolute. And this journey, from *turya* to *turyatīta*, is extremely rewarding. It is moment to moment an experience of *vismaya* (wonder, the utter amazement), comparable to nothing, nor expressible in any other way. It is the experience far more amazing than the rise of *kuňđalini*, through various *ćakrās* up to *Āġa-ćakrā* (*Brūmadhya*), or a live contact with the realms of *tanmātrās*. It is *vismaya* at its highest. Each new unfolding is wondrous. The *will* gets identified with the true *swātantrya-Śakti* of *Śiva*, the *Umā*, the virgin *ever (!)*, the *kumāri*, ever an explorer and never explored, ever captivating and never captured (!), evoking ever the sense of mystery and amazement. Beholding the perpetual projection of untouched, untainted virgin-wonder, invoking utter bewilderment with no bounds, getting devoured by it, and re-emerging, yet again for yet more of it, cannot be expressed but by silence. It is the state that of *Śiva*, experienced in the garb of a body, the perfect state of *Ćidānanda*, as *Jagadānanda!*

विस्मयो योगभूमिका:

(vismayo yogabhūmikāĥ)

...sūtra - (*ss - I – 12)*

"Introduction to the (total) communion with I-consciousness is an experience of absolute amazement."

इच्छा शक्तिरुमा कुमारी

(Iććhā Śaktir-umā kumāri)

...sūtra - (ss - I - 13)

"The will-power (of the Śāmbhava experient) is like Śiva's virgin-swātantrya-Śakti, the Umā."

शिवतुल्यो जायते

(Śiva-tulyo jāyate)

...sūtra - (ss - III - 25)

"(Such transformed) experient is like Śiva, born."

Ascending practically to the state of *Śiva* gives the experient, the entire sovereignty over everything, the ultimate *swātantrya* of *Iććhā-Śakti* and unfaltering direct understanding of all phenomena in their true essence. He identifies with the core, the essence of all that is, (and can ever be). He becomes an unstinting awareness-pue, himself. Whatever aspects of objectivity he experiences or comprehends, existent or non-existent, all, are his own body, beyond which there is nothing, not even the void. He is the essence of all embodied objectivity, the void and knowledge of it all, shining in pure subjectivity.

वितर्क आत्मज्ञानम्

(vitarka ātmaǵānam)

...sūtra - (ss - I - 17)

"He is embodiment of unfaltering knowledge of the essence."

लोकानन्दः समाधिसुखम्

(lokānandaĥ samādhisukham)

...sūtra - (ss - I - 18)

"Awareness of the ānanda of sameness of both, (the observer and the observed,) brings a wondrous delight of unity."

For him nothing is different or separate from his self, be it immanent or transcendental. It is all *Saňvid*, his intimate reality, because he, as *pārasa* (पारस) of *Saňvid*, turns everything into *Saňvit* by his touch.

दृश्यं शरीरम्

(dṛśyam śarīram)
...sūtra - (ss - I - 14)

"Everything that he sees constitutes his body"

हृदये चित्तसंघट्टाद्दृश्यस्वापदर्शनम्

(hṛdaye-ćittasamghattād-dṛśya-svāpadarśanam)
...sūtra - (ss - I - 15)

"(Because) with the immersion of ćitta into its core, the consciousness, everything that is experienced, including the void, is seen as nothing else but consciousness."

शुद्धतत्त्वसंधानाद्वाऽपशुशक्तिः

(śuddha-tattva-sañdhānādvā-apaśuśaktiḥ)
...sūtra - (ss - I - 16)

"The pure awareness can be only of the pure existence, the Śiva, the paśu-pati, or (in other words) apaśu-Śakti, and not of the paśu, the empirical existent."

Awakening into the realm of pure awareness cannot be possible unless the grip of the binding slumber of objectivity and all its associated knowledge is cast away. No trace of *ānava*, *māyiya* and *karma-mala*, the boundary conditions that define the matrix of the empirical existence must at all *remain* before this ultimate transformation occurs. As a result no experience happens through the defined versions of the reality. Everything exists in its essence and not in any of the assumed postures. The *paśu* state of experiencing yields itself to the actuality of the experiencing of transcendental reality. Every conditioned understanding is then remembered like a hazy dream.

विद्यासंहारे तदुत्थस्वप्नदर्शनम्

(vidyāsamhāre tadutth-svapnadarśanam)

...sūtra - (ss - II - 10)

"*Ascendance into the state of pure awareness means dissolution of the conditioned knowledge, the memory of which is only like a dream.*"

All the constructs of words, thoughts, prejudices, philosophies and their superstructures become redundant and irrelevant. They are surrendered, along with whatever sense of recognition or attachment existed for them, like husk or shell, and offered as oblation to the vitalizing fire of consciousness, for no return or re-use, while the essence of understanding from them, the truth of *I-consciousness*, is consumed as food which further vitalizes the fire of awareness. For a realized soul wedded to absolute *Sav̆vid*, the connotations of everything are different, as the following *Śiva-suras* declare :

शरीरं हविः

(śarīram haviḥ)

...sūtra - (ss - II - 8)

"The body, (constructs of all kinds) is his oblation (to the fire of pure awareness)."

ज्ञानमन्नम्

(Ġānam-annam)

...sūtra - (ss - II - 9)

"Ġāna (the knowledge of self, the essence 'aham',) is his food for assimilation."

कथा जपः

(kathā japaḥ)

...sūtra - (ss -III- 27)

" All his conversation is like utterance of sacred mav̆tras."

दानमात्मज्ञानम्

(dānamātmaġānam)

...sūtra - (ss -III- 28)

"He shares and gifts away the knowledge of true-self."

For one in communion with the ultimate reality of *Saňvid* everything is blazing reality of absolute and pure consciousness. He consumes it and projects it. His food or his gifts, his words and their potency, all are just this. Everything else that is illusive, delusive, confining or confined, is the refuse, the husk of non-entity. Rituals are therefore meaningless for him as are the hollow words without essence. *Kathā*, *japā*, and *dāna*, in the traditional connotations, do not hold for him. He is like *Śiva*, the master of *Śakti-ćakra*, and therefore the provider of the highest wisdom, because the whole creation is after all the unfolding of this *Śakti-ćakra.*

योऽविपस्थो ज्ञाहेतुश्च

(yo-avipastho ġāhetuśća)

...sūtra - (ss -III- 29)

"The one who is the master of Śakti-ćakra (protector of varied manifestations) surely is the provider of highest wisdom"

स्वशक्तिप्रचयोऽस्य विश्वम्

(svaśakti-praćayo-asya viśvam)

...sūtra - (ss -III- 30)

"The whole universe is the unfolding of his Śakti."

स्थितिलयौ

(sthiti-layau)

...sūtra - (ss -III- 31)

"(As is its) maintenance and dissolution. "

The absolute *ćidānanda*, the *Parama-Śiva*, as mentioned earlier and reiterated again and again, is *Prakāśa-vimarśa* composite. *Prakāśa*, the *being*, and *vimarśa*, the awareness entire. The *being* implies its 'presence' in everything, the objective as well as the transcendental domain. Objective presence is tangible existence of anything conceivable, this or that, whatever, identified through its attributes of being 'that'. It continues to be 'that', and only 'that', or else it loses its identity. It cannot be anything else. No doubt, all material things of form, animate or inanimate, are essentially formed out of the basic building blocks, the elementary particle material (as do the scientific studies reveal), with the difference only in their mutually related orientations as different patterns, which dictate the matrix of their being the specific identifiable things. For every unit, this pattern, this matrix of identity, and the intrinsic knowledge of it therein, is unique, and it is this that dictates its freedom, or limitations (all specified), to be 'that', and perform like 'that'. This, in a very gross way, represents its 'being' and 'awareness' of the potency of its being, its *prakāśa* and *vimarśa* attributes, in the empirical existence. It cannot be anything else, and that *is* the fundamental truth of the objective existence. The same is true of the building blocks, the so called elementary particles also, which represent the objective existence at infinitesimal micro-level. Their constitution (still an enigma in scientific understanding), and freedom of performance (whatever), is again dictated by some other basic matrices of intrinsic knowledge, their own *prakāśa* and *vimarśa.* Piercing deeper into the ultimate edge, the basic plasma, the building essence of all the manifested existence and beyond, we land into an absolutely indeterminate domain of existence we cannot conceive of or comprehend. At this fundamental point, *śaiva* (*Trika*) understanding, on the basis of *āgma* and *anubhav*, brings in the irreducible and un-refutable fundamental, *Śiva* and *Śakti* factor, the 'absolute' *prakāśa* and *vimarśa*, both distinct but dual aspects of a singular irreducible reality *Anuttra.* *Anuttra* , considered 'the *only* fundamental presence' (*mahā-sattā*), the absolute existence, the 'whole and unchanging' (*pūrna*), 'ever' (*nitya*), and 'self evident' (*vyāpaka*) *Śiva*, with the complete awareness (*vimarśa*) of *it* all. *Vimarśa*, the complete awareness, is not only the exact knowledge (*ġāna*) but potency of *will* (*Iććhā-Śakti*) and *action* (*Kriyā-Śakti*), entirely sovereign and free, a *pūrna-Swātantrya-Śakti.* This *Swātantrya* is the inherent potency (*Śakti*) of *Śiva*, and that is why, non-different and inseparable from it, although distinct by virtue of its expression. This *Śakti* is *Śakti-ćakra.* It ends where it begins, and it ends and begins, where it *is* ! It is inseparable from *Śiva* which is the eternal being, the ultimate being, the *being of all and everything*, and therefore *any-being* (!), because there is no other, and nothing else. This ultimate reality of inseparable *being and its potent awareness*, the absolute *I-consciousness*, is the *'soul'*, and the *'sole'* of *everything*, the grossest of the gross, and the subtlest of the subtle. The sense *'I '* , the *being*, cannot exist without its consciousness of being, and without the 'being', the consciousness can not belong. The two exist together, representing two aspects of one reality. Here it is to be reiterated clearly that *Śiva*, the being aspect, is ever *parā* (transcendental), without any attributes whatever, while *Śakti*, the consciousness is *parāparā*, both transcendental-cum-immanent. There is a third aspect of the same existence (according to *Trika*), the empirical (*ānava*) *aspect*, the *anu*, which is always *aparā* (the immanent), with all various attributes. In fact it is nothing without attributes. *Shakti*, the consciousness, the *parāparā* phase of being, therefore acts as a bridge between *anu* and *Śiva*, the *aparā* and *parā* phase of the reality. In conscious empirical beings, *anu*, the two (*being* and consciousness) are distinctly manifest, while in the inert things, the awareness aspect is dormant and intrinsic, but not non-existent. Stone or water behaves as stone or water because of an intrinsic coded *understanding* of being what each is. They are non-thinking, non-reflective but deep-inside; something inexplicit, maintains and regulates their *being*. In *ānava* experients, manifestation of their being is expressible through many aspects like *indriyās*, *mind*, *budhi*, an *ānava-entity*, etc., but in spite of their specific entities these aspects do not find expression of their being unless linked with consciousness. Unconsciousness, or temporary withdrawal of consciousness from these aspects (due to any diversion), makes their being like non-existent. Thus, whether at transcendental state or at immanent state, the being and consciousness compliment each other. At the level of *Anuttra*, however, the two, the *being* and the *awareness*, the *Ćit* and the *Ćiti* are in an indistinguishable unity. The first manifestation of *Śakti* is the *will*, the *Iććhā-Śakti*, that initiates the *ćakra of Śakti. Iććhā-Śakti* or *will* is the first s*panda* that brings in the subjective aspect of the being *I*, and its experiencing, the '*this*'. The dissolution of all experiencing is the folding back of '*this*', the *Śakti-ćakra*, again into the subject, along with even the subjectivity aspect of being, as its experient or witness. It all dissolves into the *bindu* of the indeterminate *sattatva* of *anuttra*, the absolute *Ćidānand-ghana*, the pure-consciousness-existence, which is the absolute potency, pregnant ever with *everything* that can ever manifest. The *spanda* of *Iććhā* sets the wheel of manifestation moving, and the projection of all kinds of existences endlessly continues.

" लेलिहाना सदा देवी सदा पूर्णाचभास्ते "

(lelihānā sadā devi, sadā pūrnā ća bhāste)

"The godess (the swātantriya-Śakti), always projecting manifestation out of herself, like frequent darting of the tongue, and seeming always full and complete."

Nothing is projected *out* as much as nothing is absorbed *in*. It is all ever there, in that indeterminate *existence* as an undifferentiated reality. The *spanda* of *Iććhā* *'unfolds'* the desired objective aspect of the reality, the experience of which veils the transcendental reality in that phase. The projection (*udaya*) of immanent reality means re-absorption (*parlaya*) of the transcendental reality. Whatever *Śiva* or *Śiva-pramātā* wills to experience, whether the singular, unbounded and undifferentiated reality, or the infinitely various, structured immanent reality of endless attributes, it comes to fore. From the vintage point of *Śiva-pramātā* or *Śiva* both are a reality with unbounded wonder (*vismaya*) and bliss. It is like experiencing by *Him, His body or His Hṛdaya.* It is like *His*, opening *His* eyelids, or closing them, directing *His* awareness, outward or inward. It is all the same. But for an *ānava* experient it is different. For him *Sṛšṭi* is a panorama of objective existence structured in difference, and breeding difference, while the transcendental is unknown and unreachable by any means. Unflinching penetration within, with no trace of craving for the outer objective existence, over the connecting bridge of consciousness, is the *only* means available. *Spanda* is the core of *Śiva*, (in fact *all*, as *all is Śiva*). It is the throb of *being*. It is both, the transcendental and immanent in one, the *udaya* or *pralaya* (*unmeša* or *nimeša*) of either. Succession does not hold here because it is all beyond time. It is absolute simultaneity. Both *unmeša* (unfolding) and *nimeša* (enfolding) are actually simultaneous twin aspects of it.

" युगपदेवोन्मेषनिमेषोभयरूपम "

(*yugapadevonmeša-nimeša-obhaya-rūpama*).

Unmeša (unfolding) of transcendental consciousness is actually the enfolding (*nimeša*) of the immanent consciousness, as the *udaya* of *immanent* is the *pralaya* of *transcendental* consciousness. This *saphuran* (throbbing), this *spanda* is the *Śakti-ćakra* ever in action, projecting and withdrawing, the transcendental as well as immanent aspects of its being, out of *Itself* and into *Itself.* It is the eternal *visarga,* as *parā-visarga, ānand* ever (!), the *parāparā-visarga* projecting itself as *sṛšṭi* and withdrawing itself into *Saṅvit* again, and the *aparā-visarga* maintaining the rhythm of objectivity in its creation and dissolution aspects of the varied forms of difference. It is all that. It is the beauty, the wonder, and the bliss pulsating ever. It is the *ćakra* of *Śakti* as *ma-ha-a* or *a-ha-m* , the *Śakti 'ha'* projecting from *anuttra 'a'* to *purušа 'ma'* and withdrawing from *'ma'* to *'a'* . It is *saṅkoća* (contraction) and *vikāsa* (expansion) of *Śakti* in enfolding of *sṛšṭi* into *Saṅvit,* and unfolding of *saṅvid* into *sṛšṭi,* going on eternally, the bliss (*ānanda*) of *Parā-saṅvid,* the core of *Anuttra.*

Abhinavgupta in *parātrīśikā-vivaraṇa* (PTV-99/10-13) explains figuratively what *spanda* is:

रासभी वडवा वापि स्वं जगज्जन्मधाम यत् समकालं
विकास्यैवसंकोच्य हृदि हृष्यति तथोभयमहानन्दसौषुम्णहृदयान्तरे
स्पन्दमानमुपासीत हृदयं सृष्टिलक्षणम् ॥

"As a she-ass and/or a mare, on the occasion of coitus, experiences great delight in her heart by simultaneous expansion and contraction of her female organ (the birthplace of her world); in the same way, in the interior of hṛdaya-padma (heart-lotus in kanda) of Sušumna, does the core of heart (hṛdaya-karnika), abounding in supreme ānanda, throb, (perpetually), the simultaneous expansion and contraction, characterizing Sṛšṫi. This spanda must be meditated upon!"

This perpetual *Spanda* characterizing *sṛšṫi* is represented by *sṛšṫi –bīja mantra* सौः , (स + औ + अः). स represents the *sāra*, the essence of *sṛšṫi*, the *sṛšṫi-sattaa.* स also is *Iśwara*, the *Ġāna* aspect of the *sṛšṫi*, conceived, when as *Sadāśiva*, *Anuttra's* creative *will*, the urge for immanent expression of the divine gets expression. औ is the phoneme, the *kalā* representing the complete unfolding of *swarūpa- sṛšṫi* as *Parā-vāk* within the transcendental domain of *Anuttra.* It is also the trident of *Iććhā*, *Ġāna*, and *Kriyā* aspects of *Anuttra*, the basic ingredients of all creation. सौ thus represents the complete matrix of creativity. अः is the *parāparā-visarga* , the symbol for perpetual *spanda* of creation and dissolution of *sṛšṭi* aspect of *Anuttra.* सौः therefore is the potency of the matrix of entire *sṛšṭi* representing its transcendental as well as the immanent references, the complete *bimba* and *pratibimba* of its being. Meditation on its depth and potency provides the complete panorama of its inception, culmination and dissolution aspects entirely, and shall subsequently on perseverance reveal the ultimate reality of *Śakti-ćakra.*

Tañtrika procedure of the worship of this *sṛšṭi–bīja* is very subtle and complex (that needs personal guidance and intervention of a truly realized *Guru*,) and therefore, is beyond the scope of any discussion here. A genuine aspirant may introspect, and meditate into the potency of this *sṛšṭi-bija* and get enlightenment or guidance appropriately with the unbounded *Anugraha* of *Śiva !* This *bīja* is declared to be the most potent of all the *bījas* as it is the only one with the entire potency of *Anuttra* in it. For the experient of this *spanda*, the master of the *Śakti-ćakra* of *udaya*, *sthiti* and *pralaya* of *sṛšṭi*, the knower and the source of the unfaltering, perpetual and highest wisdom; *all dualities* stand at bay because the experient is free from all the dualities breeding difference, and is *ever* established is his real self of pure consciousness alone.

तत्प्रवृत्तावप्यनिरासः संवेत्तृभावात्

(tatpravṛttāvapyanirāsaĥ sañvettṛ-bhāvāt)

...sūtra - (ss -III- 32)

"Being the knower of sthiti-laya, he is un-faltered in awareness."

सुखदुःखयोर्बहिर्मननम्

(sukha-duḥkhayorbahirmananam)

...*sūtra* - (*ss -III- 33)*

"(not being identified with puryaṣṭaka) Pleasure and pain are outside his consideration."

तद्विमुक्तस्तु केवली

(tadvimuktastu kevali)

...*sūtra* - (*ss -III- 34)*

"Freed from (the affliction of) the two, he is (immersed in) the consciousness alone."

The *kevali* state, the state of being the experient of *Śiva-vyāpti*, the *Śiva Himself* is a state of utter disregard to the duality bred by the influence of *Māyā*. It is being a *pramātā* dwelling at the state of *Śuddha-vidyā*, or *Īśwara* or *Sadāśiva* where the urge, the will, flowers into creation of *any* kind. The state where *Śakti* as *Mahā-Śakti*, is experienced as *akul-kula*, the un-manifest yet *the entire*, as *kaulikī* that dwells in the core, the *hṛdaya* (always *hṛdayestha !*)

as the source of everything, and also *kulanāyika*, the mate, the mentor and the manipulator of everything. Here, *Ġāna* is the absolute entirety of all pure understanding, the *Śuddha-vidyā*, and *Kriyā* is the entire execution of the *Śakti-ćakra* in all its expressions. The casting-away of the states of all duality, brings complete identification of the experient with *Mahā-Śakti*, giving him entire authority of creativity at the mere whimper of his will. He becomes the real *Sadaśiva*, the absolute subject, true knower of *visarga-bhāva* (!)

Creating one's own self,
from one's own self,
in one's own self.

...[tantraaloka – 3.141].

Lucid and clear do the following *Sūtras* reinfore this authority.

भेदतिरस्कारे सर्गान्तरकर्मत्वम्

(bheda-tiraskāre sargāntara-karmatvam)

...*sūtra* - (*ss -III- 36)*

"Casting away of the states of duality gives power of creativity of a different sṛšṭi."

शक्तिसन्धाने शरीरोत्पत्तिः

(Śakti-sandhāne śarīrotpattiḥ)

...*sūtra* - (*ss - I - 19)*

"Samāvesha with iććhā-Śakti results is creating any construct (body).

भूतसंधानभूतपृथक्त्वविश्वसंघट्टाः

(bhūtasandhāna-bhūtapṛthaktva-vishva-saṅghattāḥ)

...sūtra-(ss-I-20)

"Linking Consciousness with the constituents of the universe, their analysis and synthesis, (disjoining and rejoining) can be affected for reconstituting anything (anytime, anywhere)."

शुद्धविद्योदयाच्चक्रेशत्वसिद्धः

(śuddhavidyodayāććakreśatvasiddhiḥ)

...sūtra - (ss - I - 21)

"Rising to the state of Śuddha-vidyā gives complete mastery over the entire Śakti-ćakra."

करणशक्तिः स्वतोऽनुभवात्

(karaṇaśaktiḥ svato-anubhavāt)

...sūtra - (ss -III- 37)

"Power of creativity being one's personal experience."

This state of the experient, the *Maṅtra,* is not accessible unless the last shreds as well as their stitches too are discarded as non-entities. Existence of any feeblest of the feeble desire or want, remorse or expectation, doubt or inhibition, lingering in mind (*ćitta*), gives life and sustenance to the continuity of the *ānava* state of existence. A life full of duality, with likes and dislikes, pleasure and pain, good and bad, body and mind, etc., in the state of *paśu* therefore persists. *Turya* takes over intermittently while the delusion makes its grip firmer.

अभिलाषाद्वहिर्गतिः संवाह्यस्य

(abhilāšātvahirgatiḥ saňvāhyasya)

...sūtra - (ss -III- 40)

"Sense of want or a desire causes extroversion of consciousness (therefore inattention to turya), and a consequent involvement in karmic activities (dictated by delusion caused due to māyā)."

मोहप्रतिसंहतस्तु कर्मात्मा

(moha-pratisaňhatastu karmātmā)

...sūtra - (ss -III- 35)

"Compacted in delusions (brought about by karma-mala) involvement in karmic cycles results. "

One needs to guard against even the slightest of any such delusions resuing in diversion from the pure state of *turya*-consciousness. One needs to hold on firmly to the exalting state of *turya*, which is mostly prominent in the beginning and end of the (three) states of one's being. Just at the time of waking from sleep or dream-state, or at the transition from the waking to dream-state or sleep, one must remain vigilant, as at these transit points *turya* takes over. (Even for those who have no experience of *turya*, these transition points are critical, and remaining attentive to these least activity points, brings a very exalting state of mind. A perseverant and choice-less attention on such change-overs results in the experience of *turya* subsequently.) Those who have tasted of *turya*, need to infuse this nectar of *turya* steadily, with devotion and ease into their being, whenever even a sip of this nectar flows into their being. One needs to drench all the three states of one's being in it, with true yearning for it. *Sandhi* and *kāma-kalā* (mentioned earlier) should also be practiced with great zeal by the true aspirant as he progresses further. Not only the mind but *indriyās* too, and the whole body, should be surrendered to rapturous experience of *turya* so that it takes over completely to the exclusion of everything objective, (the actual contact with it or even its knowledge). Then alone does *ātma-vyāpti* get established that makes way for *turyatīta-awasthā* of *śiva-vyāpti* finally to manifest. In fact the true recognition, the true *pratyabhiġāna* happens only then. At this *Śiva-awasthā* the aspirant finds his body as a shell, a covering, maintained by the *prāṇic* forces, continuing only for the fulfillment of its *karma*. Mind dissolves into *Ćiti*, that, one with *Ćit*, the *Śiva*, basks in the bliss of *parā-bhattarika, ever !*

त्रिपदाद्यनुप्राणनम्

(tripadādyanuprāṇanam)

...sūtra - (ss -III- 38)

"Enliven the three states by (turya occurring in) their beginning."

चित्तस्थितिवच्छरीरकरणबाह्येषु

(ćittasthitivat-śarīra-karaṇa-bāhyešu)

...sūtra - (ss -III- 39)

"Body as well as ćitta, and also the external sense organs should be enlivened by the rapture of turya-consciousness."

तदारूढप्रमितेस्तत्क्षयाज्जीवसंक्षय:

(tadārūđhapramitestatkšayāj-jīvasaňkšayaĥ)

...sūtra - (ss -III- 41)

" (On) Firmly established in the subjective state without any trace of objectivity, (the full unfolding of turya), the dissolution of the empirical state takes place, along with the dissolution of (the craving for) objectivity."

भूतकञ्चुकी तदा विमुक्तो भूय: पतिसम: पर:

(bhūtakañćukī tadā vimukto bhūyaĥ patisamaĥ paraĥ)

...sūtra - (*ss -III-42)*

"Then, fully liberated and perfect like pati (Śiva), he wears his body of bhūtas as a mere covering."

नैसर्गिक: प्राणसंबन्ध:

(naisargikaĥ prāṇasaňbandhaĥ)

...sūtra - (*ss -III- 43)*

"(Having with it only) just a natural link through life force prāṇa."

नासिकान्तर्मध्यसंयमात् किमत्र सव्यापसव्यसौषुम्नेषु

(nāsikāntarmadhya-saňyamāt kimatra Savyāpasavya-saušumnešu)

...sūtra - (*ss -III- 44)*

"And what more to say, (experiencing a perpetual) Samāveśa with (the perpetual spanda of) the supreme one, the hṛt-karnika, within hṛt-padma, in the interior-most kanda of Sušumnā, (the middle one) between the right and left prāṇic channels."

Sušumnā for him is the flute, with the six holes as six *ćakras*, the mouth-piece as *Sahasrāra*, right and left *prānic-nāđīs as handlers*, the fingers, and he ever plays to *Mahā-Śakti*, the *Parā-Kuňđalinī*, *ever* enthralling her into a perpetual *Samāveśa* with Her, as His inseparable consort enjoying unbounded eternal bliss. He truly is *sampūrna* sixteen *kalā* '*Kṛśna*', ever in communion with *parā-kuňđalini* '*Radha*' and dancing with all the *śaktīs* as *gopis*. He is ever alive to the whole *sṛšŧi* as his play-field, which is an *anant-vismaya*. He is truly *jīvana-mukta*, in the world, basking in *jagadānand* of absolute *ćidānanda!*

चिदानन्दलाभे देहादिषु चेत्यमानेष्वपि
चिदैकात्मप्रतिपत्तिदाढ्‌र्यं जीवन्मुक्तिः

(ćidānandlābhe dehādišu ćetyamānešvapi
Ćidaikātma-pratipatti-dāđhryam jīvanmuktiĥ)
...sūtra - (*pbh* - *16)*

"Firmly established in perpetual ānanda of the unity with Ćit (even in vyutthān), still operating through the body, (the indriyās, taking them to be mere different coverings,). This Ćidānand-ghana state, even when still in body, is the real Jeevan-mukti ! "

समाधिसंस्कारवति व्युत्थाने भूयो
भूयश्चिदैक्यामर्शान्नित्योदितसमाधिलाभः

(samādhisaṅskāravati vyutthāne bhūyo bhūyaśćidaikyāmarśān-nityodita-smādhilābhaĥ)

...sūtra - (pbh - 19)

"Repeatedly dwelling in the sameness with Ćit, the supreme consciousness, even in vyutthaan, when the strong hang-over of it still persists, establishes (the experient) in deep perpetual samādhi."

The wondrous exploration of one's true *self* is unique, truly the only unique experience. When after having lived intensely, the worldly experience of this *sṛšṫi*, with all its agonies and ecstasies, desires and fears tearing apart the very existence of his ; enjoying its finest wealth of experiences, in all the different kinds of feelings, above all, the feeling of love, one feels forlorn by the fact of transitory-ness of everything, including life itself. Then anyone who, with a keener introspection struggles to look for something that is lasting and peeps in, looks deep and pierces sharper inside, for a long and subtle journey inward. Perseverance and devotion may lead him to finding the ultimate essence of *everything*, the pure consciousness. He gets, if he is lucky, subsequently a firmer grip on the truth and a lasting bliss, the greatest, one could aspire for, and partakes the nectar of bliss without any reserve. A journey from without to within, gives him a pedestal firm and sound, and the perspective of his true self, full of infinite beatitude and bliss. The grip of absorption into this pure *I*-consciousness is incomparably great. This introverted journey of exploration, the accomplishment of *sameness* with pure consciousness, and the establishment in it, is termed as *Nimīlana-krama.* Still wearing his body and *indriyas* as a natural sheath, which he finds not to be the essential truth of the self that he believed once it to be, but only just an assumed posture taken on itself by the reality, for the performance of just a role, he enjoys the bliss of being. Although not to be despised, this body and this universe, do not any more amuse or bind him at that stage. The grip of the recognition of, and the union with one's essential self being very great, the aspirant continues to remain in it, and enjoy the rapture of *Nimīlana-samādhi.* The rapture persists, even, whenever he comes out of it (the state called *vyutthāna*). The after-effect of the intoxication of the rapture is so great, that driven by it, he resorts to the introversion again and again. This repeated introversion and extroversion, called *krama-mudra,* continues drenching his body and senses, and the whole of *his* world, by the bliss of the rapture of *turya,* till it becomes perpetual. This, the *turyatīta-awastha,* (beyond *turya* state), this perpetual state of awareness of inner essence of pure subjectivity as *Śiva-state,* remains effulgent in and out perpetually for him. Actually there being no in and out, It is a 'no-*time*' and 'no-*space*' existence, but only the stark reality of *Śiva.* Experiencing this process of merging, of the 'within' into the 'without', is called *Unmīlana-krama*. Getting established in this *Śiva-awastha*, ever, within and without perpetually, and enjoying both, the *nimīlana* and *unmīlana Samādhi* ceaselessly, is *Pratimīlana-awastha*, the state of perfect *nirvāna* or complete *Jīvan-mukti*. Devoid of any difference, a throbbing *awastha*, simultaneously, of *jagadānanda* and *ćidānanda* is extremely rare, and experienced by the rarest of the rare aspirants. This is an experience of *parā-Kuňđalinī* for a *yogi*, who is perfectly *pure* like *Shiva* Himself. Called the state of *Niranjana-tattva* (the state, without any impression or stain of anything, but, a pure existence of *being*) this is a state of the actuality of *being*, the pure being in everything entire, the internal *Samāveśa* or external *Samāveśa* with *anything* or *any activity*. It is living in *pure being-tattva*. It is *pure being in action*. It is *Kriyā-Śakti* aspect of being !

Kāma-kalā, the process of grasping of the moment of the union of two, the *urge* and the *object*, the *rūpa* and the *vision*, the *skin* and the *touch*, the *I-ness* and the *this-ness*, is the experiencing of the *kāma-tattva*. When this *kāma-tattva* grows and permeates like poison into the entirety of being, the *urge* becomes *entire subjectivity* and the *object*, the *entire objectivity*, it is experiencing of the *viśa-tattva*. *Kāma-tattva* is the aspect of *iććhā-Śakti* and the *viśa-tattva* is the aspect of *Ġāna-Śakti*, while the actuality of the union, the total assimilation of the entire objectivity into subjectivity, such that there is no trace, whatsoever left of any shred of objectivity, then, the subject, the *pramātā*, becomes pure *pramiti*, and the *samāveśā* is of *Niranjan-tattva*, the *sameness in action*. This merging of three *tattvas*, the *kāma-tattva*, the *viśa-tattva*, and the *Niranjan-tattva*, in the purest state of *being* is actual *Bhairava-awastha* ! This is a state where it is only thunderous showers and floods of *Ānanda* drenching every pore of the being, overflowing without and within. In fact there is no without and within. It is only the *being* swinging on the flood of *Ānanda*. It is a craving and fulfillment in one. It is non-manifest and manifest in one. It is wondrous ocean of rapturous music, the player and the beholder in one, all in the utter silence of the unbounded, the *Ananta – maun* !

Thus speak the *Sūtras:*

भूय: स्यात्प्रतिमीलनम्

(bhūyaḥ syāt-pratimīlanam)

...sūtra - (*ss -III- 45*)

"There persists, again and again, the Samāveśā within and without, of Śiva-consciousness, (the experiencing of pratimīlan)."

महाह्रदानुसंधानान्मन्त्रवीर्यानुभव:

(mahāhṛdānusandhānān-mañtravīrya-anubhavaĥ)

...sūtra - (ss - I - 22)

"By uniting with the unbounded Hṛdaya, the infinite source of the absolute potency of Mañtra, the Supreme I-consciousness, the aspirant experiences the state of Śiva (becomes Śiva-pramātā)."

तदा प्रकाशानन्दसार-महामन्त्रवीर्यात्मक-
पूर्णाहन्तावेशात्सदासर्वसर्ग-संहारकारि-
निजसंविद्देवता-चक्रेश्वरताप्राप्तिर्भवतीति शिवम्

(tada prakāśānandsār–mahāmañtravīryātmaka– pūrṇāhantāveśātsadā-sarva-sarga-sañhārkāri– nijasañviddevatā– ćakreśwartāprāptir - bhavtīti Śivam)

...sūtra - (pbh – 20)

"Then, on the attainment to the status of the potency, (the highest of the experients) of the nature of mahā-mantreśwar, the essence of Ćidānanda, the perfect I-consciousness, the devourer of the entire manifestation, the achiever of the ultimate lordship of the entire Śakti-ćakra, within, He becomes Śiva Himself."

Recognition

A child grows into an adult, because it *can* grow into an adult. There *is* an adult in it. If it were not so, a child would never, ever, become an adult. All its cells within *know* how they have to proceed towards such growth. The coded information within, instructs them and coordinates their each step. The environment, inner and outer, works hand in hand for this process of unfolding. For the child the whole process is a challenge, a wonder, an experience of living and discovering, ever the new landmarks and achievements, all full of amusement and fulfillment. It is the process of recognition by him of his true potential. The child cherishes it all the way. Each impulse, each interaction with the world outside, opens a window of recognition within him. In fact there is no inside and outside. It is continuity. It is a process in unfolding. Recognition of an aspect is the end of its ignorance and an expansion of a potential. A child in its growth experiences a new potential every time and lives it, enjoys it, without ever revisiting the state of its absence. He knows exactly what it implies, because he can exercise his being that. The unknown may be a mystery but the being is the authority, the fulfillment. Recognition is not a conjuring up of anything, it is the tearing away of the layers that obscure the being of it. It is the true identity. For instance seeing a person after a long time, when much water may have flown in between, may dampen our recognition of him at first, or make it much hazy, or even inaccessible. On being reminded of some associated events and incidents, or after some fumbling, one suddenly is seized by a sense of recognition. It is not the memories of those associated events that construct the recognition, it is rather their tearing away and penetration into consciousness that unfolds the recognition. It is like pointing to a thin thread-like new moon on the horizon, the pointing only is a motivation to focus more, probe more into the depths of skies. Recognition can never be constructed, it is instantaneous. It is in present. It is, or it is not. Probing deep into memory lanes is bringing the memory into present, because the recognition is only in present, in the presence of awareness. Each experience is generally accompanied by a chain of other perceptions, related or unrelated. It is a situational phenomenon, a situational awareness. Some perceptions mark themselves as strong memories, while some others do not. All are related to the attention they have received, knowingly or unknowingly. Memories of certain things obscure those of the other feebler percepts, but all are patterns in the consciousness. Ever there ! Recognition of anything is its awareness in present, which has to be to the exclusion of everything else. To *see* it distinctly means dusting off all the other obscuring memories. That is what recognition precisely implies. Recognition is living of an experience, the full awareness of its being. The taste of anything is only in the tasting of it, not in the memory of it. Memory relates to a verbal or an 'impression tagging' of it. All objective experiences relate to *tanmātrās*. Every actual objective experience gets related within to the database of the *tanmātras* readily. When named only in words, it does not provide anyone the recognition of the experience, which only happens when one actually lives it in present. Recognition, a living experience, involves, in addition to an objective experience, a simultaneous experiencing of a non-objective factor, however transitory, depending on the intensity of awareness in experiencing. We, generally concerned with objective description and identification of the experiences, tend to overlook this, the most vital aspect of an experience. When we suddenly encounter or recognize a dear one, or place, or an old acquaintance, after some fumbling, we get a sudden, tender surge of a delight, or thrill within, but soon enough we get involved and engrossed with the numerous associated tagging aspects and other extraneous details that this *subjective* aspect of recognition is lost in these trivialities. This thrill or delight is the bliss aspect of the recognition, the touch of pure awareness that need be dwelt on for our own subjective realization, our true self. We live in it the state of our true being, when, for a feeble moment, all the dust is cast off from our consciousness and a true recognition happens. If keenly looked into, one can notice that this bliss aspect is associated with every *fresh* experience. The freshness is the clue ! Any experience, whatsoever, for the first time, brings *this* delight immensely. Every other time, a similar experience seems stale, and less or least exciting. It is, because the memory, the thought of the previous experience intervenes between the new experience and the experiencer. This dust on the mirror of perception makes the contact with the experience dull and hazy. All of us know that even the strongest and the most charming of the perceptive experiences, that of making love or having sex seems without any thrill, if the mind is dusty with extraneous involvements and not in tune with pure consciousness. When it is not keen and fresh, no experience makes a true contact with the consciousness. Nothing is truly noticed or recognized. A simple sip of tea or a drink, a tender look or a whisper, the quiver of a string or a whiff of aroma, or for that matter *any* of the feeble objective experiences can evoke a delight, a touch of bliss when consciousness offers itself to it naked. Any such experience makes an impact, and a true recognition of the experience happens. If dwelt on it, a contact with the true experiencer gets established and the subjective aspect of the experience starts dawning.

All the various states of existence, in all the varied aspects as the experiencer, are after all different commitments of consciousness. Involvement in any of these aspects creates an identification of the consciousness with that state and a delusion of considering oneself *that*. This delusion weaves the panorama of the whole creation, the *sṛšti*. The consciousness, infinite and boundless, with all its intrinsic sovereignty and freedom of action, expresses as anything it *wills*, and gets involved into expressing itself as *that*. It imbibes all the required objective attributes. It is the dust of these attributes that inhibits the vision and one considers oneself a confined experient, a specific unit, an *ānava* experient and busies one-self into the expression of that commitment. The identification becomes so strong that it *forgets* its true identity. It is entangled into a chain of cause and effect and therefore into the pursuit of its vision as a limited experient. It behaves like the chick of an eagle brought up within the chicks of an ordinary hen right from its birth. It dears not fly, least into the distant skies and is used to picking from the trash. Nothing can get this speck of consciousness out of its delusion, accept a sudden recognition of itself __ 'an eagle whose abode is the distant skies'. All empirical beings can *be* their *true-self* again on the recognition of their actuality, because all are actually the pure consciousness, only believing them-selves to be truly what the consciousness had desired to become. The difficulty is that the belief is so resilient that nothing, no effort, can obliterate it except a sustained disregard for this acquired state of an empirical being full of the experiences of differentiations, or a sudden recognition of one's *true* self as consciousness, the pure awareness!

This is what is *pratyabhiĝāna* or 'the doctrine of recognition' in the *trika* school of *śaivism.* The greatness of this school is in considering (and knowing) *everything,* the entire objective manifestation, only as an *aspect* of consciousness ; just an aspect, not the *entirety* of the consciousness. Therefore the only thing a true aspirant must seek is to experience and recognize the *entirety* even while embodied as an *aspect*, a limited perspective in the objective domain. Knowing verbally that 'I am in actuality only consciousness' is not enough, but living that reality in actuality is what is required. Again not only that, but *enjoying* the limited aspect of the objective existence even while keeping the foothold in the transcendental reality, is the true *recognition*. One can be a real *Trika* only when one lives the *awastha* (state) of *jagadānanda*. *Ātmavyāpti* is not enough, but *śivavyāpti* is the target. Consciousness, the *Śakti*, weaves the web of *sṛṣṭi* and gets entangled in this web of objectivity. Shaking off this web is not the aim, but in fact, after shaking oneself out of this web and grasping a foothold in the *prakāśa* of *śiva*, to live and enjoy the beauty and wonder of this, the *śakti*, that is, being actually in the state of complete *vimarśamaya-prakāśa awastha* of *bhairava*, the *Parama-Śiva*. This is a state of recognizing oneself as *Śiva*, as *Śakti*, and as *nara*, the entire *parā*, *parāparā*, and *aparā* existence in one. Living the transcendental in the immanent and the immanent in the transcendental as one ! it is a *pratimīlana-awastha*, a perfect *jīvanmukta* state in the body of a *nara*.

We have traced in the previous chapters the entire process of the expansion of *Anuttra*, the *Parama-Śiva* from its *perfect* state of complete *vimarśamaya-prakāśa* into the grossest of material manifestation as *sṛṣṭi*. In the light of *Sūtras* from the highly regarded texts like *Śiva-sūtras*, *Parātrīśika*, *Prathyabhigāna-hṛdayama* along with the concepts of *Parāpraveśika*, we have expounded the *trika* truth of the entire existence and found it to be a triadic expression of the *Parama-Śiva* in its creative urge for expansion. We have also considered how the withdrawal urge of *Śiva* manifests in *nara* and how the motivations and efforts lead an experient at the empirical state to rid itself of the delusions of its limited considerations and prepare for a direct contact with its true self. We have considered the *tattvic* hierarchy of the various intermediate states in this process of expansion and clearly traced the *awareness* as the *root* as also the *link* between the transcendental and the immanent expression of the divine urge of *Anuttra.* Recognition of this awareness, the unity of *prakāśa* and *vimarśa* is the only key available to every *ānava* existent to unlock the ultimate *swātantrya* of its true being. To prepare ourselves for this recognition we need to contemplate upon the entire communication that formed the text of the study that was undertaken in the previous chapters. In great detail we investigated into the *Parāvāk* aspect of creation for immanent manifestation, the *ānava* delusions and the journey within from the state of *paśu* to *pati* and *Ātma-vyāpti* to *Śiva-vyāpti,* and then to the ultimate *Bhairava-awastha.* Even then if we find ourselves asking the core of our understanding at the *parā* level exactly as *Devi* asks *Bhairava* (as is stated in the ancient scripture *Vigānā-Bhairava*), then we need to deeply contemplate on what *Bhairava* in response says to *Devi* .

Devi asks : " Even after listening to the scriptures like *Rudrayamala tantra,* and others, giving the essence of *Trika,* doubts with regard to grasping in actuality the absolute reality of the essential nature of *Bhairava*, still remain, therefore tell me my Lord, is *Bhairava* '*Śabda-rāśi-kalāmayam*' [*varṇas* from अ to क्ष with their inherent creative powers, the *Anuttra, Ānand, Iććhā, Ġāna* and *Kriyā*] or '*Navātma-bhedena*' [the various subjective aspects like *Śiva, Śakti, Sadaśiva, Iśwara, Śuddha-vidyā, Mahāmāyā, Māyā, Purušа* and *Prakṛti*] ? Is it *Triśiro-bheda-bhinnam* represented by *Mañtra* '*Sauh*' [which comprises all the 31 *nara-tattvas*, referring to the empirical aspect, represented by स् , औ , representing the three transcendental *tattvas*, the *Sadaśiva, Iśwara* and *Śuddha-vidyā* and अः , the *visarga* representing the *Śiva* and *Śakti tattvas*] or the governing *śaktis* of the three [the *Aparā-śakti, Parāparā-śakti* and *Parā-śakti*] ? Or else is it, *nāda-bindu* [the *vimarśa* and *prakāśa* aspect of the manifestation as *vākya* and *vāchaka*, the indicated and indicator of the objectivity]? Is it otherwise the various attributes of *mātṛkā* as *mañtra, mantravīrya*, and *śakti*, [the *arda-ćandra, nirodika, nāda, nādanta, śakti, vyāpni, samān*, and *unmanā*]? Is it *anaka* [the *anāhata-nāda* '*ha*' , the *prāṇa-śakti* '*hamsah*'] or the pure changeless *Parā-Śakti* ? And if it is *parā*, the *Niškala*, how is it compatible with *Sakala*, the *parāparā* and *aparā* ?"

And to this query *Bhairava* answers, " *Sakala* aspect of *Bhairava* is taught as a prop for meditation, to those engrossed in all kinds of differentiation. In fact *Bhairava* is neither *Śabda-rāshi* nor *Navātma*. It is neither the '*three Śaktis*' nor *nāda-bindu* or *arda-ćandra* etc. It is not *Śath-ćakra* nor the *prāṇa-śakti*. These are all motivations for deeper spiritual practices for finally exploring the essential nature of *Bhairava*, non-different from the true-self. *Parā* is free from direction, time, *deśa* or *uddeśa* (designation). It is indescribable (*akhyati*). Complete *vikalpa-mukti* (riddance from all alternatives) only can lead one to the real bliss of Divine *I*-consciousness. We are used to seeing *Sakala* as *parts* and thereby we miss the *bharitākāra* (the universal pervasive delight of entire creativity), the real *Bhairavai*, the *Śakti* which is 'non-different' from *Bhairava.* It is the only entrance to *Śiva.* Only by the *entry into* the state of *Śakti*, is *Śiva* recognized !"

The truth is that entire manifestation, perceptive or non-perceptive, all is *Śakti* manifested innumerably through her own *swātantrya* and perceived in multifarious ways in segments *itself* by *Her.* Penetration into itself to recognize the *Bharitākārita* of itself is the true *vimarśa*, the doorway to the real being, the *Prakāśa*, the reality of the bliss of *pūranāhaṅta*, because *Bhairava* is actually *Vimarśamaya-Prakāśa.* Any *intense penetration* or *entry* into one-self by *any* aspirant, who is *actually* an aspects of *Śakti* yields a contact with the *Bharitākārita* of *one-self*, the recognition of oneself and thus, a true *vimarśa* as *vimarśamaya-Prakāśa*, the *Aham-vimarśa.*

Bhairava, on *Devi's* query as to how *Parādevi-Śakti* can be contacted, relates in response, 112 different *Dhāranās* that a seeker can resort to, for entry into *Śakti* and thereby realize the *Bhairva* state of being. These *Dhāranās*, as given in the text of *Vigānā-*

Bhairava are actually meant for the advanced aspirants or yogis, already on the path of seeking union with their true self, but even then a deeper contemplation of these and a steady pursuit can be very beneficial for all seekers.

A keen consideration of all these *dhāranās* makes it explicitly clear that the approach to be followed is merely deep contemplations through an intensely focused mind cultivated by a clear understanding of the *Trika* truth. By now, any reader who has taken seriously whatever was considered so far, will find by deeper introspection that everything that happens within and without of any experiencer, is all a phenomenon of activity guided and coordinated by an understanding or knowledge that has sprouted from the seed of a desire. *Iććhā* is the actual potency that is the sole operator of everything. It is the creative impulse that generates and provides all the knowledge needed as also the motivation for the entire activity aspect. *Greater* the awareness of the totality of the three factors within the *Iććhā* itself, more meaningful the outcome of activity. A momentum blindly generated by a muffled awareness of the entire phenomenon in the fractured unfolding of the desire, or in fact a fragmented awareness, is bound to result in disastrous consequences. It is actually the awareness that is the essence. Awareness, the *vimarśa* focused on the being, the *Ćit*, is *ānanda* of *Ātma-vishrāňti*. It is living the *sattatva* of *ćidānanda*, while the awareness focused on *Iććhā* is *sṛšti*. It is like opening of the eyelids by *Bhairava* from its *Ātma-vishrāňti* state, only to behold itself in whatever form desired, a three-pronged materialization of *Iććhā-Ġāna-Kriyā*, a unique *parā-parāparā-aparā* reality of transcendental cum immanent aspect of itself. Every *aparā* fragment, forming an *aparā terminal* of the *parāparā-Śakti* of *vimarśa* has its core in the *parā*-ever, the reality of its pure being, the *Ćit*, which is beyond any kind of *aparā* tinge. The *parāparā* aspect, the dynamic *Śakti*, is the entrance, the conduit to cross over to that *parā*-state. This precisely forms the secret of all the *dhāraṇās* indicated in *Viġānā-Bhairava Sūtras*. These *dhārnās* lead us to the recognition of *parā* from whatever foothold of *aparā* we are at, through *Śakti*, the *parāparā* aspect of *Bhairava*. *Vikalpa-mukti* at the state of *aparā* is the sole requirement and the means for this transition. It can be resorted to by the process of *grassan*, the dissolution into the subtler and then the subtlest states of all the grosser states of *aparā* for the cross-over. Direct visualization of one's identification with pure consciousness is another approach of contemplation suggested in certain *dhāraṇās*, achieved by discarding into non-existence everything we hold on to, and by visualizing everything as vacuity by the perceiving subject, which itself is aware (and of the nature of awareness). Alternatively dwelling on, and penetrating into, any, even the feeblest of experiences of grosser aspects of *ānanda* in the form of delight or *tuśti* that may ever happen, provides a transition.

To begin with an aspirant therefore needs to remain alert and watchful, always on the watch-tower of one's subjective state, a witness unto oneself. This attitude, first theoretically grasped is to be cultivated in actuality. It becomes natural only when extraneous involvements are abandoned. Whatever one may do, or in whatever state one may be, the foothold must remain in the subjective reality, just witnessing everything through a choice-less awareness without any bias or involvement. Activities in the domain of body, mind or the world will continue and must continue, but all those belong there, outside and not at the level of the subject, who is just a watchman, watching all and even itself. When this attitude becomes spontaneous, the deliberation on any of the *dhāraṇās* can be undertaken. Just one may be enough!

Much can be said, but need not be said, about each of the 112 *dhāraṇās* under mention. What is actually needed is to grasp the spirit and the essence of what has been communicated through these *dhāraṇās*. An intuitive understanding, touched and then resorted to, in grasping and penetrating into the spirit of *dhāraṇās* is required. Words don't communicate much. The intangible reality in them cannot be explained, but can be experienced.

Ahead are presented these *dhāraṇās* arranged in several groups, each with the spirit of a single specific communication. This is done to motivate the reader to introspect for a better grasp through a deeper contemplation on these *dhāraṇās*. This reorganization changes the traditional order in which these *Sūtras* have been presented in the original texts, but the care has been taken to maintain that tag of the original *Sūtra*-number and the *dhāraṇās*-number respectively by indicating both these at the end of each *Sūtra* to maintaining their actual reference. The Original *Sanskrit* version of the *Sūtras* is not presented in these groupings resorted to here, (all those are however presented in their original order as appendix). The author has attempted to present the communication in each of the *Sūtra* in English, hopefully as lucidly as possible.

(Kindly note that in fact first dhāraṇās is presented by Bhairava in Sūtra 24, while the first 23 sūtras refer to the preliminary dialogue between Devi and Bhairava, forming the background for the communication of the dhāranās, which has already been gone into by us summarily in the previous pages [168-169].)

Group – I

Dhāraṇās that demand just an attitude of witnessing, alert watchfulness, or an intense awareness to the exclusion of everything else, are presented in this first group.

To Devi seeking 'to hear in *vaikhari* state, what she already knows in her *parā* state so as to know how *parāśakti*, the entrance to *Bhairava* state is actually realized, *Bhairava* speaks thus:

1. Parā-śakti ceaselessly expresses herself in the rise and fall of the Prāṇa-śakti as visarga-spanda at the two dwādaśāṅts in

jivas. Steady awareness of these points where the two currents 'prāṇa' and 'apāna' spring forth, provides the fullness of the parā-śakti experience. [sūtra 24 – dhāraṇā 1]

2. Breath, incoming or outgoing does not immediately return. The split-second pause of Prāṇa-śakti at dwādaśāṇts, in driving it, to and fro should be watched with steady attention at these two points. The Bhairavai śakti of Bhairava manifests there. [25 – 2]

3. Deepened awareness of the pause of Prāṇaśakti at Dwādaśāṅts unfolds into madhyā state, where the cessation of Prāṇa and Apāna currents takes place. This is associated by the cessation also of all thought-constructs into a nirvikalpa bhāva that reveals true Bhairava-bhāva. [26 – 3]

4. Retained śakti of Prāṇa and Apāna at Dwādaśāṅts manifests as tranquility-śakti. Watching this state of tranquility steadily reveals the awastha of Śānta-Bhairava. [27 – 4]

5. The fusion of Prāṇa and apāna currents, when watched steadily, leads to a complete cessation of both at either of the Dwādaśāṅts. An alert mindfulness of this state of void brings the yogi to the state of sameness with Parā-śakti. [64 – 41]

The five *dhāraṇās* cited above focus on cultivating intense awareness of the natural breathing. An objective activity, the process of natural breathing, leads through its handler the *Prāṇa-śakti* to the *visarga* aspect of the *Spanda* of *Parā-śakti.* Watching intently the creation and dissolution of *Prāṇa* currents and thereby getting dissolved into the naked *Parā-śakti,* the pure awareness, the *Vimarśa* or *Saṅvit,* the un-differentiable *Swabhāva* of *Bhairava* is recognized. *Dhāraṇās* indicated by *Bhairava* herein actually help us to take our awareness on a reversal journey back to the source. Beginning with an attitude of witnessing, the deepening of the attention leads awareness from its committed objective state through *vikalpa-mukti* to its pure and unqualified state of *Saṅvid* for final merger with the pure state of *Bhairava.*

Ecstatic delight of any kind wards off, may be transitorily, the grip of *vikalpas* on consciousness. More intense the ecstatic delight, lesser the grip of *vikalpas* or vice-versa. Witnessing the thrill keenly and dwelling on it without any deliberation of thought, yields a greater delight. An intense penetration into such delight forms a link with the *Ānanda* aspect of *Bhairavi-Saṅvit.*

यत्सुखं ब्रह्मतत्त्वस्य तत्सुखं

(this delight in actuality is that delight of the essence of Brahm).

Vismaya or *Aananda* is the perpetual *spanda* of the *Swātantrya* of *Saňvid.* Experience of any ecstatic delight, thrill, sensation, awe or wonder should not be discarded or ignored, it should rather be dwelt upon without any indulgence of thought or reason into it. Merging into it with full submission and awareness is a sure visa for transition into the *Parā*.

The *Dhāraṇās* mentioned ahead focus on watching keenly and penetrating deep into certain tangible experiences.

6. Sexual excitement, culminating through a sexual intercourse with the partner, into an intense delight of sexual orgasm is an experience of the delight of Brahman, the real self. [69 - 46]

7. Awareness of such delight flooding through the intense memory of sexual act of sucking embracing and intercourse even in absence of a woman can be dwelt on.
[70 – 47]

8. Spontaneous contemplation of the entire universe and one's own body simultaneously filled with the amrit of

Ānanda brings identification with the spiritual-bliss of Parā finally. [65 – 42]

9. Gazzelle-eyed, dwelling upon the sense of wonder through a magical feat, or an instantaneous sensation through tickling, can cause identification with the bliss.
[66 – 43]

10. Any spontaneous throb of great delight that may ever spring up within (because of any experience whatsoever) or on the occasion of seeing a dear friend or a relative after a long time should be dwelt upon and be filled by. [71 – 48]

11. Get identified with the fulfilling experience and joy arising out of rasa, the taste of eating or drinking and contemplate and dwell over that joy. Great bliss will prevail. [72 – 49]

12. Aesthetic delight that wells up within due to a touching song or the like of experiences must be identified with. Contemplating unreservedly on that state of joy unfolds it into true bliss. [73 – 50]

13. Whatever may yield 'tušti', the satisfaction, an elating joy without agitation ; remain in that state and plunge into the depth of that joy. The ultimate bliss will manifest thereby. [74 – 51]

14. Dissolve yourself into any tender sensation arising by witnessing variegated patterns of color or light as such, stretched in space by sunlight, or lamp-light or any other source. This can reveal the essence of one's real self. [76 – 53]

15. The calming of nerves by un-witting swinging of the body happening by itself or in a moving vehicle, and providing a kind of repose should be surrendered to, and watched intently, without any interference whatsoever through thoughts or otherwise. This unfolds into truly blissful state.
[83 – 60]

16. Commencement of sneeze, yawn, violent cough, terror, flight from some danger, hunger, deep sigh, sudden elation, or a state of keen curiosity or deep sorrow should be watched through, without any indulgence to the end of it. It can be revealing. [118 – 93]

17. Remaining intensely aware at the onset of a desire, greed, envy, arrogance, anger, or infatuation fills one with 'ćidānanda', the divine consciousness. [101 – 78]

18. Piercing any part of body with some sharp pointed needle etc. and then remaining steadily and one-pointedly aware

of the sensation of the prick, can lead to the singular reality. [93 – 70]

19. Due to ignorance or inability when it becomes impossible to resolve a problem and therefore one feels stilled and benumbed, remain aware and watchful of that stilled state and realize. [112 – 88]

20. If one whirls one's body round and round till the body falls down due to acute stress, the unhampered state of such complete restfulness must be watched with complete surrender. This cessation of the energy of acute commotion reveals supreme bliss. [111 – 87]

21. Beholding pure, vast sky unflinchingly with open eyes and body completely sill, O' Devi, Bhairava awastha can manifest.
[84 – 61]

22. Contemplating upon the vast sky as of the essence and form of Bhairava being dissolved in the space of one's head, floods the whole universe in the light of Bhairava.
[85 – 62]

23. In a completely dark night of the dark fortnight contemplating for long over the utter darkness as of Bhairava-rūpa can manifest actually as Bhairava-rūptā.
[87 – 64]

24. Similarly, contemplating with closed eyes over utter darkness and then contemplating the presence of Bhairava as utter darkness even with open eyes one can achieve identification with Bhairava in true sense actually. [88 – 65]

Group - II

Next we look at some *dhāraṇās* which motivate us to leave the objective aspect and attempt to grasp the intangible, non-manifest vacuity. This in fact is to relate to the un-manifest aspect of *śakti* directly. These *dhāraṇās* motivate the aspirant to visualize, everything that is present, as mere void, a vacuity, and thereby get rid of the notion of reality in terms of an objective existence. This practice or contemplation leads to non-dependence on the objective realms bringing the focus to dwelling on a pure non-tangible subjective aspect of our being. One could start with any objective point of view, visualize it as mere void and just *be*. Experiencing the pure untainted vacuity in consciousness, leads to a direct *vikalpa-mukti* right away.

25. On the onset of sleep, when external objectivity perceived through indriyās has just faded away, the state of vacuity

between wakefulness and sleep should be witnessed. Establishing awareness on this state reveals Parāśakti domain. [75 – 52]

26. One should dwell, neither on grief nor jubilation but instead remain watchful of them in a state of poise, the Madhya. This reveals the essence of true being, O' Bhairavai ! [103 – 80]

27. Listening intently to the musical notes emanating from the stringed or other instruments and carrying on with the awareness of these notes to their fading succession uninterruptedly (to the exclusion of all else) results in the absorption of awareness into highest vacuity of the attainment of Bhairava. [41 – 18]

28. Contemplation on the void existing before and after the utterance of any syllable, establishes the consciousness in the state of absolute void, the Parā-śakti, the Parāvāka repository. [40 – 17]

29. Contemplating on only void existing over the body and underneath it, and therefore visualizing oneself support-less and independent of body, one becomes void-minded, truly vikalpa-mukt. [44 – 21]

30. Contemplating that within one's body is void in all directions and a simultaneous,

complete absence of thought-constructs (a nirvikalpa state). Keen awareness of this manifests as vacuity-consciousness all around. [43 – 20]

31. One, firmly contemplating as mere void, the underneath, everything around and above, and also at heart simultaneously, experiences absolute vikalpa-mukti and there-from the dawn of pure nirvikalpa state of Bhairava. [45 – 22]

32. With an attention freed of vikalpās, if the yogi contemplates even for little while that his body considered to be the empirical subject is only pure void, he is liberated of all vikalpās and attains to the state of nirvikalpa-swarup Bhairava. [46 – 23]

33. Even if one contemplates all the constituents of one's body pervaded by mere vacuity, O' mriga-nayani (gizzalle-eyed), one gets steadied in the contemplation of vacuity-consciousness. [47 – 24]

34. A yogi contemplating that the skin of his body is a mere covering holding nothing substantial within attains a state which is beyond any contemplation or perception, a truly niškala Bhairava state. [48 – 25]

35. Intense contemplation that this whole universe is totally void dissolves the mind completely into the absolute void of Śiva state, O' Mahādevi. [58 – 35]

36. Beholding a view of vast emptiness with no trees, mountains or any other supportive existence makes mind support-less causing its dissolution into a state completely free of flux. [60 – 37]

37. Contemplating a complete absence of one's ćitta within and therefore non-existence of vikalpās, one actually experiences one's true self, the vikalpa-mukt state. [94 – 71]

38. On the occasion of any sense-organ getting obstructed naturally or due to an external or self imposed cause snapping its contact with the external world, a sense of vacuity occurs. Contemplation over that vacuity and penetration into it reveals one's real self. [89 – 66]

39. Standing above a very deep gorge or well and gazing intently without diversion into its depths develops a mental disposition of vikalpa-free state and leads to complete spontaneous dissolution of mind into vikalpa-mukti. [115 – 90]

40. Gazing with deep attention into the emptiness of any vessel ignoring its confining walls and getting absorbed into its emptiness such that one's mind gets completely dissolved into the void brings the yogi's complete identification with the supreme void. [59 – 36]

41. After looking at any object if one withdraws one's look from it along with all the knowledge and impression of it completely into the visualization of void, then O' Devi complete merger with the ultimate state of void happens. [120 – 95]

42. Perception of a specific object means vacuity with respect to every other object. Contemplation of that vacuity with a thought-free mind bestows tranquility in spite of that perception. [122 – 97]

43. Contemplation of vast outside space as being limitless, support-less, ever present, eternal, and only void dissolves the mind ultimately into the nirākāśa of Bhairava. [128 – 103]

44. On the occasion of referring to ' I ' or 'mine' , the concept ' I ' should be understood as intangible entity, the support-less nirvikalpa even with respect to its objective tangible references. [131 – 106]

[This nirvikalpa subjective contemplation in relation to the objective context can become a wormhole channel to 'that' reality.]

45. The mind should be impelled to move away from whichever object it goes to by the mind itself and thus not allowed to resort to it repeatedly. This makes the mine support-less and free from all kinds of agitation and therefore tranquil. [129 – 104]

46. Having made the mind support-less it should then be made nirvikalpa by not engaging it with any thought constructs. This way O' Mriga-nayani the self attains to its exalted Bhairava-state. [108 – 84]

47. Not dwelling on any of the two successive thoughts, objective perceptions or their knowledge but instead remaining intently aware of the gap, the intermediate void between the two, flashes forth the ultimate reality. [61 – 38]

48. On quitting one thought if the mind is not allowed to move to the next thought but made to remain intensely aware of the intermediate void between the two, the realization of the pure consciousness soon manifests. [62 – 39]

49. One should watch the mind during the birth of any desire in it and not allow that to flourish. Putting an end to it immediately and watching its submergence gives identification with void. [96 – 73]

50. At the instance of the birth of a desire or its concerned knowledge, one should look at it as the aspect of real self and witness it keenly without paying any attention to any objective existence at all. Realization of true self will dawn thereby. [98 – 75]

51. Remaining intently aware of the fading of the visarga sound when a letter with a visarga is uttered makes the mind support-less which finally gets immersed into the eternal reality. [91 – 68]

Group – III

Dhāraṇās that were considered in section II, focused all on taking the awareness from a tangible point of view to the intangible void with no objective attributes and therefore a state of no differentiations or alternatives, but only just a sense of witnessing the void and holding on to a state of pure awareness. This awareness on deepening becomes a pure witnessing or awareness of one's real subjective aspect of existence, the awareness of being aware!

Dhāraṇās that follow now in the section III, focus on beginning actually with a visualization of oneself as well as everything else as consciousness and penetrating deep into that state. This approach leads the aspirant to recognizing and then getting actually established in the state of *Ātmavyāpti*, his true state of being.

52. Visualizing oneself, vast as sky and unlimited in every direction as deep void of Ćiti, the pure consciousness, uncommitted and free reveals itself as the essential self of the aspirant. [92 – 69]

53. With mind steadied and freed of all alternatives, contemplating on oneself, one's body and the whole universe as nothing but pure consciousness, one attains supreme awakening. [63 – 40]

54. Subjective and objective consciousness is an aspect of all embodied beings. The awareness of this reality is the distinction that yogis posses. Realizing that body actually is not a need for the consciousness to operate, and contemplating that in all the bodies, the same consciousness is present

in just the same way as in one's own body exalts one to all pervasiveness.
[106, 107 – 83]

55. Consciousness, as the true self, without any difference anywhere, is present in all the bodies alike. Realizing this oneness and being mindful of it leads to liberation from birth and death. [100 – 77]

56. Transcending attachment for one's body and other things firmly and contemplating deeply that 'I exist' (as consciousness) 'ever and everywhere' results in the highest joy that can ever be.
[104 – 81]

57. Every time consciousness operates through the sensory organs, keep aware and contemplate that it is the pure universal consciousness that is revealing itself. Causing merger into the universal consciousness this way provides absolute fulfillment. [117 – 92]

Group – IV

There are certain typical practices recommended which need a deep visualization of certain subtle aspects of *Śakti* manifestation to identify the consciousness at play. These *Dhāraṇās* are based on *Tāňtrika* approach to practice and therefore some of them may need specifically the guidance of a *Guru* in person for a clearer understanding of such manifestation as also an easy transition.

58. If the aspirant visualizes that Kālāgni-Rudra, the universal destroyer aspect of Śakti, is rising from his right toe and burning his entire body and contemplates long on it, he will experience profound peace as his real nature. [52 – 29]

59. Visualizing and contemplating on Kālāgni-Rudra burning the entire world and not allowing the mind to wander out to any thing else, the aspirant exalts to the highest state. [53 – 30]

60. Visualize Prāňa-śakti rising as a lustrous candescence from mūlādhāra-ćakra and becoming subtler till its dissolution into dwādaśāňt at brahmrandhra. Such contemplation leads finally to Bhairava-awastha. [28 – 5]

61. Śakti rising like lightning from one ćakra to another, each three fists away from the other, up to dwādaśānt at the end (at Brahmrandhra) must be contemplated for Bhairava-udaya. [29 – 6]

62. Successive twelve centers of Śakti associated with twelve vowels should be contemplated upon in their gross, subtle and supreme phases for one's complete merger with Śiva. [30 – 7][15]

63. Filling Mūrdhānta (Brahmrandhra) with Prāṇa-śakti quickly and crossing the bridge over eyebrows by bhrūkśepa technique one should become nirvikalpa and rise above the dwādaśānt to the state of omnipresence. [31 – 8]

64. Sacred mantra like Praṇava recited appropriately with contemplation over the void aspect of its ending through its protracted utterance into the Śakti of void, brings identification with that Śakti of void, the Parā-Śakti. [39 – 16][16]

65. Letting go with ease one's ćitta into the middle of vahini and viša (adhaĥ and ūrdhva kundilini) as it is, or through the Prāṇic manipulation brings union with 'kāma-like' bliss. [68 – 45][17]

66. Contemplating over Piṇđamantras from gross utterance to subtler spanda's and onto the void of Samanā through ardaćańdra bindu etc. provides attainment of unmanā (Śiva) state. [42 – 19][18]

67. Stopping of all the inputs of perception causes Prāṇa-śakti to crawl slowly upward (from Mūlādhārā towards Sahasrara). This is accompanied by a feeling like that of an ant crawling over the body yielding supreme delight. [67 – 44]

68. Prāṇa-śakti contemplated upon as breath going in and out as a feeble current with sound between hṛdaya and dwādaśānt must be penetrated into. This bestows Swātantrya Śakti. [55 – 32]

69. One should deeply contemplate over the five voids of the five perceptive senses within one's heart present like five voids within five mandalās in the peacock feathers. Absorption in the absolute void will happen subsequently. [32 – 9]

70. Similarly when contemplation is made on anything, say void or a wall or any elevated one, one's complete absorption into it results into the achievement of the desired result. [33 – 10]

71. Central channel, located centrally like the stem of a lotus has an inner channel (Suṣumnā). Contemplation on an absorption into the vacuity of this channel reveals the Lord. [35 – 12]

72. A tilaka of fire like a droplet of light appearing on the occasion of an extinguishing lamp should be contemplated upon within Hṛdaya or Brahmarandhara. Absorption into it subsequently ends all vikalpās and complete absorption into supreme. [37 – 14]

73. Stopping all the sense-organ openings like eyes etc. with the astras of hands, the block in the opening between the eyebrows is shattered into the appearance of a dot of light there. Contemplation over this dot leads to its gradual fading away accompanied by one's dissolution into the void of pure consciousness. [36 – 13]

74. Deep absorption into anāhat (ha m sa) going on uninterruptedly within, develops into ability of listening with ears the uninterrupted sound of śabda-brahm, like that of a gushing river, which perfected, gives merger with the Parama-Brahm.
[38 – 15]

75. One who, without any other vikalpa, enters into the interior of the bowl of his heart-lotus within the void of one's hṛdaya, and gets completely dissolved in it acquires the supreme fortune O' beautiful one. [49 – 26]

76. By repeatedly paying attention to Dwādaśāṅt, wherever one is or whatever one is doing, all the fluctuations and disparities in mind diminish and vanish. [51 – 28]

77. Knowing that all the feelings of pain and pleasure happen to indriyās, one should detach the awareness from the indriyās and remain poised in oneself. [136 – 111]

78. Listen to the mystic tradition I am relating exactly to you Devi, "by keeping eyes wide open without blinking kaivalya is instantly achieved ". (This Dhāraṇā is referred to as Bhairava-Mudra, in which one is completely absorbed within through unwavering nirvikalpa attention on one's subjective self while all perceptive senses are unobstructed and unattended.) ...
Contracting the openings of ears, anus, and penis and contemplating on 'anackam-ahalam' , the unstruck-sound without a varṇa, brings eternal entry into Brahm. (Anuswar or visarga (·) and (:) without varṇas are the un-struck sounds representing Śiva and Śakti that cannot be uttered but should be visualized).
[113, 114 – 89]

79. Mouth steadily kept open, the backward turned tongue maintained at middle and attention on the middle of the

mouth and remaining contemplating the utterance of vowel-less un-struck sound 'ha' brings lasting dissolution in tranquility. [81 – 58]

80. Fixing gaze on any gross object and making mind free of all thoughts and thus support-less leads to Śiva-state. [80 – 57]

81. Comfortably seated, one should arch one's arm overhead and gaze into one's armpits. Absorption into the state of this posture brings great poise and peace to the aspirant. [79 – 56]

82. Supported by only one of the buttocks should one sit on a soft cushion with hands and feet dangling totally support-less. One attains great poise, ease and harmony by it. [78 – 55]

83. Yogic practice of mudraas like karankinī, krodhana, bhairavai, lelihānyā, and khećari yield supreme attainments. [77 – 54]

84. Devi, reciting akār without bindu or visargah superb wisdom manifests instantly. (This is holding on to ćakita-mudra with no apāna or prāṇa currents and mouth poised for अ) . [90 – 67]

Group – V

Dhāraṇās mentioned above focus on watching keenly and penetrating deep into certain tangible practices.

Next, comprises the process of allowing one's grosser concept to get devoured by a subtler aspect of its existence, and following this process (of *grassana*) with intense feeling of it, one attains to the state of *Parā-Shakti*, the door to the ultimate reality of *Bhairava.*

85. Contemplating that desire, knowledge etc. appear not only within me but within all existents makes one all pervasive. [105 – 82]

86. Sight of a place or view sometimes makes one go beyond the thoughts and memories turning the body support-less. Dwelling on such a state unfolds into experiencing of the Lord. [119 – 94]

87. Visualizing the universe as an act of jugglery, a painting or a fleeting show from a sliding point of view. A deep contemplation over it brings great delight. [102 – 79]

88. Contemplating that one's body and the whole universe is being absorbed into the respective subtler constituents (say Panća-

mahabhūta into Tanmātras etc.) till Parādevi is revealed. [54 – 31]

89. The whole universe in the form of bhuvanas and adhvas must be contemplated as getting dissolved into their successive subtler states up to the supreme state of pure consciousness. [56 – 33]

Group – VI

For those who have developed an attitude of *vairaġa* and are convinced of their being in actuality only *Ćidānanda*, the *Bhairava*, and are bent upon getting rid of their *malas*, there are a few *dhāraṇās* that demand a full-fledged assertion on their part for contemplating deeply on those aspects that deepen such conviction and finally lead the aspirant on his actual realization of *Bhairava.* A yogi who has actually experienced *Ātma-vyāpti* and has no doubt in his being *Śiva* actually, can by resorting to these *dhāraṇās* establish himself in true *Śiva-vyāpti* and thus in the actuality of *Bhairava-awstha.* Following *dhāraṇās* are precisely for such aspirants.

90. Due to the delusive influence of Māyā, the supreme reality reflects in the empirical state like kalā etc. as various tattvas. Contemplating over this reality with intense

attention removes the sense of separateness from the absolute. [95 – 72]

91. 'The knowledge we harbor, is without any cause or foundation, irrelevant and delusive with respect to the absolute truth' . With deep contemplation on this, my dear, one attains to Śiva. [99 – 76]

92. 'Like a magical show without a real being is this universe'. Convinced of the non-essentiality of this illusory spectacle one attains the lasting peace and freedom from the illusion. [133 – 108]

93. The Self is eternal without any alteration. Knowledge and activity therefore do not belong to it since they are only relevant to the realm of objectivity which is changeable and thus merely void. This contemplation must be resorted to for complete vikalpa-mukti. [134 – 109]

94. The concept of purity in the people of conditioned understanding is an outcome of vikalpas and therefore it is an impurity from the Śaiva perspective. Freedom from vikalpas only is the true purity and brings real happiness. [123 – 98]

95. Perfect detachment and intense devotion unfolds a spiritual understanding

in an aspirant. Contemplation over it (when sustained) leads to the attainment of Śiva. [121 – 96]

96. Uniformly poised towards a friend or a foe, and honour or dishonor due to the conviction that everything after all is an aspect of Brahma, the aspirant remains eternally happy. [125 – 100]

97. Remaining without attachment and aversion for anything whatsoever, makes the aspirant free of these conflicting vikalpas, poised and worthy of divine consciousness. [126 – 101]

98. That which is non-objective and therefore un-graspable, that which is void but pervades and penetrates everything, even non-existence, all that is Bhairava. Deep contemplation over it provides enlightenment and identification with Bhairava. [127 -102]

99. The mind may go anywhere, inward or outward, it will only find Śiva, because Śiva is omnipresent. Intense contemplation on this reality will ultimately lead to attaining to Śiva. [116 – 91]

100. 'Everything, even the most ordinary, is an expression of Bhairava, there being nothing which is not Bhairava'.

Contemplating this with conviction one attains non-duality. [124 – 99]

101. " As waves rise in water and flame emerges from fire, or else the rays of light project out of sun, so does this multi-phased universe with all the differentiation emerge out of me, the Bhairava ".
[110 – 86]

102. "The greatest Lord Śiva is all-knowing, all-doing and present everywhere ! I am that Lord Śiva ". This strong assertion brings the exaltation to this state. [109 – 85]

103. Knowing intensely (in turya consciousness) that the duality state of waking, impression state of dream and unknowing state of deep-sleep are only the forms of Bhairava one is drenched in the Amrit of Turya-consciousness. [86 – 63]

104. "When desire and knowledge do not spring up in me, what am I in that state ? " Truly am I the essence, the reality itself ! Contemplating thus one gets absorbed and identified with the ultimate. [97 – 74]

105. "Bhairava is the light of consciousness that gives the being to the entire universe by pervading and dwelling in its entirety ". With this contemplation,

reciting the word Bhairava gives actual attainment of Bhairava. [130 – 105]

106. All-pervasive, Omnipresent, Eternal, self-supporting! Knowing the Lord to be all that and contemplating ceaselessly on these aspects of Bhairava gives attainment of it. [132 – 107]

107. When the aspirant knows one's own body as well as every thing all around as pure consciousness, then, diving into dwādaśāňt with complete one pointed awareness brings unity with Śiva. [50 – 27]

108. Meditating on Śiva-tattva, the essence of everything of the entire universe to all its limits, by the technique of adhvās results in the supreme awakening. [57 – 34]

109. Seated on a seat or a bed and contemplating that one's body is support-less helps dissolve one's mental flux and all kinds of underlying thoughts subsequently vanish. [82 – 59]

110. Seated with eyes closed and the mind firm, one must focus one's attention on kapāla (interior of cranium, and as ka-pāla the domain of the union of Parā-Śakti, and Shiva). Contemplating like that one shall attain to the supreme realization. [34 – 11]

111. Bondage and liberation are not for me. These scare-crows are for the frightened. The universe is nothing more than a reflection of the reality in budhi like the sun in water. [135 – 110]

112. Ġāna is the revealer of everything, and again, self of everyone is revealer. Since both have the same swabhāv, there is no difference between Ġānī and Ġāna.
[137 – 112]

Glossary

Note-1 *(Zero-point energy, p-6)*
....For the first time in history, a lot of media attention is being paid to the sea of energy that pervades all of space. It just happens to be the biggest sea of energy that is known to exist and we're floating inside it....

....What is it? Many people are not sure what "zero point energy" (ZPE) is. Most agree that virtual particle fluctuation contributes to it and van der Waals forces don't explain everything.......

....How can the energy be converted to a usable form? What are the basic explanations of ZPE and the new discoveries, which have rocked the U.S. Patent Office, Physical Review Letters, Science, Scientific American, and the New York Times? Why is ZPE implicated in the latest confirmation of cosmological antigravity? Can the Casimir effect be a source of energy?.......

.... During the early years of quantum mechanics, Paul Dirac theorized that the vacuum was actually filled with particles in negative energy states (Proc. R. Soc. London A, 126, 360, 1930) thus giving rise to the concept of the "physical vacuum" which is not empty at all. Quantum mechanics also predicted that invisible particles could become materialized for a short time and that these virtual particle appearances should exert a force that is measurable. Hendrik B. G. Casimir (Phys. Rev. 73, 360, 1948) not only predicted the presence of such a force but also explained why van der Waals forces dropped off unexpectedly at long range separation between atoms,......

.... Another historically valid test in the verification of ZPE has been what's been called the "Lamb shift." Measured by Dr. Willis Lamb in the 1940's, it actually showed the effect of zero point fluctuations on atomic levels. The electrons are slightly shifted upwards in their atomic orbits. (The implications of the Lamb shift were never fully explained......

...Excerpts from...[© 1999 Thomas Valone, M.A., P.E., ...Ref. 1]

Note-2 *(Switches, p-10)*
....The cortical sheet contains tens of cortical areas, each with their own anatomical and functional characteristics. Cortico-cortical fibers connect these areas, such that information can flow from sensory to other sensory areas, or to motor areas, and vice-versa. These connections define a hierarchy among these areas. Primary visual cortex (V1, also striate cortex or area[17]), where visual information enters the cortex, is the lowest area in the visual sensori-motor hierarchy. From V1, information is distributed to the extra-striate areas (like V2, V3, V4, MT), and from there to areas in the parietal and temporal cortex, constituting the 'dorsal' (parietal), and 'ventral' (temporal) visual streams[12]. The dorsal stream is mainly translating sensory input into motor behavior, while the ventral stream plays a central role in object recognition[13] ..

.... Excerpts from....
["Can Neurosciences reveal the true nature of Consciousness", ... Ref 2]

Note-3 *(Quarks, p-13)*
... Quarks and Leptons are the building blocks which build up matter, i.e., they are seen as the "elementary particles". In the present standard model, there are six "flavors" of quarks. They can successfully account for all known mesons and baryons (over 200). The most familiar baryons are the proton and neutron, which are each constructed from 'up' and 'down' quarks. Quarks are

observed to occur only in combinations of two quarks (mesons), three quarks (baryons)A .....
.... Excerpts from....
["Quarks" , ... Ref. 3]

Note-4 *(Fuzzy observables, p-13)*
..... 'Ordinary objects' (i) are composed of a large but finite number of un-extended objects (particles that do not 'occupy' space),22,23 (ii) 'occupy' finite volumes of space, and (iii) are stable: they neither explode nor collapse the moment they are created. Thanks to the quantum theory, we know now that the existence of such objects hinges on the *fuzziness* of the relative position and momentum of their constituents. This, rather than our uncertainty about the values of these observables, is what 'fluffs out' matter. But the mathematically rigorous and philosophically sound way of quantifying a fuzzy observable (and of defining its 'fuzziness') is to assign probabilities to the possible outcomes of a measurement of this observable.25 This is the reason why the quantum formalism is a probability algorithm, and why measurements play a fundamental role in all axiomatizations of standard quantum mechanics.....

.... Excerpts from....
[' The Two Faces of Reality ' , ... Ref. 4]

Note –5 *(Vimarśamaya-Prakāśa, p-19)*
Trika perspective of visualizing the absolute ultimate reality as *Vimarśamaya-Prakāśa* is the core of the entire philosophy of this school. Naming, un-namable reality *Anuttra*, (the unsurpassable), the one that is an absolutely incomprehensible indeterminacy, considered from whichever perspective, while still absolutely accessible to any and every existent, and therefore the greatest enigma

that can ever be, as *Vimarśamaya-Prakāśa* , is therefore the greatest of the projections of this approach. *Prakaśa*, the presence, the being of this reality, like light needs no proof or confirmation for its being, since it is *vyāpak,* (evident in itself,) as the sense of *our being* is to us, as much as it also projects everything else into being, into presence, into its prominence by virtue of its potency in being conscious, having *Vimarśa*, the consciousness of its being, of what it is in its entirety. In fact, in *Trika* it is understood as *aham-vimarsha*, the sense of 'my being to me'. This sense is inherent in *every* conscious existent. It connotes, not only the subjective being, but also the objective as well as the entire related understanding and knowledge, not only in the immanent domain of the empirical existence, but actually beyond, into the domain of indeterminate, transcendental existence, as homogenized, absolutely undifferentiated singular in-effable reality, __ the actuality of the fundamental being differentiating into various aspects of being, the *tattvas*, down the *tattva-sopān*, in its differentiating expansion up to earth, and all that it bears, (all that this terrestrial world comprises, and is sustained by), including the empirical experient. This fundamental being, the pure absolute consciousness, the *sattatva* of everything, is an un-definable, un-locatable dot of absolute potency, the *Parma-Śiva*, the supreme-being *Maheśvara* with the absolutely un-restricted potency, its *Maheśvarya* :

(स्वात्मा महेश्वरः। माहेश्वर्यं सर्वशक्तित्वम्।
सर्वशक्तित्वम् (नाम) अहंविमर्शः ।
कर्तरि ज्ञातरि स्वात्मन्यादिसिद्धे महेश्वरे ।)
Ref. ... (IPK 1.1.2)

Its two aspects, also called *Śiva* and *Śakti* , connote the being and the potency perspectives. *Śiva* is an undifferentiating (*abheda*) and transcendental (*parā*) reality ever, while (its) *Shakti* is potency ever unrestricted in projecting itself as both, differentiated or undifferentiated (*bheda* and a*bheda*) aspects, in transcendental as well as immanent (*parā* and *aparā*) domains. In fact She projects ' all the domains ' out of Herself. This *bhedābheda* or *parāpara* visualization of *Shakti* is the greatest amazement (*Vismaya*) that the ultimate potency of *Parama-Śiva* projects, as is experienced and revealed by *Trika* sages. *Śiva,* poised within Himself, in His *ātma-viśrānti* is entirely beyond any expression or visualization, while *Śakti* expresses Herself variously. She is self-affirming *Aham-vimarśa in Śiva,* as she is His bliss awareness, the '*ānanda* of *being*' that makes Him *Ćidānand-ghana,* 'the intensely-dense bliss of being'. She springs from Him as the throb (*spanda*) of creativity, the *Ćiti,* with its potency of absolute autonomy and sovereignty (*Swatantriya-shakti*), to execute the creation. Taking the form of *Iććha* and expanding into *ġāna* and *kriyā,* She pours Herself out as *parāvāk,* to form into the *swarūpa-sṛšṭi,* the *bimba,* the matrix of creation in the transcendental domain. Becoming then the *parāparā Visarga-Śakti,* She manifests Herself as its *pratibimba* in the form of actual manifestation, the *Sṛšṭi* in the empirical domain, on transforming Herself into the *aparā Visarga-Śakti.* She is simultaneously the *Swatantriya-Śakti* in transcendental unity-consciousness as also the executor of the whole creation in the empirical difference-consciousness domains through the *Vameśwari* (that projects universe) *Śaktis* of *Khećari* (बोधगगने चरन्ति इति खेचरीय: प्रमातृभूमिस्थित: ...[Sp.S]), *Goćari* (अंत:करणभूमि ...[Sp.S]) , the *Śaktis* of inner discerning faculties, *Digćari* (दिशासु बाह्यभूमिषु चरन्ति ...[Sp.S]), the *indriya-Śakti* and *Bhūćari-Śakti* (भू:रूपादि पंचात्मकम मेयापदम् तत्र चरन्ति इति भूचरिय: ...[Sp.S]), the aspects of *pańća-mahā-bhūta,* remaining ever available for the sustenance of the empirical experient by residing in, and connected to him, allowing him the choice of getting more and more involved in the empirical delusions, or rise beyond, into the transcendental sameness with *Śiva. Śakti* therefore acts as conduit or the worm-hole for the empirical experient as *Khechari,* as well as *Mahā-prāna, or Mahā-Kuńdalini,* the postures in which She dwells in him, for his withdrawal into *Parā-Sańvid.* She

provides an empirical experient always a connection from his *savikalpa Vaikhari* state to the *nirvikalpa, Parā* state through *Paśyanti* and *Madhyamā*, always lurking there, in undifferentiated phases of consciousness without ever going on a holiday. She springs up as *Pratibhā* from time to time (प्रतिभातत्त्वं शक्तिलक्षणम् ...[NTU-I-191]). Ever there, *Śakti*, the *Guru-vaktra* (the mouth of the ultimate *Guru*, the *Parama-Śiva*) in all her aspects is accessible to us always. What is needed is Awareness, choice-less (*vikalpa-mukt*) and attentive, for the cross-over. This is what *Trika* offers ! And precisely this, we are going to investigate in the pages ahead.
[explanatory note, with quote's from Ref. 5, 6, 7.]

Note – 6 *(Abhinavagupta, p-26)*
... Abhinavagupta (approx. 950 - 1020 AD), one of India's greatest philosophers, mystics and aestheticians, also considered an important musician, poet, dramatist, exegete, theologian, and logician exercised strong influences on Indian culture.

Born in the Valley of Kashmir in a family of scholars and mystics he studied all the schools of philosophy and art of his time under the guidance of as many as fifteen (or more) teachers and gurus.[8]and completed over 35 works, the largest and most famous of which is Tantrāloka, an encyclopedic treatise on all the philosophical and practical aspects of Trika and Kaula (known today as Kashmir Shaivism). His very important contribution in the field of philosophy of aesthetics (Abhinavabhāratī), commentary of Nāṭyaśāstra of Bharata Muni,being no less important.

Abhinavgupt born into a Kashmiri Pandit family and named Shankara earned from his master, the title "Abhinavagupt" meaning "competence and authoritativeness". Jayaratha (1150-1200 AD), Abhinavagupta's most important commentator, also reveals three more meanings of this title: "being ever vigilant", "being present everywhere" and "protected by

praises". Raniero Gnoli, the only Sanskrit scholar who completed a translation of Tantrāloka in a European language, mentions that "Abhinavagupta" also means "new", as a reference to the ever-new creative force of his mystical experience.
Jayaratha comments that Abhinavagupta was in possession of all the six qualities required for being a recipient of the tremendous level of śaktipāta, as described in the sacred texts (Śrīpūrvaśāstra): an unflinching faith in God, realization of mantras, control over objective principles (referring to the 36 tattvas), successful conclusion of all the activities undertaken, poetic creativity and spontaneous knowledge of all disciplines.

Abhinavagupta himself defines his origin as "yoginībhū" - "born of a yoginī". In Kashmir Shaivism and especially in Kaula it is considered that a progeny of parents "established in the divine essence of Bhairava", is endowed with exceptional spiritual and intellectual prowess. Such a child is supposed to be "the depository of knowledge", who "even as a child in the womb, has the form of Shiva".

His mother, Vimalā (Vimalakalā) died when Abhinavagupta was just two years old; as a consequence of losing his mother, to whom he was reportedly very attached, he grew more distant from the world and all the more focused only on the spiritual endeavor.

His father, Narasiṃhagupta, after his wife's death favored an ascetic lifestyle, even while raising his three children. He had a cultivated mind and a heart "outstandingly adorned with devotion to Mahesvara (Shiva)" (in Abhinavagupta's own words). He was Abhinavagupta's first teacher, instructing him in grammar, logic and literature.

Lakṣmasṇagupta, a direct disciple of Somānanda, in the lineage of Trayambaka, was highly respected by Abhinavagupta. He taught him all the schools of monistic thought : Krama, Trika and Pratyabhijña (except Kula).

Śambhunātha taught him the fourth school (Ardha-trayambaka). This school is in fact Kaula, emanated from Trayambaka's daughter.

For Abhinavagupta, Śambhunātha was the most admired guru. Describing the greatness of his master, he compared Śambhunātha with the Sun, in his power to dispel ignorance from the heart, and, in another place, with "the Moon shining over the ocean of Trika knowledge".

Abhinavagupta received Kaula initiation through Śambhunātha's wife (acting as a dūtī or conduit). The energy of this initiation is transmitted and sublimated into the heart and finally into consciousness. Such a method is difficult but very rapid and is reserved for those who shed their mental limitations and are pure.

It was Śambhunātha who wanted him to write Tantrāloka. As guru, he had a profound influence in the structure of Tantrāloka[37] and in the life of its creator, Abhinavagupta. ...

..... Excerpts from.....
[wikipedia.org 'Abhinavagupta'. Ref. 8, 9, 10, 11.]

Note – 7 *(Devi – Bhairava Samvād, p-37)*
Āgamas, ' the teachings in the traditional scriptures' have come down to us in the form of *Sūtras* generally. *Sūtras* are crisp and very brief, potent and profound communications with multi-dimensional enlightenment that can be interpreted in lots of different ways, (अनन्तार्थसूत्रणात् सूत्रम् . PTV-102/8). The mode of '*Devi asking Bhairava*' or '*Bhairava speaking*' often resorted to in such teachings needs to be given attention to. Our channels of thoughts and introspection, comprehensions and creativity, listening and responding, etc. route from our comprehensible and differentiating understanding and speech at the *Vaikhari* level, through *Madhyama* where differentiation just begins and the thought word begin linking, and *Paśyanti*,

where the understanding percolates in an un-differentiated form and feel from *Parā* , the transcendental source and referent of all understanding absolute. The channels are both *a-ha-m* and *ma-ha-a* directional, that is, route from *parā-samvid,* the supreme consciousness through these channels up to *Vaikhari* at *aparā* level and back. The listening, evaluation, comprehension, and creativity, all follow this track of manifestation. It is *Parā-Samvid* , that becomes the seeker or questioner at *Madhyama level* and *Bhairava* , at the *Parā* level, that answers or unfolds the truth or understanding. This unfolding is recollected by it at the domain of succession and differentiation in *Madhyama,* for its onward expression at *Vaikhari.* Devi is none other than *Bhairava* Himself or the *Parā-Samvid* in various aspects of *Guru* and *śiṡya* , or *Śiva* and *Śakti* , or any other of the interacting capacities. Abhinava in *Parātrīśikā-vivaraṇa* says:
(एवं भगवती पश्यन्ती ... परोक्षतया)...[PTV-3/14-18].

<u>*Note -8*</u> (*Worm-hole, p-44*)
A hypothetical mouth, tunneling as a traversable shortcut between two separate, remotely existing time-space domains, named *worm-hole,* was first hypothesized by an American theoretical physicist John Archibald Wheeler in 1957. The concept is since being considered for its actual feasibility. Many physicists believe that Casimir effect, among certain other suggestions made so far, may hold the key for this inter-universal fastest transit. [see *Worm-hole, Wikipedia,* on net]. The word has been used here to convey the transition from the objective world-domain existence into the subjective and fundamental transcendental state of existence, one full of succession and changing finites and other the eternal, complete, and absolutely autonomous sovereign state of being.
[see *Worm-hole, Wikipedia,* on net]

Note – 9 *(New found Phonemes, p-121)*
All the phonemes in *Sanskrit* language are based on the *Mātṛkā* order and get created due to the *spanda* of creativity urge in *Anuttra 'a'* [अ] the *tithīśa*, the *Soma*, (the *saĥ-Umā*, _ always with *Umā* the *Śakti*, as the great Lord *Śiva*).This creativity-urge, His *Swabhāva*, always pulsating as *ā* , the *ānanda*, the *Parā-Visarga*, gives rise out of it, to other *tithīshās*, i, ī, & u, ū, the *Iććhā* and *Ġāna* aspects, with *sarva-sarvātmakta* in them all. These *kalās*, (the *Soma-kalās*, the *Somāmśās*, the *tithīśās*,) through *Kriyā* activity within them create other *varṇās* or *kalās* forming the *Swarūpa-sṛšti*, the *bimba* or the matrix of creation which includes the eternal *samhār-bhāva*, the *anuswār 'um'* and the eternal *parāparā Visarga –bhāva*, ' *aĥ* ' . This *bimba* through coagulation gives rise to all *vyanjans* and thus to the entire *varṇa-sṛšti*.

The *Kriyā* aspect envisaged in it all is based on the eagerness of *tithīśās* for creation. *Kriyā* for the objectivity can not be seen in isolation as creativ*ity only* without the *samhāra-bhāva*. Creativity is the aspect of *Śakti-bhāva* which is not un-accompanied by the *Śiva-bhāva*. *Visarga* connotes projection as well as the withdrawal, *sṛšti* and *samhāra bhāva* both. This observation has led to the aspect of *Śiva-bhāva*, the penetration of *Anuttra* into its *Iććhā* and *Ġāna* aspects as the inverse penetration in addition to the penetration of *Iććhā* and *Ġāna* aspects into *Anuttra*. Visualization of This *Kriyā* aspect has yielded some new phonemes. This is not a mere intellectual pursuit of an *ideal* activity. It resulted out of a necessity. The author was actually working on the phonetic logic of speech, trying to develop a transliteration script for Kashmiri language, which had no reliable script, and the fumbling for which had led to many controversies and a consequent loss confusion in the language transcription. This *Kriyā* aspect consideration has yielded a smooth development of a genuine and natural *lipi* for it. The whole consideration and growth of this *lipi* is systematically documented in the manuscript which is in the process of publication. This new-found *lipi* including these new-found phonemes can be certainly helpful also in

transcribing many other of the linguistic variations of different languages, and prevailing dialects in India.
[Ref. "*Māṭṛkā, pūrna-devanāgrī lipi*" ref.13]

<u>*Note – 10*</u> *(Bhairava-bila, p-183)*
In the ascension process of *Mahā-Kuňđalinī Śakti through Sušumnā,* there is a point above the apex of head, above the seat of *Sahasāra-ćakra,* outside the physical orientation of body, which is known as *Bhairava-bila.* The union of *Kuňđalinī-Śakti* with *Sahasrāra-ćakra* yields the experient the bliss of *Parā-Bhattarika* and the ultimate *Śiva-vyāpti* within the body while *Bhairava-bila* privides an escape route from the clutches of the body to the *yogi* at the highest pinnacle of the journey _a complete *mokša* from the worldliness, the approach contested by Abhinava from the *Trika* point of view. He says that when nothing including the body and the *sansār* is a bondage, then this approach is not in-dispensible.
(ईदृश एव नाभिहृत्कण्ठतालुब्राह्मभैरवबिलाद्यधिष्ठानकमप्राप्त ....) ... says Abhinava in *Parātrīśika-vivaraňa* .... [PTV – 7/24 onward].

<u>*Note – 11*</u> *(Lambikā, p-186)*
... Collecting together spontaneously and poised to descend *(adhomukha)* into the central channel at *Lambikā,* an area at the roof of the soft palate, the *Lambikā-sthāna,* (the loation for *Lambikā*) *apāna* and *prāṇa* initially find the right *Lambikā* closed (as it is ordinarily blocked, while the left two *Lambikā* channels are normally functional). Thus the ordinary course of breathing stops and a chocking sensation occurs. Then the right *Lambikā* opens and the breath rushes down. An internal sound like the sound of ocean is felt and the breaths pass through the central channel to *mūlādhāra-ćakra* which is set into rotation. This

channel is the pathway for the *Kuňđalinī* to rise, *ćakra* after *ćakra*, to *Brumadhya* (*the ūrdhva mārga*). There is however another channel of *Lambikā* through which, in rare cases the *Prāṇana* rises directly to *Brahmrandhra*. In all there are four *prāṇa* pathways, the four *Lambikā* channels.

.....Exerpt from ....

(*'Self-realization in Kasmir Shaivism'*...... ref. 14. - 106/22 Onwards) and (*'Pratyabhijñāhṛdayam'* ,the secret of self recognition, Ref. 16, p-151).

<u>*Note – 12*</u> *(Kaulikī Kuňđalinī, p-187)*

In *Kula** system of Kashmir *Śaivism*, *Kuňđalinī-Śakti*, the creative energy of Lord *Śiva* is described as *Kaulikī Kuňđalinī* with three-fold aspects namely *Prāṇa–Kuňđalinī*, *ćit–Kuňđalinī* and *Parā-Kuňđalinī*. *Prāṇa– Kuňđalinī* also called *Śakti–Kuňđalinī*, in Her creative mission, transforms her *Visarga-Shakti* into *Prāṇana*, the seed of *Prāṇa* the vibrating energy. On conception through a sex-act, it is this vibrating-energy of *Prāṇa– Kuňđalinī* that gets installed in the foetus and takes care of it by all the various required means, although remaining dormant in the location of *Kanda* in the forming body. This *Śakti–Kuňđalinī*, although not resting in objectivity, becomes, by merely directing Her will out (*bahir-aunmukhya*), the cause of all objectivity. Installing the aspect of *ġāna* , She gives rise to the entire system of *ġānendriya* (including subjective and objective aspects of its manifestations, providing at the same time a worm-hole for *Jivas* to achieve *pūranāhanta* through the *samāveśa* of the *kama-kalā* of these aspects [see page 192 of the main script]).

Piercing by *Samāvaśa*, into the blanks between any two thoughts or breaths (as mentioned already) yields the experience of the arousal of *Prāṇa– Kuňđalinī*, lifting the fortunate aspirants to the *Parābhattarika* experience of its unity with its *Shiva* aspect in *Sahasrāra-ćakra*. There are two more ways mentioned in scriptures in which this manifestation of arousal and its accomplishment happens in more fortunate yogis with intense urge and *vairāġa* .

Arousal of *ćit–Kuňđalinī* is experienced by yogis by intense attentive awareness between two breaths, two thoughts, two actions or between two aspects of decay and rise of any two phenomenon. As in the arousal of *Prāṇa–Kuňđalinī*, *Prāṇa* and *apāna* merging to form *Prānana* which pierces *Kuňđalinī*, the experiencing of a crawling sensation at *mūādhāra* and intense bliss like that of sexual orgasm (only more intensely) is experienced. With it dawns the recognition of the real nature of self as bliss-consciousness. Steadied on it for a while, piercing of *Brumadhya ćakra* is experienced with an abrupt breathing out once and its halting outside. Simultaneously the ascent of *ćit– Kuňđalinī* to *Sahasrāra* takes place. *Ćit–Kuňđalinī* fills the entire *Sušumnā* channel from *mūlādhāra* to *Brahmrandhara.* Yogi finds at this point his eyes opening wide and his breath halting outside. This lasts a moment when again introversion happens and he enjoys the bliss of *ćit– Kuňđalinī*. Again in a while, the eyes open and breath is pushed out to halt there and the world is experienced as drenched in bliss and ecstasy when again introversion into *ćit– Kuňđalinī* happens. This is repeated again and again providing the yogi an experience of the state of *Jeevan-mukta.* This experience is termed as *Krama-mudrā*

Yet another manifestation of the arousal of *Kuňđalinī* can happen. This kind of *tīvra-Shaktipāt* happens to very rare and most fortunate ones with no trace whatsoever of the worldly aspirations, those with complete *vairaġa* and the singular urge for *pūrnāhanta.* Divine grace descends on such rare persons instantaneously. *Samāveśa* with any of the above mentioned aspects or otherwise on an abrupt vacuity happening anyway can trigger the gush of *Prānana* towards *Kuňđalinī* causing it to rise like a fountain to *Sahasrāra* fo instantaneous *Parābhattarika* experience of the highest degree launching the fortunate one into a durable *Krama-mudrā.* He then swings back and forth like a swing into the bliss within and bliss without, experiencing *unmīlana* and *nimīlana awastha*, and thus getting established in *pratimīlana* state enjoying perpetual Jagadānanda. He attains to the *Niranjan-tattva* the actuality of *Bhairava awastha* !

(Details given above are in addition to those at pages 185-187)
(* Ref.-14, 94/6, ;)

<u>Note – 13</u> *(Piśāćāveśaĥ, p-188)*
... Due to bad luck of yogi sometimes *Kuňđalinī* rises in reverse direction. When the breath is sipped down in the central vein and reaches *Mūlādhāra – ćakra,* it does not pierce it or set it into rotation, instead it rises directly, without piercing any other *ćakra* up to *brumadhya* and sets it into rotation. Thereafter it begins descending downward and penetrate *ćakras* at throat, heart etc. in descending order up to *Mūlādhāra.* This is reverse penetration or rise of *Kuňđalinī* called *Piśāćāveśaĥ (trance of ghosts)* that makes the yogi a victim of unending series of obstacles for the rest of life. It happens when the aspirant is much involved with the objective cravings of the world or has gained utter displeasure or curse of *Guru. (These Ghoratarī energies of Rudra carry the individual entangling him in the joy of senses ...Mālinī Vijaya Tantra:III-31.)*

.....Exerpt from ....
(*'Self-realization in Kasmir Shaivism'* ...... Ref. 14. – 108/9, onwards) and
(*'Kashmir Shaivism the secret supreme'* ... Ref. 15 - 125/21 onwards)

Note – 14 *(States of being, p-211)*

A deeper visualization of the three states, as Kšemrāja in reference to this study (in the context of *Mālinī vijayā*) describes, can lead us into a wider perspective of understanding of these states, and therefore a greater penetration of *turya* into them. Waking, as considered earlier, is associated with the objective experience. In such experiencing, the experiencer has a sharp focus entirely on the objective things to the exclusion of everything else, that is, a complete identification with the object. Secondly, there can be an association or identification mainly with the *knowledge* (of any kind) of the object, while the focus on object recedes into the background. Thirdly, the attention of the experiencer mainly focused on the experiencing aspect (of an experience), with a feeble awareness of the object and the knowledge of it. This puts the experience in prominence with respect to the object and its related knowledge. Fourth, there can be a wakefulness or entire attention of the subject on himself, the experiencer, (without the slightest trace of anything else). This brings the focus entirely on the subject in the wakeful state with no involvement with the object or its knowledge whatsoever. In *philosophic* terminology, the four above-mentioned states respectively put the experiencer in *abuddha, buddha, prabuddha,* and *suprabuddha* states of awareness. These states are identified also as *jāgrat-jāgrat, jāgrat-swapna, jāgrat-suśupti* and *jāgrat-turya* respectively indicating wakefulness actually towards *i)* objects, *ii)* ideation of objects (*swapna*), *iii)* deep-sleep (*suśupti*) towards the objective existence and *iv)* the subjective aspect of existence, the consciousness. These states in other words indicate *un-awakened, awakened, well-awakened,* and *fully-awakened* attitudes towards the real-self, the consciousness aspect of being, representing respectively the *prameya, pramāna, pramātā,* and *pramiti* postures of consciousness in the manifestation. All these states of wakefulness seen in the perspective of the objective (*prameya*) world are termed *pindastha.*

Dream representing the *vikalpa* or the ideation state specific to the dreamer, irrespective of the objective existence at that instant, can similarly be seen in four different sub-states. Full wakefulness to, or focus on the dream by the dreamer provides a perception of distinct and specific dream-experience (called *swapna-jāgrat* or *gatāgat*) to the dreamer, while a dream, incoherent in its presentation (*suvikśipt*) represents a dreamy-state within the dream itself. It is a scattered focus on the *vikalpas* or ideations. This state is termed *swapna-swapna*, (*vikalpas* within *vikalpas* or ideation within ideation). Perception of a dream well-related, recognized and coherent within the dream elements and the dreamer is *samgat*. Such a dream termed *swapna-suśupti causes* no distraction or confusion to the dreamer who enjoys a peaceful sleep simultaneously. To a yogi with *turya* experience, the pure subjective state of being, a state of dream called *swapna-turya* can occur. In this state the dreamer is conscious of his *being* and *knows* that he is dreaming, remaining all the while in control of his consciousness, thus fully integrated (*susamāhit*). In whatever phase of dream, the dreamer, dwelling in ideation, *vikalpa*, or pure-self, is un-involved in the actual objective world, thus remaining *padastha*, he experiences a *vyāpti* or pervasion in one's own being.

Suśupti, the deep-sleep is withdrawal of the involvement of consciousness from all kinds of objective activities via *indriyās* or mind. Both remain in abeyance. There however remain some residual traces of certain dormant *vikalpās* lingering even in deep-sleep. Their poppings up (*udit*) in deep-sleep state, brings the focus of consciousness on them. This state of deep-sleep is called *suśupti-jāgrat*. If however, these *vikalpās* crowd up to make their presence deep and thick (*vipul*) *as* in *swapna*, the state is identified as *suśupti-swapna*. Absence of *vikalpās*, a complete abeyance of mind and *indriyās*, is a state of rest and peace, when everything is in harmony with *prāṇa*. Termed as *Śānta awastha*, it is *suśupti-suśupti* state. The fourth state of deep-sleep or *Suśupti*, is a state completely washed out of all *vikalpās*, dormant or active, a completely *vikalpa-*

mukt awastha, a state of pure *I*-consciousness, the *Śiva* state. This state is termed as *suśupti-turya* or *su-prasanna awastha*. All these four states are *pramātā* or subjective aspects of being.

A wakefulness to *turya*, the consciousness aspect of being, breaks down the boundary conditions imposed on *indriyās*, and the perception of the objective world does not remain confined in *bheda*. The differentiation in the objective existence begins melting down. Everything gets drenched in the light of consciousness, the *turyālok*, and the *sṛšti*, the objective world is viewed differently. This state is *manonmana* or *turya-jāgrat*. This breaks down the limitation of knowledge which then expands into unlimited domains presenting itself as various manifestations of consciousness in all the *vikalpās*. This state is termed as *turya-swapna* or *ananta*. This expansion ultimately encompasses everything. Everything, imminent as well as transcendental is experienced as divine, nothing but the *swatantriya Śakti* of *Śiva*. This state of *turya*, called *sarvārtha* or *praćaya* is *turya-suśupti*. All these *turya* aspects present a *rūpātīta* state in which objects and *vikalpās* are all experienced in an entirely different perspective by the subject who is transformed totally itself also. It is an *ātmavyāpti awastha*.

When this *turyābhog*, the divine rapture of *I*-consciousness becomes steady and uninterrupted, this *praćaya-awastha* becomes *mahā-praćaya-awastha*, in which perfect *Śiva-vyāpti* or *turyātīta* state is experienced. There is no within and without, no transcendental or imminent difference at this stage and *everything* is experienced as *Śiva* by the experiencer who is *Śiva Himself*!

Note – 15 *(Twelve centers of Śakti, p-278)*
Twelve successive (*karma-dvādaśakam or dwādaśasthāna*)centers of *Shakti* through *Sušumna* through which *Kuňđalinī* may rise piercing each or otherwise, are said to be correlated with the twelve vowel sounds. First four of

them are considered *aparā* or *bheda* , next five, *parāparā* or *bhedābheda*, while the last three *parā* and *abheda* centers. First, at the generative organs (*janamārga, the path of birth*) is associated with अ , and the next three, *Mūla* (*Mūlādhāra*), *Kanda, Nabhi*, are respectively assigned आ, इ, ई , while the next five the *Hṛd, Kantha, Tālu, Brumadhya* and *Lalāta* are associated with उ , ऊ , ए , ऐ , ओ . The last three, *Bramarandhra, Śakti and vyāpini* are associated with vowels औ , अं , अः . These are the centers and the vowels on which the specific *dhāranās* are focused as suggested in *dhāranās - 7, verse – 30* through *ānava etc.* approaches.
(*Vijñānabhairava or Divine Consciouness,* Ref. 16, - *p-27*)

<u>*Note - 16*</u> *(Praṇava , P - 256 & 278)*
Śaivāgamas maintain that pure consciousness (*Samvid*) on its mission of creativity transforms itself into *Mahāprāna*, and dwells in *prānis* for their maintenance providing a live link with itself. As an un-struck sound - vibration (*anāhata nāda, Hamsaĥ*) it ceaselessly continues unabated throughout the life of a living being, which by an unqualified attentive awareness (*samāveśa*) with it can take our consciousness to its source, the *Samvid. Dhāranā* 19 of *Viġānā-Bhairava* tells us that subtle contemplation on the *pindamātrās* from *bindu* to *unmanā*, arranged in order of gross letters provides *Śiva-vyāpti* to the aspirant. *Pindamātrās* letters, (ह् , र् , क्ष् , म् , ल् , व् , य् , ण् , णूँ) associated with *Bindu* , *Ardha-ćanra* , *Nirodhini* , *Nada* , *Nādānta* , *Śakti* , *vyāpini* , *Samanā* and *Unmanā* aspects of *Praṇava.* First three aspects of *Praṇava* representing *Vedic mańtra AUM* with three letters (अ उ म्) associated with *Nābhi* , *Hṛdaya* and *mukha* .This *mańtra* is recited at the gross level of *Vaikhari* , while the *pindamātrā mańtra* is contemplated upon at the subtle and subtlest levels that carries on itself into *Śakta* and *Śaiva* domains and is thus *Śākta and Śaiva Praṇava.* The utterance of *Aum* representing the intense point of light, the universal

energy at *Vaikhari* level carries the contemplation onward to the subtle *Bindu*, the *prāṇic* energy that appears at *Brumadhya* (between eyebrows) represents the *prakāśa* of the undivided objective existence. This *prāṇic spanda* later transforms into a subtle inarticulate sound vibration, which disappears subsequently assuming the form of *Ardha-ćandra*, a vibration associated with forehead (*lalāta*). This is the subtlest objective manifestation which ultimately disappears into *Nirodhini*, a demarcating line associated with the uppermost of forehead that prevents the undeserving aspirants from experiencing *Nāda* and the deserving ones from succumbing into the duality. The relative persistence of the four phases of *Praṇava* namely, *Aum*, *Bindu*, *Ardhs-ćandra*, and *Nirodhini* on the time-line is 1, ½, ¼, and 1/8 *matra*.

On crossing *nirodhini* one experiences the mystical vibration of *Nāda* the sound of *anāhata* resonating between the apex of head and the *Suśumnā*. *Nāda* sounding un-struck, un-interrupted (*abhagnśabde*) like a gushing river is experienced only by the deserving (*pātra-kaṃe*). About ten types of *Nāda* as tinkling of bells, becoming subtler and subtler into the sound of flute, *vīna* , buzzing of bees etc. manifest such that the absorption into it (*Nāda*) switches off the external world resulting in the absorption into *ćidākāśa* such that even the *Nāda dissolves*. This is *Nādanta* state manifesting at *Brahmarandhra*. Absorption into this state rids one from the body identification. There onwards an identification of self with *Śakti* residing all over the body, like skin, is experienced, which grows into the pervasion of *Śakti* all-around like sky enveloping everything. This is the state of *Vyāpini*. The relative persistence of these four states of *Praṇava* namely, *Nāda*, *Nādanta*, *Shakti* and *vyapini* are respectively 1/16 , 1/32 , 1/64 , and 1/128 of a mātra.

Deepening of *Samāveśa* with *vyāpni* results in identification with the state of *Samanā*. This is complete *ātma-vyāpti* , the state without any limitations of time, space, body, *vikalpās* or any subservience. It is a state of complete awareness (*bodha*) and action. At this level One can manipulate any aspect of universe if desired, but this is not the final state according *to Trika*. The final state is perfect *Jagadānanda* , the excellence beyond the even the next, the *unmanā* state, the complete freedom from all *vikalpās* born and borne from *māyā* and *prakriti*, with the concern only for *pūrṇa-āhanta*, the *śiva-vyāpti*, the Complete *swatantriya* , the *ānanda-ghana awastha* of *Parama-Śiva*. The relative time-line in deep *Praṇava* contemplation of these two states *samanā* and *unmanā* is put as 1/256 and 1/512 of *mātra*. Contemplation of *Praṇava* provides a touch of all these twelve states, the deepening of the *Samāveśa* of which is not a matter of effort but is spontaneous, depending only on the intensity of the urge for the recognition of ones true self, the *pūrṇa-Āhanta*, and *Vairaġa*, the absence of the last and even the least of the traces of the clutches of desire for the worldly. In fact these higher states are all considered as *śūnya* states, connoting the degree of absence of the cravings for the worldly, which reciprocally are proportionate to the presence of the urge for freedom, the transcendental *swatantriya*. There are six states of vacuity (śūnya) recognized, lowest being associated with the awareness at *Shakti* aspect, called *ūrdhava*-śūnya. Next the *adhaĥ* at *hṛdaya*, and the third at *Madhya* is the state of awareness at *kanṫha* (throat), *brumadhya*, *lalāta* , and *brahmraňdhara*. The fourth one is at *vyāpini*, the fifth at *samanā* , and last, the sixth, is at the level of *unmanā* . After dwelling in these *sūnyās*, and discarding the concern for even these, is the *Parama-Śiva awastha* achieved .

(Explained in the context of *Dhāranā 16 – verse 39 and Dhāranā 19 – verse 42. Of Viġānā-Bhairava**) [* Ref. 17].

<u>*Note – 17*</u> (*Adhaĥ and Ūrdhva Kuňđalinī*, *p-278*)
Rise of *Kuňđalinī Śakti through Sušumna nāđi* involves two distinct activities. First the *prāṇa* and *apāna* merging together as *Prāṇana* pass through the right *Lambika* and gush *down* to *Mūlādhāra* to arouse the *Kuňđalinī*. This going down to *Kuňđalinī* from *Lambika* to *Mūla* is called

adhaĥ-Kuňđalinī. This activity involves binding or shrinking together the two currents of *Prāṇa* and *apāna* (cutting of *vahas*) and a *samaveśa* on them. This process is also known as *Saňkoća* and as the *Prāṇana* is carried onto *Kuňđalinī*, it is also called *vahni* (to carry). When *Prāṇa-Kuňđalinī* rises, to mūla, and other *ćakras*, setting them into rotation, it is called *ūrdhva- Kuňđalinī* , as it is the rise (*ūrdhava*). It is also called *vikāsa*, since it is the pervasion or expansion into various *ćakrās* and expansion into the state of consciousness also. It is *vikāsa* or *permeation*, (or *prasāra*) like poison, and thus called *viša* also.

(*'Pratyabhijñāĥṛdayam'* ,the secret of self recognition, Ref. 16, p- 150, 151)

Note -18 *(pindamātrās* from *bindu* to *unmanā, p-278)*
See note 16.

References

1. " *Understanding Zero-point Energy* ", Thomas Velone, Integrity Research Institute, 1220 L , Washinton D C.

2. "*Can Neurosciences reveal the true nature of Consciousness*"
   Victor A F Lamme, Cognitive Neurosciences Group, Deptt. Of Psychology, University of Amsterdom , Netherlands.

3. "*Quarks*" ,
   http://hyperphysics.phyastr.gsu.edu/hbase/particles/quark.html

4. "*The Two Faces of Reality* ", Ulrich Mohrhoff, Sri Aurobindo Inter-national Centre of Education Pondicherry 605002 India (ujm@auromail.net)

5. "*Īśwara – pratyabhijñā – kārikā vṛtti* " (IPKV)[Utpapadeva,]
   Translation: Raffaele Torrella, (1994.)

6. "*Spanda – Sandoha,*" the commentary of Kšemarāja on the first verse of Spanda-Karika, ed. M R Shastri, KSTS, Srinagar,(1917)

7. "*Netra – tantra uddyota*" by Kšemarāja -vol-I, ed. M S Koul, KSTS.

8. "*Introduction to the tantrāloka*", Navjivan Rastogi, Pages: 20,21,30,31,34,35, 44-54,92.

9. "*Re-accessing Abhinavagupta* " , Navjivan Rastogi, Page:4.

10. "*The kula ritual* " *(chapter 29 of the Tantraaloka), Abhinavagupta*, John R. Dupuche page : 4,7.

11. "*Luce dei Tantra, Tantāloka*", *Abhinavgupta* , Raniero Gnoli page: 3,4

12. "*Parātrīśikā -Vivarana*" (Abhinavagupta vyakhyopeta- granthaḥ) [MLBD, pub. Delhi, For Th. Jaidev Singh.]

13. "*Mātṛkā, pūrna-devanāgrī lipi* " , *(for the transcription of Kashmiri Language* , Tej Rina) [under print]

14. "*Self realization in Kashmir Śaivism* "(oral teachings of Swami Lakšmanjoo, John Hughes), [Sri Satguru Publications N. Delhi]

15. "*Kashmir Shaivism the secret supreme*" Swami Lakšmanjoo, Sri Satguru Publications N. Delhi]

16. "*Pratyabhijñāhṛdayam*, the secret of self recognition", Jaideva Singh, [MLBD, pub. Delhi, For Th. Jaidev Singh.]

17. "*Vijñānabhairava or Divine Consciounes* " , Jaideva Singh, [MLBD, pub. Delhi, For Th. Jaidev Singh.]

Sutras quoted in the book.

Source	**Sutra**	**Page**
(SS – I) - 1	चैतन्यमात्मा	27
(SS – I) - 2	ज्ञानं बन्धः	30
(SS – I) - 3	योनिवर्गः कलाशरीरम्	33
(SS – I) - 4	ज्ञानाधिष्ठानं मातृका	98
(SS – I) - 5	उद्यमो भैरवः	147
(SS – I) - 6	शक्तिचक्रसंधाने विश्वसंहारः	204

(PT) – 4	कौलिकोऽयं विधिर्देवि ! मम हृद्वयोम्न्यवस्थित: कथयामि सुरेशानि ! सद्य: कौलिकसिद्धिदम्	40
(PT) – 5	अथाद्यास्तिथय: सर्वे स्वरा बिन्द्ववसानगा: तदन्त: कालयोगेन सोमसूर्यौ प्रकीर्तितौ	101
(PT) – 6	पृथिव्यादीनि तत्त्वानि पुरुषान्तानि पञ्चसु क्रमात् कादिषु वर्गेषु मकारान्तेषु सुव्रते !	132
(PT) – 7	वाय्वग्निसलिलेन्द्राणां धारणानां चतुष्टयम् तदूर्ध्वं शादि विख्यातं पुरस्ताद् ब्रह्मपञ्चकम्	132
(PT) – 8	अ-मूला तत्क्रमाज्ज्ञेया क्षान्ता सृष्टिरुदाहृता सर्वेषामेव मन्त्राणां विद्यानाञ्च यशस्विनि !	134
(PT) – 9	इयं योनि: समाख्याता सर्वतन्त्रेषु सर्वदा *(only half of 9th sūtra)*	134

Index

Appendix

(original *Sutras* of *Viġānā-Bhairava*)

श्रीदेव्युवाच
श्रुतं देव मया सर्वं रुद्रयामलसम्भवम्
त्रिकभेदमशेषेण सारात्सारविभागशः १
अद्यापि न निवृत्तो मे संशयः परमेश्वर
किं रूपं तत्त्वतो देव शब्दराशिकलामयम् २
किं वा नवात्मभेदेन भैरवे भैरवाकृतौ
त्रिशिरोभेदभिन्नं वा किं वा शक्तित्रयात्मकम् ३
नादबिन्दुमयं वापि किं चन्द्रार्धनिरोधिकाः
चक्रारूढमनच्कं वा किं वा शक्तिस्वरूपकम् ४
परापरायाः सकलमपरायाश्च वा पुनः
पराया यदि तद्वत्स्यात् परत्वं तद्विरुध्यते ५
नहि वर्णविभेदेन देहभेदेन वा भवेत्
परत्वं निष्कलत्वेन सकलत्वे न तद्भवेत् ६
प्रसादं कुरु मे नाथ निःशेषं छिन्धि संशयम्
भैरव उवाच
साधु साधु त्वया पृष्टं तन्त्रसारमिदं प्रिये ७
गूहनीयतमं भद्रे तथापि कथयामि ते
यत्किञ्चित्सकलं रूपं भैरवस्य प्रकीर्तितम् ८
तदसारतया देवि विज्ञेयं शक्रजालवत्
मायास्वप्नोपमं चैव गन्धर्वनगरभ्रमम् ९
ध्यानार्थं भ्रान्तबुद्धीनां क्रियाडम्बरवर्तिनाम्
केवलं वर्णितं पुंसां विकल्पनिहतात्मनाम् १०
तत्त्वतो न नवात्मासौ शब्दराशिर्न भैरवः
न चासौ त्रिशिरा देवो न च शक्तित्रयात्मकः ११
नादबिन्दुमयो वापि न चन्द्रार्धनिरोधिकाः
न चक्रक्रमसंभिन्नो न च शक्तिस्वरूपकः १२
अप्रबुद्धमतीनां हि एता बालविभीषिकाः
मातृमोदकवत्सर्वं प्रवृत्त्यर्थमुदाहृतम् १३
दिक्कालकलनोन्मुक्ता देशोद्देशाविशेषिणी

व्यपदेष्टुमशक्यासावकथ्या परमार्थतः १४
अन्तः स्वानुभवानन्दा विकल्पोन्मुक्तगोचरा
यावस्था भरिताकारा भैरवी भैरवात्मनः १५
तद्वपुस्तत्त्वतो ज्ञेयं विमलं विश्वपूरणम्
एवंविधे परे तत्त्वे कः पूज्यः कश्च तृप्यति १६
एवंविधा भैरवस्य यावस्था परिगीयते
सा परा पररूपेण परादेवी प्रकीर्तिता १७
शक्तिशक्तिमतोर्यद्वत् अभेदः सर्वदा स्थितः
अतस्तद्धर्मधर्मित्वात्पराशक्तिः परात्मनः १८
न वह्नेर्दाहिका शक्तिः व्यतिरिक्ता विभाव्यते
केवलं ज्ञानसत्तायां प्रारम्भोऽयं प्रवेशने १९
शक्त्यवस्थाप्रविष्टस्य निर्विभागेन भावना
तदासौ शिवरूपी स्यात् शैवी मुखमिहोच्यते २०
यथालोकेन दीपस्य किरणैर्भास्करस्य च
ज्ञायते दिग्विभागादि तद्वच्छक्त्या शिवः प्रिये २१
श्रीदेव्युवाच
देवदेव त्रिशूलाङ्ककपालकृतभूषण
दिग्देशकालशून्या च व्यपदेशविवर्जिता २२
यावस्था भरिताकारा भैरवस्योपलभ्यते
कैरुपायैर्मुखं तस्य परादेवी कथं भवेत् २३
यथा सम्यगहं वेद्मि तथा मे ब्रूहि भैरव
श्रीभैरव उवाच
ऊर्ध्वे प्राणो ह्यधो जीवो विसर्गात्मा परोच्चरेत्
उत्पत्तिद्वितयस्थाने भरणाद्भरिता स्थितिः २४
मरुतोऽन्तर्बहिर्वापि वियद्युग्मानिवर्तनात्
भैरव्या भैरवस्येत्थं भैरवि व्यज्यते वपुः २५
न व्रजेन्न विशेच्छक्तिर्मरुद्रूपा विकासिते
निर्विकल्पतया मध्ये तया भैरवरूपता २६
कुम्भिता रेचिता वापि पूरिता या यदा भवेत्

तदन्ते शान्तनामासौ शक्त्या शान्तः प्रकाशते २७
आ मूलात्किरणाभासां सूक्ष्मात्सूक्ष्मतरात्मिकाम्
चिन्तयेत्तां द्विषट्कान्ते शाम्यन्तीं भैरवोदयः २८
उद्गच्छन्तीं तडिद्रूपां प्रतिचक्रं क्रमात्क्रमम्
ऊर्ध्वं मुष्टित्रयं यावत्तावदन्ते महोदयः २९
क्रमद्वादशकं सम्यग्द्वादशाक्षरभेदितम्
स्थूलसूक्ष्मपरस्थित्या मुक्त्वा मुक्त्वान्ततः शिवः ३०
तयापूर्याशु मूर्धान्तं भङ्क्त्वा भ्रूक्षेपसेतुना
निर्विकल्पं मनः कृत्वा सर्वोर्ध्वे सर्वगोद्गमः ३१
शिखिपक्षैश्चित्ररूपैर्मण्डलैः शून्यपञ्चकम्
ध्यायतोऽनुत्तरे शून्ये प्रवेशो हृदये भवेत् ३२
ईदृशेन क्रमेणैव यत्र कुत्रापि चिन्तना
शून्ये कुड्ये परे पात्रे स्वयं लीना वरप्रदा ३३
कपालान्तर्मनो न्यस्य तिष्ठन्मीलितलोचनः
क्रमेण मनसो दार्ढ्यात् लक्षयेल्लक्ष्यमुत्तमम् ३४
मध्यनाडी मध्यसंस्था बिससूत्राभरूपया
ध्यातान्तर्व्योमया देव्या तया देवः प्रकाशते ३५
कररुद्धदृगस्त्रेण भ्रूभेदाद्द्वाररोधनात्
दृष्टे बिन्दौ क्रमाल्लीने तन्मध्ये परमा स्थितिः ३६
धामान्तःक्षोभसंभूतसूक्ष्माग्नितिलकाकृतिम्
बिन्दुं शिखान्ते हृदये लयान्ते ध्यायतो लयः ३७
अनाहते पात्रकर्णेऽभग्नशब्दे सरिद्द्रुते
शब्दब्रह्मणि निष्णातः परं ब्रह्माधिगच्छति ३८
प्रणवादिसमुच्चारात्प्लुतान्ते शून्यभावनात्
शून्यया परया शक्त्या शून्यतामेति भैरवि ३९
यस्य कस्यापि वर्णस्य पूर्वान्तावनुभावयेत्
शून्यया शून्यभूतोऽसौ शून्याकारः पुमान्भवेत् ४०
तन्त्र्यादिवाद्यशब्देषु दीर्घेषु क्रमसंस्थितेः
अनन्यचेताः प्रत्यन्ते परव्योमवपुर्भवेत् ४१

पिण्डमन्त्रस्य सर्वस्य स्थूलवर्णक्रमेण तु
अर्धेन्दुबिन्दुनादान्तःशून्योच्चाराद्भवेच्छिवः ४२
निजदेहे सर्वदिक्कं युगपद्भावयेद्वियत्
निर्विकल्पमनास्तस्य वियत्सर्वं प्रवर्तते ४३
पृष्ठशून्यं मूलशून्यं युगपद्भावयेच्च यः
शरीरनिरपेक्षिण्या शक्त्या शून्यमना भवेत् ४४
पृष्ठशून्यं मूलशून्यं हृच्छून्यं भावयेत्स्थिरम्
युगपन्निर्विकल्पत्वान्निर्विकल्पोदयस्ततः ४५
तनूदेशे शून्यतैव क्षणमात्रं विभावयेत्
निर्विकल्पं निर्विकल्पो निर्विकल्पस्वरूपभाक् ४६
सर्वं देहगतं द्रव्यं वियद्व्याप्तं मृगेक्षणे
विभावयेत्ततस्तस्य भावना सा स्थिरा भवेत् ४७
देहान्तरे त्वग्विभागं भित्तिभूतं विचिन्तयेत्
न किञ्चिदन्तरे तस्य ध्यायन्नध्येयभाग्भवेत् ४८
हृद्याकाशे निलीनाक्षः पद्मसम्पुटमध्यगः
अनन्यचेताः सुभगे परं सौभाग्यमाप्नुयात् ४९
सर्वतः स्वशरीरस्य द्वादशान्ते मनोलयात्
दृढबुद्धेर्दृढीभूतं तत्त्वलक्ष्यं प्रवर्तते ५०
यथा तथा यत्र तत्र द्वादशान्ते मनः क्षिपेत्
प्रतिक्षणं क्षीणवृत्तेर्वैलक्षण्यं दिनैर्भवेत् ५१
कालाग्निना कालपदादुत्थितेन स्वकं पुरम्
प्लुष्टं विचिन्तयेदन्ते शान्ताभासस्तदा भवेत् ५२
एवमेव जगत्सर्वं दग्धं ध्यात्वा विकल्पतः
अनन्यचेतसः पुंसः पुंभावः परमो भवेत् ५३
स्वदेहे जगतो वापि सूक्ष्मसूक्ष्मतराणि च
तत्त्वानि यानि निलयं ध्यात्वान्ते व्यज्यते परा ५४
पीनां च दुर्बलां शक्तिं ध्यात्वा द्वादशगोचरे
प्रविश्य हृदये ध्यायन्मुक्तः स्वातन्त्र्यमाप्नुयात् ५५
भुवनाध्वादिरूपेण चिन्तयेत्क्रमशोऽखिलम्

स्थूलसूक्ष्मपरस्थित्या यावदन्ते मनोलयः ५६
अस्य सर्वस्य विश्वस्य पर्यन्तेषु समन्ततः
अध्वप्रक्रियया तत्त्वं शैवं ध्यात्वा महोदयः ५७
विश्वमेतन्महादेवि शून्यभूतं विचिन्तयेत्
तत्रैव च मनो लीनं ततस्तल्लयभाजनम् ५८
घटादिभाजने दृष्टिं भित्तीस्त्यक्त्वा विनिक्षिपेत्
तल्लयं तत्क्षणाद्गत्वा तल्लयात्तन्मयो भवेत् ५९
निर्वृक्षगिरिभित्त्यादिदेशे दृष्टिं विनिक्षिपेत्
विलीने मानसे भावे वृत्तिक्षीणः प्रजायते ६०
उभयोर्भावयोर्ज्ञाने ध्यात्वा मध्यं समाश्रयेत्
युगपच्च द्वयं त्यक्त्वा मध्ये तत्त्वं प्रकाशते ६१
भावे त्यक्ते निरुद्धा चिन्नैव भावान्तरं व्रजेत्
तदा तन्मध्यभावेन विकसत्यतिभावना ६२
सर्वं देहं चिन्मयं हि जगद्वा परिभावयेत्
युगपन्निर्विकल्पेन मनसा परमोदयः ६३
वायुद्वयस्य संघट्टादन्तर्वा बहिरन्ततः
योगी समत्वविज्ञानसमुद्गमनभाजनम् ६४
सर्वं जगत्स्वदेहं वा स्वानन्दभरितं स्मरेत्
युगपन्स्वामृतेनैव परानन्दमयो भवेत् ६५
कुहनेन प्रयोगेण सद्य एव मृगेक्षणे
समुदेति महानन्दो येन तत्त्वं प्रकाशते ६६
सर्वस्त्रोतोनिबन्धन प्राणशक्त्योर्ध्वया शनैः
पिपीलस्पर्शवेलायां प्रथते परमं सुखम् ६७
वह्नेर्विषस्य मध्ये तु चित्तं सुखमयं क्षिपेत्
केवलं वायुपूर्णं वा स्मरानन्देन युज्यते ६८
शक्तिसङ्गमसंक्षुब्धशक्त्यावेशावसानिन्कम्
यत्सुखं ब्रह्मतत्त्वस्य तत्सुखं स्वाक्यमुच्यते ६९
लेहनामन्थनाकोटैः स्त्रीसुखस्य भरात्स्मृतेः
शक्त्यभावेऽपि देवेशि भवेदानन्दसंप्लवः ७०

आनन्दे महति प्राप्ते दृष्टे वा बान्धवे चिरात्
आनन्दमुद्गतं ध्यात्वा तल्लयस्तन्मना भवेत् ७१
जग्धिपानकृतोल्लासरसानन्दविजृम्भणात्
भावयेद्भरितावस्थां महानन्दस्ततो भवेत् ७२
गीतादिविषयास्वादासमसौख्यैकतात्मनः
योगिनस्तन्मयत्वेन मनोरूढेस्तदात्मता ७३
यत्र यत्र मनस्तुष्टिर्मनस्तत्रैव धारयेत्
तत्र तत्र परानन्दस्वरूपं सम्प्रवर्तते ७४
अनागतायां निद्रायां प्रणष्टे बाह्य गोचरे
सावस्था मनसा गम्या परा देवी प्रकाशते ७५
तेजसा सूर्यदीपादेराकाशे शबलीकृते
दृष्टिर्निवेश्या तत्रैव स्वात्मरूपं प्रकाशते ७६
करङ्किराया क्रोधनया भैरव्या लेलिहानया
खेचर्या दृष्टिकाले च परावाप्तिः प्रकाशते ७७
मृद्वासने स्फिजैकेन हस्तपादौ निराश्रयम्
निधाय तत्प्रसङ्गेन परा पूर्णा मतिर्भवेत् ७८
उपविश्यासने सम्यक्बाहू कृत्वार्धकुञ्चितौ
कक्षव्योम्नि मनः कुर्वन् शममायाति तल्लयात् ७९
स्थूलरूपस्य भावस्य स्तब्धां दृष्टिं निपात्य च
अचिरेण निराधारं मनः कृत्वा शिवं व्रजेत् ८०
मध्यजिह्वे स्फारितास्ये मध्ये निक्षिप्य चेतनाम्
होच्चारं मनसा कुर्वस्ततः शान्ते प्रलीयते ८१
आसने शयने स्थित्वा निराधारं विभावयन्
स्वदेहं मनसि क्षीणे क्षणात्क्षीणाशयो भवेत् ८२
चलासने स्थितस्याथ शनैर्वा देहचालनात्
प्रशान्ते मानसे भावे देवि दिव्यौघमाप्नुयात् ८३
आकाशं विमलं पश्यन् कृत्वा दृष्टिं निरन्तराम्
स्तब्धात्मा तत्क्षणाद्देवि भैरवं वपुराप्नुयात् ८४
लीनं मूर्ध्नि वियत्सर्वं भैरवत्वेन भावयेत्

तत्सर्वं भैरवाकारतेजस्तत्त्वं समाविशेत् ८५
किंचिज्ज्ञातं द्वैतदायि बाह्यालोकस्तमः पुनः
विश्वादि भैरवं रूपं ज्ञात्वानन्तप्रकाशभृत् ८६
एवमेव दुर्निशायां कृष्णपक्षागमे चिरम्
तैमिरं भावयन्रूपं भैरवं रूपमेष्यति ८७
एवमेव निमील्यादौ नेत्रे कृष्णाभमग्रतः
प्रसार्य भैरवं रूपं भावयंस्तन्मयो भवेत् ८८
यस्य कस्येन्द्रियस्यापि व्याघाताच्च निरोधतः
प्रविष्टस्याद्वये शून्ये तत्रैवात्मा प्रकाशते ८९
अबिन्दुमविसर्गं च अकारं जपतो महान्
उदेति देवि सहसा ज्ञानौघः परमेश्वरः ९०
वर्णस्य सविसर्गस्य विसर्गान्तं चितिं कुरु
निराधारेण चित्तेन स्पृशेद्ब्रह्म सनातनम् ९१
व्योमाकारं स्वमात्मानं ध्यायेद्दिग्भिरनावृतम्
निराश्रया चितिः शक्तिः स्वरूपं दर्शयेत्तदा ९२
किञ्चिदङ्गं विभिद्यादौ तीक्ष्णसूच्यादिना ततः
तत्रैव चेतनां युक्त्वा भैरवे निर्मला गतिः ९३
चित्ताद्यन्तःकृतिर्नास्ति ममान्तर्भावयेदिति
विकल्पानामभावेन विकल्पैरुज्झितो भवेत् ९४
माया विमोहिनी नाम कलायाः कलनं स्थितम्
इत्यादिधर्मं तत्त्वानां कलयन्न पृथग्भवेत् ९५
झगितीच्छां समुत्पन्नामवलोक्य शमं नयेत्
यत एव समुद्भूता ततस्तत्रैव लीयते ९६
यदा ममेच्छा नोत्पन्ना ज्ञानं वा कस्तदास्मि वै
तत्त्वतोऽहं तथाभूतस्तल्लीनस्तन्मना भवेत् ९७
इच्छायामथवा ज्ञाने जाते चित्तं निवेशयत्
आत्मबुद्ध्यानन्यचेतास्ततस्तत्त्वार्थदर्शनम् ९८
निर्निमित्तं भवेज्ज्ञानं निराधारं भ्रमात्मकम्
तत्त्वतः कस्यचिन्नैतदेवंभावी शिवः प्रिये ९९

चिद्धर्मा सर्वदेहेषु विशेषो नास्ति कुत्रचित्
अतश्च तन्मयं सर्वं भावयन्भवजिज्जनः १००
कामक्रोधलोभमोहमदमात्सर्यगोचरे
बुद्धिं निस्तिमितां कृत्वा तत्तत्त्वमवशिष्यते १०१
इन्द्रजालमयं विश्वं व्यस्तं वा चित्रकर्मवत्
भ्रमद्वा ध्यायतः सर्वं पश्यतश्च सुखोद्गमः १०२
न चित्तं निक्षिपेद्दुःखे न सुखे वा परिक्षिपेत्
भैरवि ज्ञायतां मध्ये किं तत्त्वमवशिष्यते १०३
विहाय निजदेहास्थां सर्वत्रास्मीति भावयन्
दृढेन मनसा दृष्ट्या नान्येक्षिण्या सुखी भवेत् १०४
घटादौ यच्च विज्ञानमिच्छाद्यं वा ममान्तरे
नैव सर्वगतं जातं भावयन्निति सर्वगः १०५
ग्राह्यग्राहकसंवित्तिः सामान्या सदेहिर्वनाम्
योगिनां तु विशेषोऽस्ति संबन्धे सावधानता १०६
स्ववदन्यशरीरेऽपि संवित्तिमनुभावयेत्
अपेक्षां स्वशरीरस्य त्यक्त्वा व्यापी दिनैर्भवेत् १०७
निराधारं मनः कृत्वा विकल्पान्न विकल्पयेत्
तदात्मपरमात्मत्वे भैरवो मृगलोचने १०८
सर्वज्ञः सर्वकर्त्ता च व्यापकः परमेश्वरः
स एवाहं शैवधर्मा इति दार्ढ्याद्भवेच्छिवः १०९
जलस्येवोर्मयो वह्नेर्ज्वालाभङ्गयः प्रभा रवेः
ममैव भैरवस्यैता विश्वभङ्ग्यो विभेदिताः ११०
भ्रान्त्वा भ्रान्त्वा शरीरेण त्वरितं भुवि पातनात्
क्षोभशक्तिविरामेण परा संजायते दशा १११
आधारेष्वथवाऽशक्त्याऽज्ञानाच्चित्तलयेन वा
जातशक्तिसमावेशक्षोभान्ते भैरवं वपुः ११२
संप्रदायमिमं देवि शृणु सम्यग्वदाम्यहम्
कैवल्यं जायते सद्यो नेत्रयोः स्तब्धमात्रयोः ११३
संकोचं कर्णयोः कृत्वा ह्यधोद्वारे तथैव च

अनच्कमहलं ध्यायन्विशेद्ब्रह्म सनातनम् ११४
कूपादिके महागर्ते स्थित्वोपरि निरीक्षणात्
अविकल्पमतेः सम्यक् सद्यश्चित्तलयः स्फुटम् ११५
यत्र यत्र मनो याति बाह्ये वाभ्यन्तरेऽपि वा
तत्र तत्र शिवावस्था व्यापकत्वात्क्व यास्यति ११६
यत्र यत्राक्षमार्गेण चैतन्यं व्यज्यते विभोः
तस्य तन्मात्रधर्मित्वाच्चिल्लयाद्भरितात्मता ११७
क्षुताद्यन्ते भये शोके गह्वरे वा रणाद्द्रुते
कुतूहले क्षुधाद्यन्ते ब्रह्मसत्तामयी दशा ११८
वस्तुषु स्मर्यमाणेषु दृष्टे देशे मनस्त्यजेत्
स्वशरीरं निराधारं कृत्वा प्रसरति प्रभुः ११९
क्वचिद्वस्तुनि विन्यस्य शनैर्दृष्टिं निवर्तयेत्
तज्ज्ञानं चित्तसहितं देवि शून्यालयो भवेत् १२०
भक्त्युद्रेकाद्विरक्तस्य यादृशी जायते मतिः
सा शक्तिः शाङ्करी नित्यं भावयेत्तां ततः शिवः १२१
वस्त्वन्तरे वेद्यमाने सर्ववस्तुषु शून्यता
तामेव मनसा ध्यात्वा विदितोऽपि प्रशाम्यति १२२
किंचिज्ज्ञैर्या स्मृता शुद्धिः सा शुद्धिः शम्भुदर्शने
न शुचिर्ह्यशुचिस्तस्मान्निर्विकल्पः सुखी भवेत् १२३
सर्वत्र भैरवो भावः सामान्येष्वपि गोचरः
न च तद्व्यतिरेकेण परोऽस्तीत्यद्वया गतिः १२४
समः शत्रौ च मित्रे च समो मानावमानयोः
ब्रह्मणः परिपूर्णत्वादिति ज्ञात्वा सुखी भवेत् १२५
न द्वेषं भावयेत्क्वापि न रागं भावयेत्क्वचित्
रागद्वेषविनिर्मुक्तौ मध्ये ब्रह्म प्रसर्पति १२६
यदवेद्यं यदग्राह्यं यच्छून्यं यदभावगम्
तत्सर्वं भैरवं भाव्यं तदन्ते बोधसंभवः १२७
नित्यं निराश्रये शून्ये व्यापके कलनोज्झिते
बाह्याकाशे मनः कृत्वा निराकाशं समाविशेत् १२८

यत्र यत्र मनो याति तत्तत्तेनैव तत्क्षणम्
परित्यज्यानवस्थित्या निस्तरङ्गस्ततो भवेत् १२९
भया सर्वं रवयति सर्वदो व्यापकोऽखिले
इति भैरवशब्दस्य सन्ततोच्चारणाच्छिवः १३०
अहं ममेदमित्यादि प्रतिपत्तिप्रसङ्गतः
निराधारे मनो याति तद्ध्यानप्रेरणाच्छमी १३१
नित्यो विभुर्निराधारो व्यापकश्चाखिलाधिपः
शब्दान् प्रतिक्षणं ध्यायन् कृतार्थोऽर्थानुरूपतः १३२
अतत्त्वमिन्द्रजालाभमिदं सर्वमवस्थितम्
किं तत्त्वमिन्द्रजालस्य इति दार्ढ्याच्छमं व्रजेत् १३३
आत्मनो निर्विकारस्य क्व ज्ञानं क्व च वा क्रिया
ज्ञानायत्ता बहिर्भावा अतः शून्यमिदं जगत् १३४
न मे बन्धो न मोक्षो मे भीतस्यैता विभीषिकाः
प्रतिबिम्बमिदं बुद्धेर्जलेष्विव विवस्वतः १३५
इन्द्रियद्वारकं सर्वं सुखदुःखादिसङ्गमम्
इतीन्द्रियाणि संत्यज्य स्वस्थः स्वात्मनि वर्तते १३६
ज्ञानप्रकाशकं सर्वं सर्वेणात्मा प्रकाशकः
एकमेकस्वभावत्वात् ज्ञानं ज्ञेयं विभाव्यते १३७
मानसं चेतना शक्तिरात्मा चेति चतुष्टयम्
यदा प्रिये परिक्षीणं तदा तद्भैरवं वपुः १३८
निस्तरङ्गोपदेशानां शतमुक्तं समासतः
द्वादशाभ्यधिकं देवि यज्ज्ञात्वा ज्ञानविज्जनः १३९
अत्र चैकतमे युक्तो जायते भैरवः स्वयम्
वाचा करोति कर्माणि शापानुग्रहकारकः १४०
अजरामरतामेति सोऽणिमादिगुणान्वितः
योगिनीनां प्रियो देवि सर्वमेलापकाधिपः १४१
जीवन्नपि विमुक्तोऽसौ कुर्वन्नपि न लिप्यते
श्री देवी उवाच
इदं यदि वपुर्देव परायाश्च महेश्वर १४२

एवमुक्तव्यवस्थायां जप्यते को जपश्च कः
ध्यायते को महानाथ पूज्यते कश्च तृप्यति १४३
हूयते कस्य वा होमो यागः कस्य च किं कथम्
श्रीभैरव उवाच
एषात्र प्रक्रिया बाह्या स्थूलेष्वेव मृगेक्षणे १४४
भूयो भूयः परे भावे भावना भाव्यते हि या
जपः सोऽत्र स्वयं नादो मन्त्रात्मा जप्य ईदृशः १४५
ध्यानं हि निश्चला बुद्धिर्निराकारा निराश्रया
न तु ध्यानं शरीराक्षिमुखहस्तादिकल्पना १४६
पूजा नाम न पुष्पाद्यैर्या मतिः क्रियते दृढा
निर्विकल्पे महाव्योम्नि सा पूजा ह्यादराल्लयः १४७
अत्रैकतमयुक्तिस्थे योत्पद्येत दिनाद्दिनम्
भरिताकारता सात्र तृप्तिरत्यन्तपूर्णता १४८
महाशून्यालये वह्नौ भूताक्षविषयादिकम्
हूयते मनसा सार्धं स होमश्चेतनास्रुचा १४९
यागोऽत्र परमेशानि तुष्टिरानन्दलक्षणा
क्षपणात्सर्वपापानां त्राणात्सर्वस्य पार्वति १५०
रुद्रशक्तिसमावेशस्तत्क्षेत्रं भावना परा
अन्यथा तस्य तत्त्वस्य का पूजा कश्च तृप्यति १५१
स्वतंत्रानन्दचिन्मात्रसारः स्वात्मा हि सर्वतः
आवेशनं तत्स्वरूपे स्वात्मनः स्नानमीरितम् १५२
यैरेव पूज्यते द्रव्यैस्तर्प्यते वा परापरः
यश्चैव पूजकः सर्वः स एवैकः क्व पूजनम् १५३
व्रजेत्प्राणो विशेज्जीव इच्छया कुटिलाकृतिः
दीर्घात्मा सा महादेवी परक्षेत्रं परापरा १५४
अस्यामनुचरन् तिष्ठन् महानन्दमयेऽध्वरे
तया देव्या समाविष्टः परं भैरवमाप्नुयात् १५५
सकारेण बहिर्याति हकारेण विशेत् पुनः
हंसहंसेत्यमुं मंत्रं जीवो जपति नित्यशः १५५

षट्शतानि दिवा रात्रौ सहस्राण्येकविंशतिः
जपो देव्याः समुद्दिष्टः सुलभो दुर्लभो जडैः १५६
इत्येतत्कथितं देवि परमामृतमुत्तमम्
एतच्च नैव कस्यापि प्रकाश्यं तु कदाचन १५७
परशिष्ये खले क्रूरे अभक्ते गुरुपादयोः
निर्विकल्पमतीनां तु वीराणामुन्नतात्मनाम् १५८
भक्तानां गुरुवर्गस्य दातव्यं निर्विशङ्कया
ग्रामो राज्यं पुरं देशः पुत्रदारकुटुम्बकम् १५९
सर्वमेतत्परित्यज्य ग्राह्यमेतन्मृगेक्षणे
किमेभिरस्थिरैर्देवि स्थिरं परमिदं धनम् १६०
प्राणा अपि प्रदातव्या न देयं परमामृतम्
श्रीदेवी उवाच
देवदेव महादेव परितृप्तास्मि शङ्कर १६१
रुद्रयामलतन्त्रस्य सारमद्यावधारितम् ।
सर्वशक्तिप्रभेदानां हृदयं ज्ञातमद्य च १६२
इत्युक्त्वानन्दिता देवी कण्ठे लग्ना शिवस्य तु १६३